MW00561484

D.H. Lawrence's
Final Fictions

D.H. Lawrence's Final Fictions

A Lacanian Perspective

Ben Stoltzfus

LEXINGTON BOOKS
Lanham • Boulder • New York • London

Published by Lexington Books
An imprint of The Rowman & Littlefield Publishing Group, Inc.
4501 Forbes Boulevard, Suite 200, Lanham, Maryland 20706
www.rowman.com

86-90 Paul Street, London EC2A 4NE

British Library Cataloguing in Publication Information Available

Library of Congress Cataloging-in-Publication Data

Names: Stoltzfus, Ben, 1927- author.
  Title: D.H. Lawrence's final fictions : a Lacanian perspective /
  Ben Stoltzfus. Description: Lanham : Lexington Books, [2022] | Includes
  bibliographical references and index. |
Summary: "Shows how Lawrence and Lacan can change beliefs and practices, oppose
  the Anthropocene, and restore cosmic balance. Stoltzfus brings literature and
  psychoanalysis together in readings that are both aesthetic and epistemological"--
  Provided by publisher.
Identifiers: LCCN 2022007935 (print) | LCCN 2022007936 (ebook) |
  ISBN 9781666903676 (cloth) | ISBN 9781666903683 (ebook)
Subjects: LCSH: Lawrence, D.H. (David Herbert), 1885-1930--Criticism
  and interpretation. | Human ecology in literature. | Psychoanalysis and
  literature.
Classification: LCC PR6023.A93 Z6233866 2018 (print) | LCC PR6023.A93 (ebook)
  | DDC 823/.912--dc23/eng/20220216 LC record available at https://lccn.loc.
  gov/2022007935 LC ebook record available at https://lccn.loc.gov/2022007936

For Juliet Flower MacCannell

Contents

Foreword

D.H. Lawrence's Final Fictions: A Lacanian Perspective is an exploration of how literature thinks, more specifically, how Lawrence infuses his writings with deeply held beliefs about people and the world. He writes about cultural dysfunction and alienation from the cosmos, not only in his short stories and novels, but also in essays such as *Apocalypse, Reflections on the Death of a Porcupine,* and *Sketches of Etruscan Places.* He speaks eloquently about social dislocations caused by the Industrial Revolution and World War I; and he sees an urgent need for mankind to reorient its priorities away from an industrial dominance of the physical world toward a more intuitive acceptance of "blood-consciousness," Lawrence's term for a renewed awareness of nature, the erotic body, and the unconscious.

Lawrence wants to bring mind and body together so that, psychoanalytically, the Id and the Ego (*It* and *I*) become one entity. In this endeavor there is a remarkable convergence between Lawrence's writings and those of Jacques Lacan, the French psychoanalyst and author of *Écrits.* In saying that the unconscious is structured like a language Lacan shifts the emphasis from Freud's dreams to linguistics; the unconscious, however, remains a central concern insofar as Lawrence's and Lacan's goal is to meld consciousness with the unconscious. They both want humans to lead happier and more productive lives.

Lacan compares human dysfunction to a knot. Lawrence compares it to a tangle. Both men strive to cut through the knot in order to cure the emotional tangle, Lawrence in his fiction, and Lacan in psychoanalysis. In this sense Lawrence's fiction is both descriptive and prescriptive. Lacan's cut is the talking cure itself.

My study of Lawrence focuses on his desire to restore the harmony and balance between humans and nature, a relationship between people and the cosmos that was once the hallmark of all things Etruscan. Lawrence intuits this harmony from the frescoes and sarcophagi of the Etruscan tombs he visited and wrote about. In this endeavor his essays and late fictions reflect the

Etruscan charm of natural proportion, its simplicity, its ease, and abundance of life. Because they embody these qualities, the short stories that Lawrence wrote during the last five years of his life illustrate his mature thinking about how fiction works and the state of the world. They embody his hope of restoring sanity and spontaneity to the social fabric.

The first part of my Introduction, "A Prelude: Cultural Dysfunction," is conversational in tone because I'm trying to mirror some of the spontaneity of Lawrence's writing in *Reflections on the Death of a Porcupine;* also the urgency that he infused into *Apocalypse.* After that, I analyze the complexities of Lawrence's oeuvre and that of Lacan. Accordingly, the style and tone of my writing shifts into standard academic discourse.

The seven chapters of my study are Lacanian readings of five stories and two novellas. Bringing them together and analyzing them as a group gives Lawrence's art and thought a holistic thrust that parallels the urgent message of his essays. Also, the seven fictions and my chapter subtitles are instructive because they describe a progression from malady to remedy, as both writers address the disruptive effects of cultural aberrancy.

Acknowledgments

Generous sabbaticals and annual research-travel grants from the University of California made it possible for me to write this book and also to present papers on D.H. Lawrence at scholarly meetings in the United States and abroad. I am indebted to Vonnie Tessier for her help in processing the necessary moneys for these endeavors. I am also grateful to Seabrook Mendoza for his help in finding a student research assistant, Amy Hough-Dugdale, whose assistance has been invaluable.

My largest debt goes to the late Virginia Hyde who solicited and edited two essays for *D.H. Lawrence Studies*—essays that appear in this volume as chapters 1 ("The Sun") and 3 ("None of that!"); my thanks also extend to *D.H. Lawrence Studies*, the journal, for permission to reprint this material. I thank Doo-Sun Ryu for his role in overseeing their publication.

I am grateful to Holly Buchanan, Lexington's acquisitions editor, for her help and guidance through the final stages of the publication process. Thankful acknowledgment also goes to Megan White, Lexington's assistant acquisitions editor, for her editorial expertise in helping to prepare the manuscript for publication and to Anna Keyser, assistant production editor, for overseeing the production of the book.

I am indebted to M.J. Muratore who edited a somewhat different version of Chapter 2 (*The Woman Who Rode Away*) for her volume entitled *Hermeneutics of Textual Madness: Re-Readings—Herméneutique de la folie textuelle: re-lectures.* Thanks also to Giovanni Dotoli, general editor of the Bibliotecca Della Ricerca series, for permission to reprint this essay on world madness and cosmic sanity. Additional thanks go to Etienne Barnett for soliciting my contribution to the two-volume edition on textual madness.

I am grateful to Juliet Flower MacCannell for her insights into the enigmatic writings of Jacques Lacan. Thanks also to SUNY Press for permission to reprint two chapters from *Lacan and Literature: Purloined Pretexts:* "The Rocking-Horse Winner," and *The Escaped Cock.* I also thank the *D.H. Lawrence Review* for permission to reprint my articles on "The Man Who

Loved Islands" and "Glad Ghosts." All these materials have been substantially revised for the present volume.

Finally, I would like to acknowledge the long-standing support of Keith Cushman, Jill Franks, Juliet Flower MacCannell, and the late James Cowan. My wife Judith has been cheerfully tolerant while D.H. Lawrence occupied so much of my time and space. My sons, Jan and Andrew, and my daughter, Celia, have gladly made room as well.

Additional Parenthetical References

Écrits I and II   Jacques Lacan, the French edition
Écrits   Sheridan translation

Introduction

A PRELUDE: CULTURAL DYSFUNCTION

One hundred years ago D.H. Lawrence was writing historical and cultural books and essays such as *Apocalypse, Reflections on the Death of a Porcupine*, and *Sketches of Etruscan Places*—writings that were addressing urgent social issues. He was analyzing the effects of the Industrial Revolution on people's lives and the progressive mechanization of the means of production that were being imposed on men and women in the Western World. He was describing people's alienation from themselves, each other, and society while also contrasting this estrangement with the more harmonious relationship with people and the cosmos that was cultivated by earlier Chaldean, Greek, and Etruscan cultures.

One hundred years later Lawrence's rants against industrialization seem prescient and, insofar as the technological revolution has exacerbated them, solutions to the problems raised by mechanization have become more urgent. Scientists tell us that we are now in the "Anthropocene Era"—from *anthropos*, for "man," and *cene*, for "new"; that we are witnessing the sixth great extinction of species, and that it is a man-made calamity. Flora and fauna on all the continents of the globe and in all the oceans are under siege. It is an unprecedented threat due to the unrelenting pursuit of economic growth; and it has already affected over one million species. Many are already extinct. More than half of the vertebrate extinctions since 1500 have occurred since 1900 (the First Industrial Revolution began in the eighteenth century). Scientists are saying that greenhouse gas emissions from industry, human action, and commercial practices are responsible for these extinctions. They also contribute to climate change. Unless nations act in concert to curb noxious discharges into the environment, the accumulation of gases and waste will exacerbate global warming to a point of no return. Oceanographers say that the oceans have already absorbed as much carbon dioxide as they can hold; because forests also absorb carbon dioxide, geographers say that

1

deforestation in the Amazon, the Congo, Indonesia, and elsewhere, in order to make room for more people, farming, and industry, is moving the planet further away from a solution to the problem of climate change. We are already witnessing the effects of rising seas, higher temperatures, more frequent hurricanes, severe droughts, wildfires, and increased rainfall. Global warming seems to have intensified these phenomena. Primitive man would have said, "The gods are angry."

Lawrence is also angry. In the third version of *Lady Chatterley's Lover* Sir Clifford rages against the madness of World War I—a war that killed millions of soldiers and wounded many more. He is dismayed that young men in their prime have been sacrificed to the money-machine of greed, that the abstractions of Mind, *that is*, the Cartesian "cogito," have triumphed over *blood-consciousness;* and that the fundamental intuition of the body's senses—senses that constitute the unconscious—have been neglected. He is appalled that men and women are no longer in touch with nature and that our much-vaunted reason is destroying life itself. In *Psychoanalysis and the Unconscious* Lawrence denounced the very idea of *Mind*—the repository of abstract ideals—for not being in touch with the body's vital impulses. In his essay, "Democracy," he wrote: "An ideal is superimposed from above, from the mind; it is a fixed arbitrary thing, like a machine control. The great lesson is to learn to break all the fixed ideals, to allow the soul's own deep desires to come direct, spontaneous into consciousness" (Lawrence 1988b, 78). Lawrence's critique of ideals that have denatured people and society is also the linguistic sub-text in his fiction. His emphasis is always on "life-blood," a term for the bodily center of unconscious feeling and behavior. In *Phoenix* he says that the self-conscious phase of our mental evolution has produced repressive social systems; and these repressive social systems are the very ideals that he despises (Lawrence 1936, 378).

Had Lawrence lived to see the civil war in Spain (he died in 1930), Mussolini's invasion of Ethiopia, World War II, the Holocaust, the Gulags, the Cold War, the Korean War, the Vietnam War, the Iran-Iraq War, the wars in Iraq, Afghanistan, Ukraine, terrorism, and the civil wars in Syria, Yemen, and Africa, as well as the extraordinary developments and innovations in digital technology of the past several decades, he would have been horrified by the effects of human activity and the suicidal madness of a world that has lost its moral compass; of a world that has elevated death over life.

During the wars of the twentieth century millions of soldiers and civilians died. In World War I, generals and officers ordered their men on the front lines to attack, despite the withering effects of machine-gun fire that killed them the moment they emerged from the trenches. Lawrence deplores the blood that was shed in the battles of the Somme and Verdun in France, and he rejects the ideals of nationalism, patriotism, and self-sacrifice that value death more than life. Hours away from the signing of the armistice in 1918, and in full knowledge of the forthcoming ceasefire, British commanders ordered their soldiers to attack. More soldiers died. Why were such orders given, and where was good judgment? In contrast, Lawrence's blood-consciousness opposes the bloodlust of war. He believes that elevating *Mind* over body and reason over blood-consciousness has led to the mechanization and dehumanization of life. Ideological automatisms have formed patterns of behavior that are self-destructive; they lead to types of conduct that go against the grain of love.

Despite the fact that F.R. Leavis's critiques of Lawrence's work are now one-sided and outmoded, in *D.H. Lawrence: Novelist,* he praises his "vital intelligence" and "creative spirit," qualities that are "informed by an almost infallible sense for health and sanity" (Leavis 1955, 81). He praises Lawrence's novels as paeans to erotic love, even though *Lady Chatterley's Lover* was censored by the "authorities" for its alleged obscenity. For Lawrence this censorship was further proof that *Mind* and the money-machine had triumphed over blood-consciousness. Although sexual behavior in the Western World has changed radically since Lawrence's time, it has not led to an improvement of social behavior. Today sex censorship is minimal, compared to what it was then, and we no longer have to smuggle copies of *Lady Chatterley's Lover* across the border, but our inability to communicate with each other is extreme. Smart phones fragment our time and interrupt conversations. Trolls on social media bully people, insult them, and threaten them. Conspiracy theories multiply. Suicides among teenagers have been rising, the opioid epidemic has been staggering, and sex among teenagers is on the decline. Some pundits argue that the decline in teenage sex is salutary, while others point to the fact that it reflects their inability to connect face-to-face. College students are fearful: they require "safe" places, they shun new ideas that challenge their received ideas, and their professors' syllabi contain trigger alerts for information that may offend them. Whereas Lawrence speaks of the "blue light of the sun" that streams between a man and a woman whenever the spark of love ignites their senses, today's teens, instead of having a meaningful relationship with a partner, would rather go to sleep with the blue light of their cell phones streaming across the ceiling of their bedrooms; they are more intimate with the new technologies than with people.

When Lawrence says, "Start with the sun, and the rest will slowly, slowly happen" (Lawrence 1979, 149), he is asking men and women to connect with nature by opening themselves to the full rays of the cosmic orb, and, like Juliet in the short story, "Sun," to experience the penetrating power of love. Lawrence is speaking metaphorically, but the urgency to connect with nature is no less real because, unless men and women realign their sensibilities with the power of the sun and the tug of the moon, with day and night, with sleep and wakefulness, and with each other, the planet is doomed. In *Fantasia of the Unconscious* Lawrence addresses these binary systems that flow naturally from mind-consciousness into blood-consciousness and back into mind-consciousness in a continuous cycle of day/night, male/female, mind/blood, and so on. His critique of *Mind* is that in dominating blood-consciousness it has denatured humanity's relationship with the cosmos (Lawrence 2004b, 170–73).

Two key word-images in Lawrence's lexicon are the sun and the dandelion. I have already defined the metaphorical role of the sun. As for the dandelion, Lawrence sees in this lowly flower not only the metaphorical power of union with the sun, but also the flower's union with the vital, dark forces that reside deep within the earth (the cosmos) and ourselves (the unconscious) (Lawrence 1969, 210–12). The dandelion connects with both, and its yellow flower opens to the sun in the sky while its taproot goes down into the earth where it draws nutrients and power from its dark sun. Both suns are necessary and, if we open ourselves to the orb in the sky and tap into the blood-consciousness beneath the earth's surface, we will not only restore the balance within ourselves, a balance that has been sundered, but also restore the balance of a cosmos that has been misaligned. There is urgency in Lawrence's writings. He implores us to change our behavior and to listen to the "glad ghosts"—the title of a short story—within ourselves whenever they urge us to connect with the Holy Ghost of life, that is, with what he calls the "fourth dimension" of self-realization. Lawrence eulogizes the earth and the humus that the dandelion's root taps into and from which his fiction, like the dandelion, draws its sustenance (Lawrence 1969, 213–15).

Each one of Lawrence's stories, like the dandelion, opens with love toward the sun; and each story combines the brevity of a poem with the length of a novel. A sporting metaphor would say that a short story sprints to the finish line with the sinews of a long distance runner. Once there, the corolla of the flower, like the story, blossoms briefly, even as its brevity depends on the long taproot that sustains it over the time of its gestation. And then, in due course, when the flowering life of a dandelion is spent, its pale stem shoots upwards, seemingly overnight, and the bright flower becomes a round, white bundle of seeds waiting for the wind to disperse them to the four corners. Sometimes the seeds of these stories take root in the consciousness of men and women.

A good short story is based on omission and compression. The writer omits everything that might have gone into a novel, but that which remains possesses the intensity of a poem. It must have punch, and provide that flash of insight that captures the reader's attention. When speaking of omission and compression in fiction I am referring primarily, although not exclusively, to Ernest Hemingway's theory of writing. According to his theory, a story is both the tip of the iceberg and its submerged part. The submerged portion is not described, but it is there, nonetheless, beneath the surface, buoying up the visible portion. For Lawrence the fictional metaphor is not so much the iceberg as it is the dandelion—the lowly flower nestled in the grass where it shines with yellow radiance. This radiance is the visible portion, while the invisible taproot, like the seven-eighths of Hemingway's iceberg, is below the surface. Unlike Hemingway's fiction, however, Lawrence's short stories, without exception, narrate the visible flower and the invisible taproot, together. In Chapter One I discuss "Sun," Lawrence's story that comes closest to illustrating the iceberg theory of writing. The ideas in his essays buoy the fiction, and the two are inseparable. He himself says that the fiction came first, and the ideas later, although the ideas must have been there all along, subliminally, for the story to express them at all, even metaphorically.

In his *Studies on Hysteria* Sigmund Freud says that there is a link between theory and imagination because when writing a psychiatric case history, he wanted it to be judged as such, but, dismayingly, it read like a short story. He concluded that a short story conveys information that is superior to psychoanalysis because theory relies on the story in order to make itself heard. Lawrence, like Freud, extrapolates essays from his fiction—essays that are comparable to Freud's theory, and he combines them in works such as *Apocalypse*, *Reflections on the Death of a Porcupine*, and *Fantasia of the Unconscious*. In *Reflections on the Death of a Porcupine*, the porcupine and the dog are real, but in his essay they become symbols. The dog's snout is a metaphor for the sun, and the porcupine becomes mankind that is sticking "quills into the face of the sun" (Lawrence 1988b, 376). Metaphorically, the two animals, in their antagonism, as we shall see in Chapter Two, represent Lawrence's railings against humanity's global misalignment—a misalignment that is the source of humanity's dysfunction.

According to Lawrence, mankind is sick, and, like the doctors in his fiction, he wants to cure his ailing protagonists. His prescriptions are not pharmaceutical. Instead, as we shall see, they are metaphoric and psychological. In order to understand what is going on in Lawrence's short fictions, in addition to examining them as craft, I have analyzed seven stories from a Lacanian perspective: two novellas (*The Woman Who Rode Away* and *The Escaped Cock*) and five short stories ("Sun," "None of That," "The Rocking-Horse Winner," "The Man Who Loved Islands," and "Glad Ghosts"). The protagonists are three women, three men, and one boy.

Throughout these fictions Lawrence's characters go about their daily lives buffeted by destructive elements that have enmeshed them in forces beyond their knowledge or control. Knowing this, the stories that Lawrence wrote at the end of his life—1925 to 1930—become parables whose purpose was to counter the dehumanizing legacy of reified greed; and, in order to shape a better world, Lawrence creates situations that dramatize the events in which people find themselves enmeshed. Only those who connect with blood-consciousness survive. Blood-consciousness, that is, the voice of the unconscious, manifests itself in dreams and in enhanced states of awareness of nature and the cosmos, as well as actual contact with other people.

We, like Lawrence's characters, need to understand what blood-consciousness is, and then connect with it. As Jane Costin points out, Lawrence believed in the duality of human consciousness, and he often referred to the polarity between blood and mental consciousness. Mental consciousness was characterized by the exertion of human will and the emphasis on science, whereas blood-consciousness was intuitive, attuned to place, nature and the environment, places where "the blood remembered older religious ideas than those imposed by Christianity" (Costin 2012, 151–52). For Lawrence, will, *Mind,* mechanization, and materialism are all linked. By contrast, blood-consciousness indicates a preference for an intuitive rather than a scientific response to humanity's place in the world. In the story "Sun," Sicily will be the place where Juliet connects with nature and blood-consciousness.

In "Sun," Juliet, the protagonist, lives in New York, and she is not well. She creates herself anew, however, by going to Italy and communing with nature and the sun. In "None of That," Ethel Cane, an American, falls for Cuesta, a Mexican bullfighter. She is governed by *Mind* without the tempering effects of blood-consciousness, and, because of that, she loses the battle of wills between them. Unlike Ethel, Juliet discovers the healing power of nature, the bright sun in Italy, and the dark sun of the earth beneath the lemon groves. She gets in touch with her unconscious and is reborn, whereas Ethel Cane dies because she tries to rule her body with willpower, that is, with her *Mind.*

The plight of "the woman who rode away," in the novella of that name, is somewhere in between that of Ethel Cane and Juliet. Like Juliet, she leaves a dead marriage behind in search of renewal but, like Ethel, she too dies. In her search for that something that will restore meaning to life, she rides her horse into the remote mountains of Mexico where she is captured by the Chilchui Indians. After many rituals they immolate her on the altar of cosmic renewal because they believe that the white race is responsible for the disarray in their lives. The Indians' blood-sense tells them that the white woman must be sacrificed in order to realign the sun and the moon. They believe that this realignment will restore their lost power, a power that has been usurped by the white man.

The boy in "The Rocking-Horse Winner," like so many of Lawrence's characters, is not well. He has been infected by his mother's mendacity and her inability to love. To please her and earn the money she craves, he rides his hobbyhorse compulsively. Riding enables him to predict the winning horse at the races. Although he wins big money, he cannot regain his mother's love. He dies trying.

Cathcart, "the man who loved islands," is a human being in search of meaning. He flees not only from other humans and connectedness with them but also from one island to another. In his efforts to escape from people, love, and fatherhood—civilization itself—he removes all traces of language, the bond between him and humanity: he blocks mail from coming to his island, and he even detaches the nameplate on the stove.

Unlike Cathcart, who eschews social contact, Mark Morier, in "Glad Ghosts," does all he can to bring people together. Indeed, he is the only sane person at the Riddings Estate. "Glad Ghosts" puts him in touch with the erotic presence of his unconscious. Indeed Morier's unconscious is described as a woman-ghost—blood-consciousness itself—and she comes to him in the middle of the night. His dream of her visit enables him to restore sanity to a house that has been in the grip of hysteria. He cures the symptoms of everyone.

In *The Escaped Cock,* Christ does not die, and, having survived his crucifixion, he offers humanity a different kind of salvation: erotic love. It will replace charity, the love of God for mankind, and man's love for God. The trauma of the crucifixion prompts him to reevaluate his life. He concludes that he cared too much for others and not enough for himself. Nonetheless, despite having survived the ordeal, he finds himself bound in the loincloths of his earlier convictions. Eventually he cuts through the tangle that was hobbling him. The story's climax is his sexual union with the priestess of Isis. His erection is his resurrection. Unlike the Biblical resurrection, it enables "the man who died" to discover the erotic potential within himself—his blood-consciousness. Union with the priestess brings the Id and the Ego together. In Lacanian terms *I* will be where *it* was, that is, the conscious self and the unconscious self will have fused into one entity. The man, like his cock, has risen, and his two selves are now one fully-healed entity. Erotic love was the prelude to the fulfillment of the self.

Unlike "the man who died," and his coming into contact with his discovery of erotic love, Cathcart, "the man who loved islands," eschews love, community, and union with others. He longs for the perfect oneness of an egg, that is, isolation, and, on the third and last island in the North Sea, he is entombed in the cocoon-whiteness of snow. The rocking-horse-winner wants money, the man who loved islands rejects it, and, both he and the boy engage in compulsive behaviors that are deadly. But there are survivors, and the fictions I discuss in the following seven chapters narrate the lives of three characters who endure: "The man who died" and who, having found love, survives; Juliet, who is sick, opens herself to the sun and thrives; and Morier, after his erotic union with the lovely ghost, spreads a healing touch to all his friends.

The three victims in these stories are Ethel, Paul, and Cathcart. As for" the woman who rode away," she dies, but from Lawrence's point of view she is immortal because she will have saved the world. What are we to make of these contradictions?

In my discussion of *The Woman Who Rode Away* (Chapter Two) I argue that in Lawrence's eyes the modern world is insane but that his characters are not. They may act irrationally, but they are coping with circumstances over which they have little control; they are striving to adapt as best they can to a life that has been shaped by parents, culture, and history. In many cases industry, the money-machine, and war have pushed them to the brink of inadaptability. Those who adapt to the insanity of the modern world may survive, but their actions define a death-in-life existence. Lawrence's survivors—Christ, Juliet, and Morier—reject the unauthentic existence of their peers. The rebellion of these characters is based on a new awareness of self—erotic love, nature, and contact with the cosmic forces of the world that are in play around them. The three victims are shaped by constraints, and governed by compulsions that end their lives prematurely: Ethel uses *Mind* to control desire, and fails; Paul wants to please his mother's mendacity, and fails; and Cathcart, disillusioned by the world around him, returns to a prenatal, less threatening place: the womb-tomb, snow-covered rock-island on which he dies.

Fiona Becket phrases it aptly when she says that Lawrence's final fictions, as fables, "draw attention to [his] highly successful handling of the form and demonstrable authorial control. At their best each is a finely crafted text, which synoptically and directly apprehends much that is dealt with in more exploratory fashion in the novels" (Becket 2002, 91). In the chapters that follow, and with Becket's praise of Lawrence's short fictions in mind, I discuss why certain characters adjust to situations of adversity and succeed in overcoming them, and why others fail to do so. Each chapter addresses the whys and wherefores of the protagonists' dilemmas using Freudian, Lacanian, Derridian, Barthesian, and Saussurean strategies. My primary emphasis will be on Lacanian solutions because Lawrence, like the author of *Écrits,* wants to connect the mind and the body—consciousness with the unconscious. This is why figuring the unconscious in his stories is essential. When read for its sub-text, literature renders it visible. It "figures" it. Figuring out how it works within each story is the next step. I analyze the psychology of Lawrence's characters in order to develop insights into and conclusions about his craft and how it works. In order to understand his craft we also need to know how Lawrence's "survivors" manage to integrate their conscious selves with their unconscious selves. Morier, the protagonist of "Glad Ghosts," is a prime example. In his dream, the plum-blossom scented one comes to him in the middle of the night. She is his unconscious self, and their union is illuminating. Deirdre Barrett, a professor of psychiatry at the Harvard Medical School, says: "Dreaming is, above all, a time when the unheard parts of ourselves are allowed to speak. We would do well to listen" (qtd. by Jarvis 2021, 45).

PREVIOUS STUDIES OF D.H. LAWRENCE'S FINAL FICTIONS

In his letters and articles Lawrence wrote extensively about the novel as form. He also wrote more than sixty pronouncements about the short story—pronouncements that address the same creative spark that animated his novels. When comparing his short fictions with the chiseled prose and story-plots of a Poe, Chekov, or Hemingway, it becomes evident that Lawrence created new forms, narratives essentially without plot, in which feeling and the senses float free of constraint.

Between 1917 and 1921 Lawrence was searching for new narrative forms with which to express his ever-widening concepts—his "pollyanalytics" as he called them; and he began linking the actions of individual characters to larger historical, social, political and religious forces. In his final period of formal inventiveness—the fabulation period—he imbued his fictions with the genres of myth and the fairytale. Because the structure of Lawrence's final fictions are free flowing, Eudora Welty, in "The Reading and Writing of Short Stories," compares each fiction to a tropical bird that may be clumsy on the ground but that when in flight, "all that clumsiness and outrageousness is gone. Its body becomes astonishingly functional and iridescent" (Welty 1949, 55). Ronald P. Draper calls Lawrence's "fabulistic" stories "poems in prose" (Draper 1964, 120).

The variety of subject and form found among the tales has been analyzed in studies by scholars and published in many literary journals in the United States and abroad. The classic, critical book studies of Lawrence's fiction, however, discuss his novels primarily; sometimes they list a chapter or a section on one or two of his short stories. The books that have been published on his short fiction have, most often, focused on the realistic tales. Unlike these earlier studies mine dwells on Lawrence's fabulations, his final fictions.

A list of the books that have been published on Lawrence's short fiction is as follows: In 1962 Kingsley Widmer published *The Art of Perversity: D.H. Lawrence's Shorter Fictions*. In 1964 Ronald P. Draper published "The Tales," in *D.H. Lawrence*. In 1973 Frank Kermode concluded that all of Lawrence's short fictions were "allegories of personal regeneration" (Kermode 1973, 139). In 1978 F.B. Pinion published "Shorter Stories," in *A D.H. Lawrence Companion: Life, Thought, and Works*. Except for Widmer's book, the other two are not full-length studies of Lawrence's short stories.

In 1978 Keith Cushman published *D.H. Lawrence at Work: The Emergence of the* Prussian Officer *Stories,* a carefully researched study of the stories that were published in 1914. Cushman traces the creative process that gave birth to six of Lawrence's best short stories composed during his early years as a writer: "The Odour of Chrysanthemums," "Daughters of the Vicar," "The Shades of Spring," "The White Stocking," "The Prussian Officer," and "The Thorn in the Flesh." His excellent study analyzes Lawrence's early short stories. Unlike Cushman's study, mine is devoted to seven stories written at the end of Lawrence's career, stories he wrote between 1925 and 1930, the year he died.

In 1984 Janice Hubbard Harris published *The Short Fiction of D.H. Lawrence,* a study in which she analyzes Lawrence's short stories in relation to each other, his life, and his novels. Harris begins by situating Lawrence's early tales in relation to the continental short story, defining them as moving away from the nineteenth-century conventions of Flaubert, Maupassant, Gogol, Turgenev, Dostoevsky, and Tolstoy. She also situates Lawrence's short fiction in relation to that of more recent practitioners of the genre, namely Chekov, Verga, Conrad, Katherine Mansfield, Joyce, and Woolf, even as she traces Lawrence's fiction from realism to visionary fiction and fabulation. Hubbard prefers his realistic tales, however, and she criticizes the fabulation in "Glad Ghosts," as well as the visionary mode in *The Woman Who Rode Away,* unaware perhaps that narrating the uncanny and the implausible allows Lawrence to explore social issues and the unconscious, unaware also that Lawrence's primary goal is to bring the Ego and the Id together. He believes that the human species cannot survive unless it unites the conscious mind with the unconscious body. Fusing *It* and *I* is also Lacan's agenda in *Écrits.* My goal, therefore, is to show how Lawrence's seven short stories dovetail with Lacan's psychoanalytic writings. Both men are engaged in healing social ills and personal ills. For Lawrence, cultural dysfunction was already a reality in the early twentieth century.

In 1990 James C. Cowan published *D.H. Lawrence and the Trembling Balance,* a monograph in which he suggests that Lawrence's "balance" is not a static polarity of opposites but a dynamic equilibrium of life (Cowan 1990, 16). Cowan argues that the way Lawrence presents ideas in his fiction invites the reader's unconscious collaboration in creating meaning and generating conclusions. He refers to Melanie Klein's, Heinrich Hacker's, and Heinz Kohut's psychoanalytic theories of "projective identification"—theories that describe the reader's own unresolved affective needs—needs that are then projected onto the reality of the text. As a reader himself, Cowan emphasizes a necessary "psychic distancing" that must move beyond the projection of unresolved personal needs toward "understanding and interpretation." Cowan says that many critics have distorted Lawrence's work because it has been the object of negative as well as positive "overidentifications." He also suggests that the critical reading of a text is comparable to the psychoanalytic situation in which the text projected by the author is the equivalent of the patient's projective identification onto the analyst; that, in this situation, the critic takes on the role of empathetic analyst; also that the reader-critic must be alert to and acutely aware of *"unwitting,* unconscious projective identification." Essentially, Cowan is asking for a balanced reader-response theory that recognizes that the artist-writer, through his work, connects the reader with "the affective structures that govern our lives and define our needs (Cowan 1990, 1–11). This is Cowan's methodology, and he goes on to apply it to selected readings of Lawrence's novels. I should note that although Cowan does not refer to Lacan or postmodern critical theories, his Freudian approach is, nonetheless, similar to mine. Using Freud, he does for Lawrence's novels what I, using Lacan, do for his short stories. Lacan cuts through the knot of dysfunction, Lawrence cuts through the tangle.

In 2002 Fiona Becket, echoing Kermode, stated: "If Lawrence had never written novels, poetry, or plays, or philosophy, the body of short fiction and novellas would constitute an organic and coherent *oeuvre"* (Becket 2002, 87). She goes on to note that Lawrence is "one of the key short-story writers of the modernist period," and that the stories "are central to an understanding of Lawrence's major preoccupations" (Becket 2002, 91).

In 2020 John Turner published *D.H. Lawrence and Psychoanalysis,* a book in which he narrates the history of Lawrence's engagement between 1912 and 1921 with the psychoanalytic ideas of Otto Gross, Sigmund Freud, Carl Jung, and Trigant Burrow. Turner focuses on their theoretical debates and their influence on Lawrence, applying their psychoanalytic concepts to four major novels that he wrote during that period: *Sons and Lovers, The Rainbow, Women in Love, Aaron's Rod.* Turner also discusses Gross's influence on Frieda Weekley and her influence on her future husband, but he does not apply the psychoanalytic concepts to Lawrence's short stories.

Since the early 1970s feminist critics of Lawrence's fiction such as Kate Millet (*Sexual Politics,* 1969), Marianna Torgovnick (*Gone Primitive,* 1990), Simone de Beauvoir (*The Second Sex,* 1988), Sheila MacLeod (*Lawrence's Men and Women,* 1985), and Fiona Becket (*D.H. Lawrence,* 1985), among others, have disparaged Lawrence's indulgence of phallic power, female submissiveness, and his fascination with "the primitive" (Torgovnick 1990, 164–65). They critiqued his representation of women, his misogyny, the phallocentricity of his thought and language (MacLeod 1985, 11), and, on a more general level, the oppressive manifestations of patriarchy (Becket 2002, 14). In "Post-Modernizing Lawrence," Peter Widdowson stresses the key role that feminist criticism played in the history of Lawrence studies:

> If sex and sexuality had been a key issue in the sixties—both generally and
> in relation to Lawrence—it was rapidly reinflected thereafter as gender, and
> Lawrence who had been perceived as a guru of sexual liberation became the
> phallocratic opressor of gender politics. (Widdowson 1992, 10)

However, as Robert Burden notes, Lawrence has been viewed as both sen-
sitively sympathetic to women and a male chauvinist. He goes on to point
out that these versions of him were constructed by opposed points of views,
and, that in the history of reception, in order to understand and situate his
oeuvre we also need a criticism that accounts not only for the play of meaning within a text but also the "interplay between text, history and criticism."
That, he says, will explain the changing contexts of production and reception
of Lawrence's work (Burden 2000, 14). We need to keep in mind that the
early feminist attacks on Lawrence's oeuvre rarely went beyond biographical
and essentialist readings of his works. Fortunately, since the 1970s, theoretical investigations of literature have rejected both the Leavisite approach to
Lawrence's work and that of the feminists. The struggle over Lawrence has
been a long one. Indeed it is no longer possible to agree with Leavis that
he is exclusively a modernist or that he belongs to the tradition of moral
realism; or with the feminists who fail to account for the complexity of his
characters and the indeterminism of his fiction. For some readers Lawrence
is a moralist, for others he is an offender of public taste. He has been hailed
as the first working-class writer while also being critical of that class. He
favors sexual emancipation but is viewed, nonetheless, as a misogynist. He
is either a religious vitalist or a proto-fascist (Burden 2000, 2–3). When
viewing Lawrence through the lens of post-structuralist theory we have to
conclude that Lawrence's fiction is not only complex and contradictory but
that the binary oppositions that define it, coexist. The instability of his writing
transforms it into sites where the play of language encourages multiple, even
contradictory readings.

   In *D.H. Lawrence: Aesthetics and Ideology,* Anne Fernihough suggests
that with Lawrence's didacticism in mind we should read him "against the
grain" because doing so is both "productive and liberating" (Fernihough
1993, 14); and Jacques Derrida, with James Joyce in mind, when writing
about the deconstructive effects of certain texts, is also implicitly addressing
Lawrence's misogyny:

> For instance, some works which are highly "phallocentric" in their semantics,
> their intended meaning, even their theses, can produce paradoxical effects,
> paradoxically anti-phallocentric through the audacity of a writing which in fact
> disturbs the order or the logic of phallocentrism or touches on limits where

things are reversed: in that case the fragility, the precariousness, even the ruin of order is more apparent. (Derrida 1992, 50)

In Lawrence's final fictions, however, except perhaps for *The Plumed Serpent,* his previous insistence on phallic power, female submissiveness, and a return to the primitive have been replaced by his quest for the integration of the two selves, the It and the Ego—*It* and *I* (Lawrence capitalizes *It,* Lacan does not). When the melding occurs, as it does in *Lady Chatterley's Lover,* Lawrence writes love scenes of unusual tenderness, such as those between Oliver and Connie. Furthermore, in Lawrence's *Late Essays* he says: "Man or woman, each is a flow, a flowing life. And without one another, we can't flow [. . .] We Need One Another" (Lawrence 2004a, 300). As Jill Franks points out: "For Lawrence, marriage was the single most important relationship of life" (Franks 2007, 153). In the twenty-first century, however, marriage may no longer be the criterion for self-fulfillment, as long as a man and a woman in a sexual relationship and in touch with their blood-sense treat each other with tenderness as equals.

For Lawrence, both in life and in art, it is essential to understand that blood-sense is a metaphor for the vital impulses of the unconscious. In his *Studies in Classic American Literature,* an idiosyncratic critique of a body of texts, the word "blood" in Lawrence's discourse is an omnipresent metaphor; and, in "The Spirit of Place" he suggests that art should provide an emotional experience, which, in turn can become a trove of practical truth. We, as readers, when responding to the emotional experience, and, encouraged by our feelings, can dig the truth out of them. This process translates into Lawrence's desire to right wrongs. He waned to be a healer, to correct personal and cultural misalignments. Understanding how he crafted that process is what I propose to do.

In 1993 Weldon Thornton published *D.H. Lawrence: A Study of the Short Fiction.* In it he focuses on selected stories from both the realistic and fabulistic periods. For the latter he discusses "The Rocking-Horse Winner," and *The Woman Who Rode Away*—two fictions that I also discuss. Although Thornton praises the inventiveness of both stories, his analyses are relatively short, and they are not in the psychoanalytic mode.

In 1998 Martin F. Kearney published *Major Short Stories of D.H. Lawrence: A Handbook.* It is a reference guide that examines what has been written about six short stories: "Odour of Chrysanthemums," "The Shadow in the Rose Garden," "Daughters of the Vicar," "The Prussian Officer," "The Horse Dealer's Daughter," and "The Rocking-Horse Winner." The only overlap between my study and Kearney's is "The Rocking-Horse Winner." Kearney chose stories that had been the focus of critical studies and frequently published in anthologies. With reference to "The Rocking-Horse-Winner" he summarizes the psychological studies that have been published, and he describes what these studies say about it. By contrast, my chapter on "The Rocking-Horse Winner" is analytical. It focuses on the psychoanalytic link between Lawrence's fiction and the theories of Freud, Lacan, Derrida, and Saussure.

In another study, published in 2001, *D.H. Lawrence, Desire, and Narrative,* Earl G. Ingersoll uses Lacanian readings to analyze Lawrence's major novels. In that sense his book is closer to mine. He makes no mention, however, of Lawrence's short fiction. In 2003, N. Reeve published *Reading Late Lawrence,* a study of several of his works that were published during his so-called "last period." The focus is on Lawrence's revisions and the insights they offer into the complexity of his writing processes. Reeve's two overlapping stories with those in my study are "Glad Ghosts" and "Sun." *Reading Late Lawrence* also draws extensively upon the manuscript and its variant material.

Radicalizing Lawrence: Critical Interventions in the Reading and Reception of D.H. Lawrence's Narrative Fiction (2000) by Robert Burden, like Ingersol's study, uses postmodern critical strategies—French feminist, Lacanial, Foucauldian, Bakhtinian, and Derridian—to analyze Lawrence's novels. Like Ingersol, however, he does not address Lawrence's short fiction. Therefore, insofar as my book covers new and different ground, there would seem to be a place for it in Lawrentian studies. Let us, therefore, turn to literature as narration in order to find out how and why the unconscious uses metaphor and metonymy to veil its subterfuges even as conscious narration, i.e., plot, suspense, and characters, is there to charm the reader.

Lawrence wanted to reinvent the language of fiction, and, in dealing with language, Michael Bell's study, *D.H. Lawrence: Language and Being,* has been useful because it focuses on Lawrence's ontology. Bell analyzes the difficulties Lawrence experienced in crafting a language that would adequately express the complexity of his characters' feelings. His study focuses on Lawrence's novels and the author's determination to find the right language for the many nuances of emotion. Not surprisingly, Lawrence experienced similar difficulties when writing his short stories, and that may explain why, toward the end of his life, he moved from realism to fabulation. The fabulation inherent in myth and the fairy tale gave him the freedom to craft a language beyond the confines of realism. When reading stories such as "Sun," "The Woman Who Rode Away," 'The Man Who Loved Islands," and "Glad Ghosts" we sense each character's heightened state of emotional presence and response: their feelings and senses float free of constraint in narratives almost devoid of plot.

In his late short stories Lawrence crafted a language that does in fact express complex feelings. For example, in "The Man Who Loved Islands," as Peter Balbert, in "From Relativity to Paraphrenia in D.H. Lawrence's 'The Man Who Loved Islands:' Speculations On Einstein, Freud, Gossamer Webs, and Seagulls," points out, Lawrence charts the steps in Cathcart's collapse of body, mind, and spirit by employing metaphors that connect to Einstein's theories of relativity (Balbert 2020, 65–67). Indeed Lawrence's prose conveys the shifting ellipses and bending of spacetime:

> Strangely from your little island in space you were gone forth in the great realms of time where all the souls that never die veer and swoop on their vast strange errands. The little earthly island has dwindled, like a jumping-off place into nothingness, for you have jumped off, you know not how into the dark mystery of time, where the past is vastly alive, and the future is not separated off. (Lawrence 1995, 152)

Lawrence also relates the decline of Cathcart's equilibrium and the patterns of his anxiety and depression to the pathologies that Freud describes when analyzing neuroses, melancholia, and paraphrenia, a late-life psychosis that encompasses delusions and visual and auditory hallucinations (Balbert 2020, 70–72). Balbert's article, like my Lacanian reading of Cathcart's decline, describes the behavior of a man who is unable to recognize the essential function of language in communicating with other human beings (Balbert 2020, 72).

In her article on "The Man Who Loved Islands" Zahra A. Hussein Ali attributes Cathcart's decline and loss of desire to his dilettantism, dandyism, and the devolutionary, i.e., a return to the primitive (Ali 2016, 83–84). Her study contradicts Balbert's, and it exemplifies the possibility of simultaneous readings that oppose each other. Mark Kinkead-Weekes, in "A Lawrence who loved islands" (Kinkead-Weekes 2004), analyzes Lawrence's response to Trigant Burrows's notion that contact with other people is essential to a full life. Lawrence admired Burrows's work because he had broken away from Freud's psychotherapeutic ideas based solely on the relationship between analyst and analysand. Kinkead-Weekes also analyzes Lawrence's rejection of Earl Brewster's Buddhism because it advocates a withdrawal from society, as well as Lawrence's own *Weltanshauung* (Kinkead-Weekes 2004, 193).

Inez Martinez, in "Ego Readings vs Reading for Psyche," uses Carl Jung's collective unconscious to suggest that the visionary, imaginative writing in stories such as "The Rocking-Horse Winner" has the power to help our collective psyche self-regulate. This concept dovetails with Lawrence's desire to change individuals and society and also with Cowan's "projective identification," an overidentification that Martinez, like Cowan, rejects. Furthermore, Martinez argues that Lawrence's efforts to craft a language with which to express deep feelings is crucial for his writing to succeed in communicating its message.

In "The Blood-Consciousness and Lawrence's Silent Ghosts," Matt Foley privileges Lawrence's emphasis on the unconscious forces governing what Lawrence called the "will-to-life" (Foley 2017, 171). In a letter to his friend and publisher, Edward Garnett, Lawrence wrote: "you mustn't look in my novel for the old stable *ego* - of the character. There is another *ego,* according to whose action the individual is unrecognizable" (qtd. by Foley 2017, 171). This other ego—the *it*—as Lawrence calls it in *Psychoanalysis and the Unconscious,* is blood-consciousness, a consciousness that he situates in the body. After reading Sir James George Frazer's *Golden Bough* and *Exogamy* Lawrence stated that this other seat of consciousness "exists independently of the ordinary mental consciousness, which depends on the eye as its source or connector" (qtd. by Foley 2017, 172). With blood-consciousness in mind, Foley, in his "Silent Ghosts" article, refers, as I do, to the "clear resonances between Lawrencian corporeality and later Lacanian psychoanalytic thought" (Foley 2017, 171). Although we differ in our approaches to the subject, we both draw connections between Lacan's theories and Lawrence's blood-consciousness.

In conclusion, the short fictions of Lawrence's final period are more successful artistically than his novels because he was able to balance art and message in a way that makes the two indistinguishable. Critics have noted that Lawrence combined prophecy and artistry in *The Escaped Cock and The Woman Who Rode Away,* saying that these tales are sometimes prophetic; indeed, as a prophetic writer, Lawrence wanted to change society and the lives of people. His essays make this ambition abundantly clear, and, although present in his fictions, we feel it less because his desire to change behavior was crafted into the fabric of each tale. That's why it's important to analyze these fictions in sequence and together, as a group. We want to know why some characters fail to achieve self-fulfillment while others succeed in doing so. That's my purpose. I analyze the poles of Lawrence's creative dialectic in order to foreground the message that is embedded in the tissues of his art. The subtitles of my chapters are indicative: "Madness and Cosmic Sanity," "Pleasing the Mother," "A Return to the Womb," "Cutting through the Tangle," and "Salvation."

I should note that *D.H. Lawrence's Final Fictions: A Lacanian Perspective* is a sequel to my previous study, *Lacan and Literature: Purloined Pretexts,* in which I discuss works not only by Lawrence and Lacan but also works by Roland Barthes, Camus, Hemingway, and Robbe-Grillet. The present study builds on the previous one, and, I believe it adds significant new material to our understanding of Lawrence as a short story writer. In this endeavor my own writing bears the imprint of Lawrence's, Lacan's, and Roland Barthes's organic styles, styles that are metaphorical and allusive rather than purely academic. Their styles are also creative in that they strive to convey feeling as a pathway toward insight.

TOWARD A LACANIAN DISCOURSE

Literature as narration is language functioning at a higher level where connotation overrides denotation, where form obscures meaning, where ambiguity devalues message. In fact literature and the unconscious enjoy a special affinity because language is the magnetic field that joins the two; but it is a union that can function only when a reader activates the circuit between them. Jacques Lacan says that the unconscious is structured like a language (Lacan 1971a, 112, 158–59, 232–33) and James Mellard, in *Using Lacan, Reading Fiction,* argues that by focusing on language and the mechanisms of language found in tropes, "Lacan brings his analysis immediately into the domain of literary analysis" (Mellard 1991, 56). Within this domain, says Ellie Ragland-Sullivan in "The Magnetism Between Reader and Text," the literary work represents a reader's ego to itself through the language of the text—a text that exerts a "magnetic pull" on the reader "because it is an allegory of the psyche's fundamental structure" (Ragland-Sullivan 1984, 381).

But consciousness is also structured like a language, i.e., "language is the one agency that 'contains' the author, reader, work, and world in the only way available to the critic" (Mellard 1991, 36). Language not only structures our perception of reality, it is, says Anika Lemaire in *Jacques Lacan,* "the precondition for *the act of becoming aware of oneself as a distinct entity*" (Lemaire 1977, 54). Like a Klein bottle, in which the outside and the inside are reversible, we contain language, but language also contains us. In tropes there is neither an inside nor an outside and it is this reversibility that allows the unconscious, when veiled by figural language, to reveal itself. Psychoanalysis as theory is analogous to the conscious *I* (ego), and the latent content of literature as body is analogous to the unconscious *It.* Furthermore, the *It* (*ça*) and the *I* (ego) are not destined to remain separate entities. According to Juliet Flower MacCannell it is the very idea of boundaries that is constantly at issue in Lacan's texts. "We do not [. . .] have a sense that we are trapped in the prison-house of language" (MacCannell 1986, 14).

Lacan says that although language has a material reality it also contains the reality of the unconscious (Lacan 1966a, 136, 183). Lacan's work thus provides the basis for a theory of narration within the context of an unconscious discourse that he calls the "discourse of the Other." It derives from the Symbolic presence of paternal authority—the figure of the Law or the *non/nom du père*—a Law that is responsible, in the early stages of the child's development, for the repression of desire. Repression, in turn, enables us to understand, as Robert Con Davis phrases it in *Lacan and Narration*, "how language in literary texts is constituted, buoyed up, permeated, and decentered by the unconscious" (Con Davis 1983, 848).

When Lacan stated that the unconscious is structured like a language, he opened a royal road between literature and the unconscious, one for which Freud had already cleared the way with, among other essays, his psychoanalytic reading of E.T.A. Hoffman's "Sandman." Freud's analysis of dreams was essential in drawing attention to linguistic structures, but he was unfamiliar with Saussure's seminal work in linguistics (Saussure 1967) which was to have such a profound influence, despite subsequent modifications, on the oeuvre of Claude Lévi-Strauss, Lacan, Roland Barthes, Jacques Derrida, Michel Foucault, and many others. Therefore, in bringing together Lawrence's fiction and psychoanalysis we need to incorporate Freud's *Interpretation of Dreams*, Saussure's *Course in General Linguistics,* and Lacan's *Écrits* as the triad from which a psychoanalytic theory of reading can be developed.

In dreams, Freud's theories of condensation and displacement match Lacan's definitions of metaphor and metonymy because dreams as tropes are signifiers pointing to the presence of an absence. Figures of speech coalesce in the life of the subject (the author, his characters, and the reader) both as dreams dramatizing unconscious imagery, as narration veiling the unconscious, or as somatic manifestations of rhetorical functions. Bodily acts such as hysteria are comparable to the so-called manifest content in dreams because, says Lacan, "the symptom *is* a metaphor whether we like it or not, as desire *is* metonymy, however funny people may find the idea" ("le symptôme *est* une métaphore, que l'on veuille ou non se le dire, comme le désir *est* une métonymie, même si l'homme s'en gausse" (Lacan 1977a, 69, 1966a, 160). A condensed and displaced symptom in the dream or in the text is visible, even as it veils the presence of the unconscious—the unseen. Because of this veiling, the manifest symptom (be it somatic, dreamed, or narrated) corresponds exactly to its latent meaning. Lawrence's short stories contain similar veilings. The manifest content—the story we are reading—veils the latent content of the sub-text.

Lacan's analysis of narration begins with language and proceeds to rediscover the discourse of the Other that is embedded in speech and literature. The blockage of desire, along with its corollary, repression, produces a neurosis whose narrative symptoms are metaphorical. The symptom (metaphor) is a manifestation of unconscious speech (*parole*) and it contains all the idiosyncrasies of an individual utterance. For example, in somatic symptoms a hysterical pregnancy is an unconscious trope. It mimes the real thing and the figure swells but there is no fetus. It is all an act and the symptom is *parole* treating the body as language (*langue*). Since we all have bodies and use them, sometimes individually in sports or collectively in the body politic, these bodies are comparable to English as a language. We use English or French in order to communicate with each other or to write a set of laws with which to govern a state. Violations of the law are symptoms of unrest and examples of a criminal *parole*. In sociology the collective body of society or a group is the text, in *Tristes Tropiques* the kinship relations of the Nambikwara are Lévy-Strauss's anthropological text, and in the case of conversion hysteria, as Freud has demonstrated, a person's body is the text. Likewise, Lawrence's fiction is a text, and its subtext is the unconscious. Because the latent meaning is erotic love—desire—and the industrial world governed by the money-machine represses erotic desire, need is displaced and it manifests itself as a symptom of loss. Lawrence's fiction dramatizes these symptoms and, in the production of narrative (his stories), the symptoms are condensed as metaphor and displaced as metonymy. This narrative process embodies the same characteristics of Freud's dream work, and the function of the analyst or the literary critic is to show how conscious discourse veils unconscious meaning, that is, how the signifiers resolve simultaneously into manifest signified (metaphor and metonymy) and latent referents (the repressed). Lacan's formula, S_1 over S_2, means that the signifier can have two signifieds. If the dream is the iconic, although masked mirror of the unconscious, fiction is its linguistic reflector. I will be analyzing these processes in the coming chapters.

If we accept the premise that the unconscious is structured like a language, then literature contains repressed material that engenders a never-ending dialog with the Other—a fictitious self made up of the confluence of the Imaginary and Symbolic. The Symbolic is the Law, the father (*le non/nom du père*), in essence all *doxa*. In any culture, says Roland Barthes, *doxa,* or encratic language, is produced and disseminated by the voices of power, such as schools, churches, sports, advertising, popular songs, and news. These official institutions of language are repeating machines. They are stereotypes, a political reality mouthing ideology (Barthes 1975b). China has its ideology, Iran has its own, and so does the United States. As ideologies go, in the Western World, China, and in many other countries, a consumerist ideology is pervasive. The industrial revolution and technology have made it possible to mass-produce goods that appeal to a populace governed by the language of encratic desire. The Symbolic is everywhere. In contrast to the Symbolic, the Imaginary is that displaced self that must come to terms with the postponement of satisfaction, the repression of desire, and the nurturing of discontent. A repressed Imaginary manifests itself in symptoms and, it manifests itself in literature for ill or for good as the melding of the conscious body of the text with the unconscious psyche of the sub-text.

The reading of a short story is a rhetorical activity, and, when analyzing its unconscious, the reader's task is to construct a latent text from the manifest one. It is the evocative power of literature, rather than its message, that communicates its magic to the reader. After a fiction tells its story we need to focus on the story of telling, a procedure that foregrounds language and the enchantment of the text. The reader's accomplices in this endeavor are the tropic, symbolic, and homonymic traces that are embedded in its tissues. Because Lacan privileges metaphor and metonymy we will be looking mainly at their programmatic disguises but also, when appropriate, at synecdoche, irony, and humor. Language in literary texts, like the images in Freud's dreams, is constantly being displaced, condensed, deformed, and dramatized. Indeed, rhetorical language is a second sign system that functions along with character, plot, and suspense, but is also independent of them. Moreover, the literariness of the text, in Jakobsen's sense, gives us free access to the voice of the Other which, in Lacanian terminology, is the voice of the unconscious.

Whenever we focus on the literariness of a text we focus primarily on how meaning is circulating throughout it. In essence, the reader produces meaning, and in order to do so the reader's creative role is indispensable. Without an active reader a trope is inert. It remains a lifeless combinatory presence waiting for someone to animate it, to give it form, to make it sing. The frequent indeterminacy of texts suggests that the reader must step in to give plausible explanations for redundancies, gaps, and contradictions. Textual aporia—the gaps—usually means that something has been repressed. Whenever this happens the magnetic field of this black hole in the body of the text needs to be explored and its energy brought into play.

In "The Magnetism Between the Reader and Text," Ellie Ragland-Sullivan notes that the aim of Lacanian poetics is not to psychoanalyze a text but to "study the paralinguistic points of join between visible language and invisible effect" (Ragland-Sullivan 1984, 382). This invisible effect has its origin in the "mirror stage" and Oedipus complex when the subject's fragmented self is unified in the specular image of its m(Other). The subject gains access to language during that moment of misrecognition (*méconnaissance*) when the boy or girl is, in effect, being constituted by language. They subsist, says Mellard, in a system of differences, that is, in the gap between the signifier and the signified (Mellard 1991, 16–17). The subject, like language, is defined by difference, and it is this affinity between fictional aporia and the gaps in the structure of the self that no doubt explains in part the magnetism between the reader and the text.

The reader's unconscious responds to the writer's unconscious, that is, the voice of the Other in both parties. The ego and the id of the writer (the story) is read by the ego and id of the reader (the act of reading). The manifest content of the text is in the reality of its immediate discourse: plot, structure, and character. The invisible thread that links the text's latent content with the reader's desire to know is the force that binds the two in a symbiotic relationship. The text has found an audience, and the reader's unconscious is listening to the voice of the Other that is embedded in the text.

Tropes and traces are the flesh and blood of this figurative body. The reader must work through the different levels of the written and unwritten text (Freud's *durcharbeiten*) in order to weave a network of associations. The warp and woof of this weave are metaphor and metonymy; and metonymy, says Lacan, is "the one side of the effective field constituted by the signifier" ("le premier versant du champ effectif que le significant constitue"—Lacan 1977a, 156, 264). His example is the substitution of "thirty sails" for "thirty ships." In rhetoric, however, the substitution of one part for the whole defines synecdoche, that is, one of the signified is also a semantic feature of the other signified. A sail is part of a ship, and this is its semantic feature, whereas in the example "he assaulted her vengeance in hand," the word "vengeance," in association with the word "assault," describes the man's intention, but the signifier obscures the weapon. Was it a knife, a stick, or something else? We don't know, because the word "vengeance" may be substituted for any one of these hypothetical weapons without being a semantic feature of any of them. The substitution, in this example, is a whole—one signifier for another in its entirety—and not for any of its parts. Lacan, however, makes no distinction between metonymy and synecdoche, but he does distinguish between metonymy and metaphor, metaphor being the other side (*versant*) of the effective field.

Metaphor and metonymy occupy an intermediary zone between the plot of the macrotext and parts of the microtext. As tropes they inscribe their mnemonic traces on the reader's mind, and it is these tracings embedded in the text and in the reader that invite re-readings so that a polyphony can heard, "for it to become clear that all discourse is aligned along the several staves of a score" ("pour que s'y fasse entendre une polyphonie et que tout discours s'avère s'aligner sur les plusieurs portées d'une partition" (Lacan 1977b, 154; Lacan 1966b, 260–61). Lacan's musical analogy is an apt one because tropic traces coexist in the reader's mind, and it is their simultaneity that allows the reader to move back and forth along a horizontal axis. The scoring of a text resonates with the connotations and contexts that Lacan says are suspended vertically (Lacan 1977b; Lacan 1966b, 261), but I would say also horizontally, because it is the simultaneity of these horizontal units that gives the text its musical presence and vertical reality. All this is analogous to a pianist striking chords with both hands so that the vibrations of every note will be heard in unison.

Between 1950 and 1970 psychoanalytic critics were analyzing the characters in novels and plays because these personae were seen as projections of the author's psyche. Over the years, however, psychoanalytic criticism has shifted its emphasis from psychoanalyzing the author, as Marie Bonaparte did in 1933, in *The Life and Works of Edgar Allan Poe: A Psychoanalytic Interpretation*, to privileging the text. But in moving from author to the text, Freudian theory has never been comfortable with the textual limitations of the New Criticism of the 1930s and 1940s and, when Ernest Jones's study of *Hamlet* was published in *Hamlet and Oedipus*, it transgressed the confines of intrinsic or internal information to include extrinsic or external references to the Oedipus complex. Fortunately, criticism today is no longer trapped within the prison of the intrinsic text. This means that extrinsic knowledge is now viewed as indispensable material for the elucidation of a text. Today it is possible, indeed essential, for psychoanalytic criticism to apply the same kind of distortion, condensation, and displacement to texts that Freud described in 1900 in his *Interpretation of Dreams* (Freud 1953b, 277–338). Although formalist criticism has its place, it is more interesting when linked with other fields and theoretical considerations, be they anthropological, historical, Marxist, mythic, or psychoanalytic. According to MacCannell, Lacan's appeal to readers of literature derives from his emphasis on the cultural context of the inter-human situation (MacCannell 1986, 39).

Today, the influence of the cultural dimension on literary criticism is omnipresent. We have Ferdinand de Saussure and Roman Jakobson in linguistics, Lévi-Strauss in anthropology, Foucault in cultural history, Derrida in philosophy and deconstruction, Roland Barthes with his eclectic socioliterary criticism, and Lacan in psychoanalysis. There are many other luminaries transgressing boundaries in order to include information from other disciplines. We are in fact in the midst of an interdisciplinary explosion, and this dissemination of information is a fertile one for the practice of literary criticism.

Because readers bring different sensibilities and varying degrees of knowledge to their reading, the emphasis since about 1970 has shifted from the text to the reader's response to it. Marcel Duchamp once said that there is no masterpiece without an audience. Although we can argue that within the interpretive community there are masterpieces by consensus, they still need someone to activate them. Consequently psychoanalytic critics such as Norman Holland began to look at the way a work generates wishes and fantasies in the reader's mind. Whereas the act of reading actualizes a work's fictive referents, the act of interpretation completes the process. Only then do the world of fiction—and art generally—and that of the reader coalesce. It is important to understand, using Roman Ingarden's term, how this *concretization* takes place (see Ingarden 1973). Shoshana Felman, Barbara Johnson, and others have shown in different ways that although a critic may analyze a text, a text can also "read" the reader. Although we don't always know why a work will touch us so profoundly, Mellard believes that this "power of affect is the one that comes from the unconscious, whether it lies in us or in the texts that seem to bring it up or from which we bring it up" (Mellard 1991, 55). According to Peter Brooks it is *transference* that allows the reader to activate a text. A transferential model, says Brooks, "allows us to take as the object of analysis not author or reader, but *reading,* including, of course, the transferential-interpretive operations that belong to reading" (Brooks 1987, 345).[1] Meaning, he says, comes not only from the text, nor is it the exclusive fabrication of the reader, but from "the dialogic struggle and collaboration of the two" (Brooks 1987, 345). This struggle activates textual possibilities during the process of reading. Holland, however, is more concerned with the reader than with the text. In an essay entitled "The 'Unconscious' of Literature" he does not analyze Robert Frost, the man, but his poem "Mending Wall," because the poem, whatever Frost's intentions may have been, may be read as an appeal to the psychology of readers and the latent wishes or fantasies of their unconscious (Holland 1970, 131–54). Despite degrees of interpretive difference among critics, the approach they share is an insistence on the active role of the reader. I too, following in the footsteps of Cowan's earlier study of *D.H. Lawrence and the Trembling Balance,* will use this strategy in order to concretize meaning from the texts I will be analyzing. We need to remember that narration figures plot, character, and action, whereas hearing the voice of the Other figures the unconscious.

The short stories that Lawrence wrote at the end of his life are not only fabulations; together they are more than the sum of each story, or, as in this study, an assemblage of my previously published essays. They become a recipe for survival in a dysfunctional age. Like Edgar Allan Poe's "Purloined Letter," and Lacan's admiration for the craft and implied meaning of the story, Lawrence's missive is also hidden in plain view. All the reader has to do is read it and listen to the urgency of the message.

CHAPTER SYNOPSES

Chapter 1. "Sun:" Writing the Iceberg with Lawrence and Hemingway

This chapter compares Lawrence's expansive and more inclusive fabulistic writing with Hemingway's "iceberg theory," Camus's "degree zero," and Roland Barthes "body writing." It shows why Juliet, the heroine of the short story "Sun," goes to Italy, and how she recovers from her illness. It analyzes the sun as a metaphor and signifier—a phallic power that restores her health. Lawrence describes Juliet as a lotus flower and the sun as a lover who ignites her repressed eroticism. It awakens her blood-consciousness by putting her in touch with earlier civilizations—Etruscan and Phoenician—and their sense of cosmic oneness that modern humans have lost.

Keywords: Fabulistic writing - iceberg theory - writing degree zero - the sun - the body erotic - blood-consciousness - cosmic sanity – recovery

Chapter 2. *The Woman Who Rode Away*: Madness and Cosmic Sanity

In his essays and his fiction Lawrence dramatizes the plight of modern men and women enmeshed in cultural forces that have deadened their sensibilities. They are alienated from themselves, from others, from nature, and from the cosmos. Lawrence rails against the dehumanizing legacy of reified greed that has cost men and women their sense of selfhood. To counter these destructive forces he asks us to create ourselves anew by reshaping the modern world, and by opposing its madness. More specifically, his estranged heroines (Juliet, in the story, "Sun," and "the woman who rode away," in the novella so entitled) discover the healing power of the sun, cosmic realignment, and the unconscious. Their unconscious selves are touched by the sun, and for the woman who rode away, also by the moon, and this contact imbues them with a sense of renewal. In his art Lawrence works with metaphors that allow his characters to eschew *Mind* by returning to a more primitive, pre-intellectual human condition. Accordingly, he advocates an intuitive relationship of the self with the world, a reorientation designed to alter the nightmare of an insane, industrialized society governed by the abstractions of *Mind* and technology. He believes that when the dark sun of each individual's inner self (the *It*) encounters the radiance of the cosmic sun (the *I*)—with phallic love as the mediator—then the world will be reborn. The fragmented self will have been healed and its sanity restored. Lacan's dictum: *"Wo Es war, soll Ich verden* (Where It was, there I must be") also identifies a new consciousness formed by the melding of *It* and *I*. Such is the regenerative power of Lawrence's tropic suns.

Keywords: Alienation - mind - madness - sun - phallic consciousness - cosmic consciousness - immolation

Chapter 3. "None of That": Lawrence and Hemingway at the Bullfights with Ethel and Brett

In the aftermath of World War I both Ernest Hemingway and D.H. Lawrence use the bullfight as a background against which to highlight the love-lives of two liberated women: Brett Ashley in *The Sun Also Rises,* and Ethel Cane in "None of That." Both women fall in love with bullfighters—Pedro

Romero for Brett and Cuesta for Ethel. Brett has had many lovers and makes no attempt to repress her sexuality, while Ethel strives to repress her sexual desires with her mind, and dies trying. Hemingway's visual style, his iceberg technique, displays "more than meets the eye" even as Lawrence probes the depths of psychological realism beneath the surface.

Keywords: Gender - machismo - mind - love - bullfighting - art - psychology

Chapter 4. "The Rocking-Horse Winner": Pleasing the Mother

This chapter provides in-depth Lacanian, Freudian, Saussurian, and Derridian analyses of a boy's obsessive need to please his mother. In doing so, he is undone by his mother's mendacity and social climbing—the *doxal* patterns that govern her life. Roland Barthes defines *doxology* as a manner of speaking that adapts to appearances and public opinion. *Doxa,* he says, encourages inert repetition. Indeed "The Rocking-Horse Winner" foregrounds the tragic consequences of a repetition-compulsion that kills; riding his hobbyhorse frenetically enables the boy to predict the next winner at the races. Although he succeeds in his predictions, and wins, he loses his life. My exegesis frames this story within Freud's "Jokes and Their Relation to the Unconscious" and Lacan's essay "The agency of the letter within the unconscious or reason since Freud." These two texts explain linguistic and metaphorical slippages in relation to jokes and the unconscious. I analyze this semantic "free play" of language and the paronomasia of words such as "luck" and "lucre"; also the meaning of the Lacanian terms "jouissance," "signifiance," and "symbolic lesions."

Keywords: Rocking - mendacity - desire - language - luck/lucre - the unconscious - the pleasure principle - death instinct - paronomasia - "jouissance"—"signifiance"

Chapter 5. "The Man Who Loved Islands": A Return to the Womb

Cathcart, the man who loved islands, moves from one island to another, three islands in all, each one smaller than the previous one. The third one is a rocky outcropping in the North Sea where he dies entombed in the snow. His misanthropy prompts him to flee toward the smallest island where he banishes all living contact—human and animal—as he strives to erase the signs of language, including the nameplate on the stove. On the first island he discards money, on the second one he says farewell to love, and on the third one, he abandons life itself. He longs for the oneness of an egg, and is entombed in the cocoon-whiteness of snow. The theme, structure, and language of this story replicate psychoanalytic concepts of Lacan's Other, castration, desire, and aphanasis or the loss of sexual desire. Aspects of Saussurian linguistics and Freudian theory (the touchstones of Lacan's thought) are embedded in the title: To love "I-lands" is to dwell within the split self, a division that mimes the splitting (*Spaltung*) during Lacan's so-called "mirror stage" of the infant's development. Lawrence foregrounds not only the islander's fragmented identity but also his progressive misanthropy. Arrested desire repudiates all contact with men, the islander's wife and daughter, even life itself.

Keywords: "I-lands" - arrested desire - misanthropy - death drive - aphanasis - "mirror stage" - the Other

Chapter 6. "Glad Ghosts": The Cure—Cutting Through the Tangle

In "Glad Ghosts" Lawrence moves away from death toward life. This move represents an important progression in his strategy of unveiling the untapped resources of the erotic body. In the beginning, the aristocratic residents of Rathkill are unhappy because they have been immobilized by *doxa*—the rigidity of their social class and the tangle of conformity. Lawrence's tangle is the equivalent of Lacan's knot; and no cure of the Lathkills will be possible until the knot of their repressed selves is severed. At the end of the story, the ghost visiting Morier in the middle of the night is the voice of his unconscious. It is an annunciation that adumbrates the reconciliation of the *It* and the *I*—a reconciliation that both Lawrence and Lacan dream of; and Morier's erotic dream of the ghost's visitation, with her silkiness of touch and her scent of plum blossom, helps him cut through the hysterical tangle that has deadened his friends. Furthermore, Lawrence's rhetorical poetics infuses the narrative with intentional oxymorons—conscious signifiers connoting unconscious signifieds: The Riddings estate represents "the obscene triumph of dead mater"; Carlotta's breasts lift "on a heaving sea of rest." Morier becomes a narrator-analyst who engages the Lathkils and the Hales—the analysands— in "the talking cure" that will free them from their hysterical symptoms. The ghost is the messenger of rebirth, and Morier, the savior, announces the good news to his friends. In narrating "Glad Ghosts" Lawrence melds literature and psychoanalysis, story and theory, *it* and *I*.

Keywords: ghost - tangle/knot - repressed eroticism - *doxa* - narrative unconscious - fabulation - social unconscious - intentional oxymorons - reconciliation of *it* and *I* – annunciation

Chapter 7. *The Escaped Cock:* Salvation

The Escaped Cock is Lawrence's fictional treatment of Jesus's life after his "resurrection." He describes a Christ repudiating the Law of the Father. It is a story of repressed sexuality (symbolic death) and repressed desire that reenacts the tenets of Lacanian theory. At the height of his newfound sexual identity, as the man-Christ "rises" to the Father in the temple of Isis, Lawrence gives us a formulaic image of a mythical union worthy of the Oedipus Complex. The difference, however, is that instead of castration, the son recovers his manhood, possesses the mother symbolically, and ascends toward the sun that is illumining his ego with the "dark rays" of the id. Christ recovers from impotence and is redeemed. His erection is his resurrection. This story becomes a free-floating construct in which denotation, connotation, metaphor, metonymy, synecdoche, homonymy, aporia, puns, indeed every combination possible, contribute(s) to the artistic space that defines the work. Lawrence's novella provides the answer to Lacan's question: "What does the unconscious want for me?" The answer being that it wants me to live.

Keywords: Cock - the Law of the Father - castration - the sun - touch - love - Isis/Osiris - anthropomorphism - *it/I* union - metaphorical slippage – redemption

Chapter One

"Sun"

Writing the Iceberg with
Lawrence and Hemingway

Ernest Hemingway originated the "iceberg" method of writing, and Albert Camus wrote his novel, *L'Étranger,* using Hemingway's technique. As for D.H. Lawrence, he is perhaps the last writer we would ordinarily associate with Hemingway's stylistic economy and Camus's unembellished writing. Lawrence's penchants for repetition and description, as well as "doctrinal" viewpoints, seem to distance him considerably from this terse way of writing, but as a master of the short story, Lawrence had his own version of an "iceberg" technique and its devices of brevity. As Camus was to do, Lawrence often expressed his ideology or "psychoanalytics" in philosophical essays, leaving some of his stories relatively unencumbered with "dogma" while still conveying the sense of it subliminally, under the surface—under the tip of the iceberg that is his story. In this connection Lawrence's short story, "Sun," exemplifies his version of the iceberg, and he makes the underlying depths intelligible, as do Hemingway and Camus in their works, even without related essays. Each fiction stands on its own, and the essays are there, should we want to consult them for historical background, or to confirm our intuitive reading of the story. Generally speaking, except for the most informed readers, the essays elucidate depths that might otherwise remain inaccessible. Lawrence, unlike Hemingway, is not a pure iceberg writer.

In a 1945 interview published in *Les Nouvelles littéraires,* Camus wrote that he had adopted Hemingway's style while writing *L'Étranger* because he wanted to describe "a man with no apparent sentience" (Camus 2006c, 658, my translation); and Simone de Beauvoir, in *La force de l'âge*, states that a great many of the rules she and Sartre observed in their own novels were inspired by Hemingway (Beauvoir 1960, 145). Wilfred Sheed goes so far as to say that *L'Étranger* is "the best Hemingway novel [. . .] written by Camus"

(Sheed 1977, 34). In an essay in *The Atlantic Monthly,* and in praise of Hemingway's writing, Sartre noted that psychological analysis, the hallmark of the French style from Madame de LaFayette to Marcel Proust, could no longer mirror the complexities of the new era or the sense of the absurd generated by the events of World War II. For Sartre "the greatest literary development in France between 1929 and 1939 was the discovery of Faulkner, Dos Passos, Hemingway, Caldwell, and Steinbeck" (Sartre 1966, 117).

Hemingway's influence seems to imply that *L'Étranger* was written using the American's iceberg theory of writing—a theory based on descriptive omission and stylistic compression—that allows the reader to see only the tip of the iceberg whereby the remaining seven-eighths of its mass remains submerged. In 1932, in *Death in the Afternoon,* Hemingway wrote that a good writer gives the reader a feeling for the topography below the surface where a character's feelings and state of mind reside: "If a writer of prose knows enough about what he is writing about he may omit things that he knows and the reader, if the writer is writing truly enough, will have a feeling of those things as strongly as though the writer had stated them. The dignity of movement of an iceberg is due to only one-eighth of it being above water" (Hemingway 1932, 192).

Furthermore, in a 1958 interview with George Plimpton for *The Paris Review,* Hemingway said that he always wrote on the principle of the iceberg (Plimpton 1958, 84). In practice, this means that he omitted stream of consciousness and authorial commentary because he believed that "degree zero" writing, when well crafted, would give the reader the true feeling of lived experience.

In *Le Degré zéro de l'écriture* Roland Barthes calls Camus's writing in *L'Étranger, une écriture blanche* (white writing), which he defines as a form of writing that is both innocent and neutral (Barthes 1953, 108–9), and he credits Camus with inventing this new technique, forgetting or perhaps not knowing that Hemingway's iceberg writing predates *L'Étranger* (1942), and that it was Hemingway's style in *The Sun Also Rises* (1926) that influenced Camus. Unlike Hemingway's theory, however, Barthes's degree zero seems more concerned with the dangers of "ideology" than the virtues of a telegraphic style, but his advice that a writer should hold a neutral stance, eliminating extraneous, ideological slants, can be linked to the iceberg because reducing the subject matter to its bare essentials achieves a powerful immediacy with readers. Nonetheless, in *Le Degré zéro de l'écriture,* Barthes realized that style is always individual (issuing from the very body of the author), and we should therefore not be surprised to find that Lawrence sometimes makes choices that would not come from a Hemingway or Camus. Yet all four writers would surely agree that the artist's task is to communicate with the reader in a way that maximizes audience impact. The treatment will no doubt depend on what the writer finds essential. Lawrence, in "Sun," adds more phallic images to his story in the second of two versions because, for him, phallic imagery was essential, not tangential. There is also more authorial commentary in both versions than in *The Sun Also Rises* or *L'Étranger*. The following passage from "Sun," one of many, is illustrative: Juliet's "joy was when he [the sun] rose all molten in his nakedness, and threw off blue-white fire, into the tender heaven" (Lawrence 1995b, 23). Unlike Lawrence neither Hemingway nor Camus tells the reader what a character is thinking or feeling. The iceberg mandates that we infer thoughts and feelings from dialogue or narrative description.

In a 1942 letter to his friend Blanche Balain, Camus wrote that Meursault, early on in *L'Étranger* was at "point 0" because his deeds in the first part of the novel would only become clear to him in the second part (Todd 1966, 309). Camus's point zero became the location of Barthes's "degré zéro," the iceberg. In lieu of inner monologue, Camus, like Hemingway, focuses on recurring images, objective correlatives, and tropes, all of which provide a network of interrelated associations whose presence constitutes the submerged portion—the portion that supports the visible tip. People and events are described but not interpreted and, if the medium exhibits stylistic harmony in all its parts, then the characters' feelings will be felt by the reader and the message understood. The reader provides the meaning that seems to be absent, and it requires different sensibilities and a new way of reading. Claude-Edmonde Magny, in *L'Âge du roman américain*, calls it "the objective technique in the American novel" ("la technique objective dans le roman américain" (Magny 1948, 44). Many commentators refer to it simply as *le style américain* wherein the absence of authorial commentary is replaced by the intensity of unfiltered experiential immediacy. Early on Lawrence recognized this style and, in his review of Hemingway's *In Our Time*—a review published in *The Calendar* in April 1927—he calls the stories in the collection "short, sharp, vivid, and most of them excellent"—"so short, like striking a match, lighting a brief sensational cigarette, and it's over." The feeling is there, in the story, despite the brevity, and Lawrence gets it. Furthermore, these Hemingway fictions exemplify to Lawrence a "fragmentary novel" of someone's life: "we need know no more" (Lawrence 2005a, 311–12).

Should we want to know more, in Camus's case, his philosophical essay, *Le Mythe de Sisyphe,* infuses *L'Étranger* with all of Meursault's omitted sentience. He acts out his feelings but never describes them. The novel is the tip of the iceberg whereas the essay probes the depths of *the absurd* below its surface thereby contributing to our understanding of Meursault's state of mind. In *Le Mythe* Camus distinguishes between the notion of the absurd and the feeling of the absurd, and he says that the feeling is not the idea. Apropos, in his essay on *L'Étranger,* entitled "Camus's *The Outsider,*" Sartre says that *The Myth of Sisyphus* gives us the idea of the absurd, whereas the novel gives us its true feeling (Sartre 1957, 32). Accordingly, the philosophical *ideas* that Camus develops in *The Myth of Sisyphus* correspond to Meursault's *feelings* of the absurd as he experiences them in *L'Étranger*: "Getting up, tram, four hours of work, meal, sleep, and Monday, Tuesday, Wednesday, Thursday, Friday, Saturday, in the same routine" (qtd. in Sartre 1957, 26). This is Meursault's daily life and it constitutes one small portion of the visible one-eighth of the iceberg. The repressed and invisible aspect of the absurd is Meursault's love affair with the world, his rebellion against finitude (his quarrel with mortality), and his sense of exile: "This divorce between man and his life, the actor and his surroundings, constitutes the feeling of the absurd" (Camus 2006a, 223, my translation). The novel is the tip of the iceberg and Camus's essay on the absurd contributes to its submerged mass. Although there is a difference between the unstated feelings of Meursault in *L'Étranger* and knowledge gleaned from Camus's discursive writings, the two shade into each other, and the richness of the reading will depend on the knowledge each reader brings to the experience. In similar fashion, Hemingway's iceberg, as he presents it in *Death in the Afternoon,* alerts the reader to the network of stylistic connections that support the visible tip of his fiction.[1] In "Hemingway's Iceberg Theory," Toshihiro Maekawa says that both parts of the iceberg need to be present simultaneously. Singling out "Big Two-Hearted River" as the most successful example of such simultaneity, Maekawa notes that the story never mentions the war yet succeeds in communicating the stress and anxiety Nick Adams feels while fishing (Maekawa 2001). Although invisible and submerged, his state of mind is objectified in the descriptions of the river, the trout, and the marsh. Scene and sensory detail manage to communicate Nick's distress. Hemingway's brilliant use of rhetorical devices crafts the visible tip of the iceberg even as the invisible portion (Nick's war trauma) is implied. Another example of stylistic compression and omission is the short story, "Hills Like White Elephants," in which the word *abortion* is not mentioned, even as it floats beneath the narrative surface, constituting the underlying and indeed central theme of the story.[2]

As for Lawrence, perhaps his best example of iceberg writing is the story, "Sun," which, like "Big Two-Hearted River," achieves a "world view" despite the short story form. The metonymy in the titles, in itself, is instructive. Hemingway sketches the river of life and death—the visible counterpart to Nick's trauma. Similarly, Lawrence's title stands for all the life enabled by the sun, as opposed to the deathliness of sunlessness. Each story presents life and death stakes as both protagonists need to deal with the threatening dilemmas arising from their past sufferings, Nick in the war, and Juliet in the illness occasioned by her troubled marriage and its city milieu. Both characters go to nature for help and healing. They need not "think out" all their problems for the reader, but the reader senses their grappling with them by various signs of change. Both stories (though neither is exceptionally short) are notable for the symbolism that allows so much to be conveyed despite the limits of the genre.

"Sun" is thus the *visible* tip of a narrative that is buoyed up by *invisible* ideas—ideas that Lawrence expresses in *Apocalypse, Sketches of Etruscan Places, Reflections on the Death of a Porcupine*, and other texts. They provide information that enriches the story. His essays are for "Sun" what *The Myth of Sisyphus* is for *L'Étranger,* again with the proviso that a story, when well crafted, can be read and felt independently of the essays. Of course, the works of any writer usually resemble each other in a kind of family likeness and therefore resonate with each other to some extent. In Lawrence's case, however, the relation of fiction to non-fiction is especially striking because of the general consistency and intensity of philosophy that underlies many of the pieces. He was aware of these interconnections, which he discusses in his 1921 "psychology" book, *Fantasia of the Unconscious.* Lawrence states that his "pseudo-philosophy," as he calls it, "is deduced from the novels and poems, not the reverse":

> The novels and poems come unwatched out of one's pen. And then the absolute need which one has for some sort of satisfactory mental attitude towards oneself and things in general makes one try to abstract some definite conclusions from one's experiences as a writer and as a man. The novels and poems are pure passionate experience. These 'pollyanalytics' are inferences made afterwards, from the experience. (Lawrence 2004, 65)

Even so, which comes first—the philosophy or the fiction itself—need not concern us here. The possible cross-references go in both directions with "Sun."

"Sun" is the ideal story for a study of the relationship between the two kinds of writing because it encapsulates, in a short space and a simple fable-like tale, more of the high points of Lawrence's thinking about the cosmos than most of his other short stories. Through synecdoche it sketches in a microcosm of the universe according to Lawrence, complete with the heavens (sun) and underearth (where a snake dwells) as well as an earthly refuge (primarily, under Juliet's cypress tree, standing like a "guardian," Lawrence 1995b, 21). Almost all the characters are essential, even rather symbolic. Lawrence speaks in non-fiction of the sun as vital, and it is actually the main character in "Sun," as the lover and healer of Juliet.[3] She originally exemplifies the human damage that the urban, mechanized modern world causes to people; and her businessman husband Maurice is an even more discouraging representative of that valueless world. In non-fiction, Lawrence is concerned about the future human race in the face of the deadening circumstances that threaten it. The story's child (and the future child) therefore are not incidental to the author's purpose but have particular significance in the scheme. Since the son is initially much like the father, the human future looks bleak until the boy is rescued by the sun, as was his mother. It is important, too, that the setting is Italy (Sicily) with its lingering aspects of ancient cultures.[4] Lawrence's entire belief in accepting the cosmos as the "ancients" did underlies the story, as does his belief in the importance of sexuality in tune with the elements (the penetrating sun) and the possibility of sensual fulfillment. In this story it is especially easy to sense how much of the "iceberg" of Lawrence's meaning is implied—how much is revealed by recurrent images or tropes, atmosphere, gesture, symbolism, and metonymy. It is precisely these techniques that ally this particular Lawrence story with the "iceberg" method of writers like Hemingway and Camus. All of them allow the reader to feel the circumstances and choices of their protagonists in ways that break through the surface presentation to deeper issues beneath. This story happens to be a particular repository of Lawrence's most cherished topics.

Those who know Lawrence's other writings may speculate further—they may wonder, for instance, if the "ancient" knowledge Juliet gains may be that of the Etruscans, whom Lawrence describes as the vital early inhabitants of Italy, or of the Chaldeans, whose vision he praises. He also refers to the setting as part of "the old Greek world" (Lawrence 1995b, 32) since Magna Graecia entered early into Etruscan regions. Juliet's servant is a woman of Magna Graecia, who has "far memories" (Lawrence 1995b, 24), and Juliet herself begins to think of a Greek saying about those who lack the sun. But at least as early as 1919 or 1920 Lawrence considered Italy essentially Etruscan, and he was still working on his *Sketches of Etruscan Places* just months before turning to his second version of "Sun." "Italy today is far more Etruscan in its pulse, than Roman: and will always be so," states Lawrence in *Sketches* (Lawrence 1992, 36). Moreover, the cypress tree, associated with death memorials and rebirth, is one of his special shorthand images for the surviving Etruscan spirit in Italy. In the poem "Cypresses" (Lawrence 2013, 249–51) the ancestral voices of Etruscans linger in these trees, and Aaron Sisson hears Italian cypresses "communicating" from "old races, old language, old human ways of feeling and knowing" (Lawrence 1988a, 265). Now Juliet's transformation occurs primarily under the "guardian" cypress tree. In *Sketches* Lawrence infers what the Etruscans were like from the frescoes they left behind on the walls of their tombs. He admires their vitality, their openness, and their "desire to preserve the natural humour of life" (Lawrence 1992, 32–33). In "Lawrence's Ontological Vision in *Etruscan Places*, *The Escaped Cock*, and *Apocalypse*," Jack Stewart says that the Etruscans cultivated the fluid, ever-changing rhythms of the senses, as opposed to the rigid, mechanistic rhythms of Rome (Stewart 2003, 44); and Donald Gutierrez, in "DHL's Golden Age," says "Etruscan society [. . .] symbolized a deeply realizable potential of enhanced being" (Gutierrez 1976, 406). But the story "Sun" itself is mute on such details—and does not need them—while still conveying the life values Lawrence assigns to ancient Mediterranean peoples.

By happy coincidence, the sun illuminates the point of contact between the visible and the invisible in the works of all three authors. In *The Sun Also Rises* it shines on the fragmented lives of characters damaged by World War I, the people Gertrude Stein referred to as "the lost generation." In *L'Étranger,* Meursault blames the sun for his unmotivated killing of the Arab. Camus's network of tropes allows the reader to feel Meursault's distress on the beach, at two in the afternoon, when the sky splits open and the sun rains down fire (Camus 1988, 59). He feels under attack, the pistol trigger gives, and a man dies. The murder can be attributed to the blinding light of the sun, to Meursault's alienation from society, and to his quarrel with mortality. During the trial, however, the presiding judge sees only the surface—a murder and Meursault's indifference to cultural codes; and he condemns him to death in the name of the French people. *L'Étranger* is an ironic novel, and the reader's indignation is aroused by the magistrate's arrogance and the court's incompetence. Irony also plays a part in *The Sun Also Rises* as Jake Barnes and Bill Gorton toss the notion of irony and pity back and forth even as the lost generation seeks satisfactions in booze, bullfighting, and sex. The critique of a consumer society by the two friends is epitomized in the statement: "Road to hell paved with unbought stuffed dogs" (Hemingway 1926, 73). Also, Jake's physical impotence (he was wounded in the war) corresponds to the psychological wounds of the other expats; and the word "impotence," like the word "abortion" in "Hills like White Elephants," is never mentioned; it too floats below the narrative surface of the novel. "Sun" has its own irony and it too can be read in light of the iceberg theory, although Lawrence's authorial intrusions describing Juliet's feelings and attitudes make his short story a less consistent example.

Both versions of "Sun" have their admirers, although the first one (with Julie as the heroine), because it is shorter, seems closer to the iceberg technique than the later revised version (with Juliet as the heroine).[5] Yet the longer one, which is my primary text here, is only partly consonant with Lawrence's impulse to expand, for it is interesting to note that the most striking additions are not really discursive passages but are created to convey a silent "body language" of the phallus (not mentioned in the first version) and of the more responsive womb. Lawrence, as in Barthes's description of a writer in *Degree Zero*, is someone who writes from and with the body. Nevertheless, instead of subtracting, Lawrence amplifies, and the later version of "Sun" moves slightly toward the greater complexity of his novels. Furthermore, he made substantial revisions during the *Lady Chatterley* period, and the two works have similar themes: initially, both Juliet and Connie are in deadly health crises from debilitating marriages and both come back "to life" in natural environments with new sexual vitality—except that Juliet, ironically, does not launch a new love life, as Connie does. Maurice is to return to New York, Juliet to stay in Sicily, and the new child will be her husband's, not that of a neighboring Italian worker. The social entanglements and real-world problems, like those of the novel, with its more numerous characters and sub-plotting, are generally avoided (though hinted at) in the story, although Lawrence's authorial intrusions make his short story stylistically different.

Despite Juliet's final compromise, early on in the story she finds the sun and the cosmic consciousness of the ancients. "Start with the sun," says Lawrence, "and the rest will slowly, slowly happen" (Lawrence 1979, 149). Juliet also manages to distance herself from the mercantile mentality of a grey, sunless husband, thereby shielding herself from the "madness" of the modern world in which he does business. The remedy for the deadness afflicting mankind, and Juliet in particular, according to Lawrence, is to rekindle the sensual awareness of the cosmos and the sense-knowledge of the ancients. Modern man, he says, is going mad because he is no longer "in touch," and this lack of meaningful contact is the real cause of Juliet's illness. She consults doctors, and they prescribe the sun—though of course they could not surely foresee the expansive way in which it does turn out to be the cure for her malaise. As Lawrence puts it in *Apocalypse*, "What we want is to destroy our false, inorganic connections, especially those related to money, and re-establish the living organic connections, with the cosmos, the sun and earth, with mankind and nation and family" (Lawrence 1979, 149).

In *Apocalypse* Lawrence also tells us that the ancients had an intuitive knowledge of the world grounded in instinct, not in reason; and this "blood-sense" was based on images, not words. The ancients' connection with the cosmos was emotional and intuitive, not logical, whereas modern man, says Lawrence, no longer feels the cosmos because he has stripped himself of imaginative examples that connect him to it—a paucity leading to the deadness and insanity already mentioned, and, eventually, to self-destruction. For ancient people such as the Chaldeans, Etruscans, and Mithraists life was full of mystery (Lawrence 1979, 130), and it was alive with cosmic power, a power that Lawrence equates with the phallus, blood-sense, love, and potency (Lawrence 1979, 171). In *The Escaped Cock* a man who resembles Jesus survives the crucifixion, rises from his tomb, discovers the phallus, repudiates his former life of sexual abnegation, and goes forth into the world with a sense of cosmic power: "A new sun was coming up in him, in the perfect

inner darkness of himself. [. . .] 'Now I am not myself. I am something new'"
(Lawrence 2005b, 150). In discovering the sun he realizes the divine in the
sexual union between himself and the priestess of Isis. For Lawrence, this
power of love or empathy is the Holy Ghost as a symbol of redemption. (See,
for example, "On Being Religious" 191; "The Crown" 300; "Reflections on
the Death of a Porcupine" [359, all in Lawrence 1988b.]) Lawrence's idiosyncratic vocabulary and imagery are designed to get us back into the cosmic
groove, to move us emotionally toward the sensibilities and vitality of the
ancients. As for Jake Barnes, even if "the sun also rises," he could never
recover his potency because he is maimed physically, not psychologically.
Meursault, however, although indifferent to society's conventions—manifest
in the burial of his mother or the weekend sporting rites of the residents of
Algiers—is in tune with the cosmos. He loves swimming in the sea, basking
in the sun, and making love to Marie. He loves nature and he refuses a job
promotion to Paris because the city is gray, ugly, and has too many pigeons.
The killing of the Arab (four pistol shots), however, slams the door shut on
all the physical pleasures in life that he loves. Indeed, he understands immediately the tragic implications of the act: "it was like knocking four quick
times on the door of unhappiness" (Camus 1988, 59). Meursault's sentience
shifts instantly from degree zero writing to the introspection that characterizes the second part of the novel. Despite the trial and courtroom theatrics, he
thinks about the meaning of freedom, incarceration, life, and death. Unlike
Camus, Hemingway never goes below the narrative surface, while Lawrence
moves back and forth between the tip and the submerged meanings without,
however, elucidating important segments of the seven-eighths that the essays
talk about.

Today, says Lawrence in his non-fiction, our culture views
machine-technology as the necessary destiny of mankind. Men and women
now seem to believe that the "supreme Mind" (Lawrence's term) can conquer
the cosmos and, if that is true, Lawrence is not sanguine about the future of
mankind (Lawrence 1979, 182). According to him, the only antidote to exces-
sive and unbridled *Mind* is love, the erotic experience that repairs the damage
done by abstract thought. Because the danger is immanent, he would have us
restore our lost sense of wonder—a religious wonder of sense-impressions
unconstrained by *Mind.* Mankind is unhappy—indeed, mankind is dead—
and unless men and women regain their senses and reject the madness of
money-greed and machine-technology, the world is doomed (Lawrence 1979,
199). People today, says Lawrence, have stripped themselves of emotional
and imaginative reactions and feel nothing. God may be dead, if Nietzsche
is right, but so also is mankind. Oedipus, in his day, at least had the riddle of
the Sphinx, whereas today we have only "the riddle of the dead-alive man"
(Lawrence 1979, 92). The death of mankind is immanent, says Lawrence,

because mankind has lost contact with the true meaning of the sun, which, in rational, purely scientific terms, is no more than an orb of burning gas. Ancient man, however, viewed the sun as a blazing reality, and the Chaldeans drew forth strength and splendor from it, and felt honored by the cosmos and gave back to it both homage and thanks (Lawrence 1979, 76). We, however, have lost our sense of wonder because we have been using our minds to dissect nature, and we have reduced it to formulae: physics and mathematics. We view the cosmos as an entity to be conquered, forgetting that it is "a vast body" and that "we and the cosmos are one" (Lawrence 1979, 77). We worship *Mind* without the *Blood* (Lawrence's two antithetic metaphors), and we are therefore permanently out of touch, even with ourselves, not to mention each other. Real consciousness (blood-consciousness) is in touch, not reason; and by wanting to dominate the cosmos with *Mind*, we have alienated the sun (Lawrence 1979, 199–200). Science and machine-worship have turned people against the cosmos and, since the Industrial Revolution—and I would add the technological revolution—they have been the source of man's undoing. Men and women have lost the cosmos, and they need to get back to it, but they can do so only by "*going forth* to worship the sun, a worship that is felt in the blood" (Lawrence 1979, 77–78). In "Sun," Juliet's body and mind feel the erotic power of the sun, she experiences it in her blood, and this is what saves her. She is restored. Similarly, in *The Escaped Cock*, the Priestess of Isis is resplendent because "suns beyond suns had dipped her in mysterious fire," and when, after the crucifixion, she soothes Jesus's wounds, and the risen Christ touches her, it is like touching the sun because her desire for him is like sunshine (Lawrence 2005b, 155). Aroused by her presence, and now truly risen, he discovers phallic consciousness. His erection is his resurrection.[6]

The submerged portion of the iceberg in "Sun" is alive with such ideas and they constitute the invisible mass of Juliet's consciousness. She is ill because she is dead-alive, and while Maurice is good at making money, that is not what she needs or wants. She is unhappy because, among other things, she perceives a "white core of fear" in the clothed body of her husband (Lawrence 1995b, 25). She herself has been "spectral and vengeful," and her marriage has settled into a climate of hostility (Lawrence 1995b, 35). Juliet must discover her "naked sun self," shed her modern, nervous and personal consciousness, and experience the "blazing interchange" of communion with the world. In due course she rediscovers her body, and her womb opens to the sun like a lotus flower, the sun penetrates and *knows* her in the carnal sense of the word, and she is now "in the spell of a power beyond herself" (Lawrence 1995b, 23–32). This is where Lawrence fully anthropomorphizes the sun and describes "him" as full and naked, and Juliet's symbolic intercourse with the sun imbues her with "his" phallic power. It is in order to communicate this heightened awareness that Lawrence, in the second version, adds the phallic images mentioned earlier.

Although Lawrence's essays enhance our understanding of issues that are touched upon in the story, it is important to note that he surrounds Juliet with a host of living things, thus allowing us to infer cosmic allusions from the story itself. He also gets great mileage out of pitting illness (or near-death) against life and forcing his characters to choose the way of life or death. Juliet chooses life, and when she is likened to a white gourd ripening, or her womb to a burgeoning lotus flower, we are reminded of organic life functions and the suggested correspondence between human and non-human, both earthly and cosmic. On the earthly level a Sicilian peasant surprises her sunbathing naked and, as they look into each other's eyes and the man's phallus rises under his clothing, the fire flows between them "like the blue streaming fire from the heart of the sun" (Lawrence 1995b, 29). At last, Juliet feels in touch not only with herself and the cosmos but also with a man. The phallic circle is now complete and, in Lawrence's mind, Juliet's awakening could be a necessary prelude to the rejuvenation of humanity. Having discovered her sexual self, Juliet can lead a new life basking in the "fourth dimension," and her enlightened state of consciousness, like that of "the man who died," is raised to another level which some call "heaven" (as in Lawrence 1988b, 358). (On this "fourth dimension," see also, e.g., "Him with His Tail in His Mouth," in Lawrence 1988b, 313–14.)[7] Although her husband has the "eyes of a creature that has been caught young, and reared entirely in captivity" (Lawrence 1995b, 36), Juliet will, nonetheless, bear his child, not the peasant's. The fact that the future child will be Maurice's has prompted some readers to say that for all the sun's efforts, Juliet unites again with her hopeless husband, thereby gaining only a few ironic concessions while losing the main battle. I would argue, on the contrary, that she gains a significant victory in order to remain in Italy where she is happy. While he may return to New York and the life she despises, she is free. Free to do whatever she wants to without him or his mercantile world.

A realistic reading of Juliet's compromise may construe it as an ironic choice on her part, but a "visionary" reading of the story—a reading that the essays themselves encourage—situates Juliet (as we have seen) inside a cosmic curve, in the almost-legendary land of the ancient Etruscans where possibilities may seem less constrictive than elsewhere.[8] Certainly, as Izabel F. O. Brandão points out, the story hints at a possible affair with the Italian peasant (Brandão 2013, 136), but it also affirms hope for the existing child. As soon as Juliet feels like another being, she wants her infant son to absorb the sun and be transformed. They frolic together, naked in the garden, and neither is afraid of the snakes that live there. Of course, Lawrence readers will be reminded that Lawrence the poet calls this creature "one of the lords

/ Of life" in "Snake" (Lawrence 2013, 305) and suggests in "The Hopi Snake Dance" that the snake represents the mysterious life-spirit because it lies in "the dark, lurking, intense sun at the centre of the earth" which is the source of potency (Lawrence 2009, 84). But the story conveys enough by itself to show that humans and non-humans, however different, can share the environment in harmony and that a nature-friendly upbringing can conquer fear. Like Juliet, the child starts to draw strength from the potency of nature and the inner sun inside the self, and this stream of life, like the nutrients from the earth that are absorbed through the tap root of a plant, flows up toward the sun in the sky, and the sun blazes back animating body and soul. The child with "burnt gold hair and red cheeks" is quick like a young animal absorbed in life (Lawrence 1995b, 27). Readers who know *Sketches of Etruscan Places* may even be reminded of Lawrence's descriptions there: "When the Italian of today goes almost naked on the beach, he becomes of a lovely dark ruddy colour. [. . .] And the Etruscans went a good deal naked. The sun painted them with the sacred minium" (Lawrence 1992, 51). Lawrence associates vermilion with royalty, for the ancient kings of Italy, "who were probably Etruscan," painted their faces with it to signify their power and glory (Lawrence 1992, 50). Knowing this, we might guess that the sun-tanned boy has become something like a little red god because he has absorbed the gleaming vitality of the cosmos; and now he too is "shining like the morning, blazing like a god" (Lawrence 1992, 58). In Italy, Juliet and her son find what Lawrence calls the eternal quick of all things. They find pure pleasure in life and in the dance of living.

Lawrence imagines this dance of life to have been present in the Etruscan tombs and their artifacts. Having seen them he envisions a life of the body capable of countering the sterility of the modern, mechanized world. In *Sketches of Etruscan Places* Lawrence finds a "phallic consciousness" to supplement or even supplant the inadequacies of "mental consciousness." He pictures an animated and sensual life expressed in the symbolic phallus ("lingam') and arx (womb) that are represented in the stone entrance to tombs for men and women (Lawrence 2002, 20).

In addition to its Etruscan subtext "Sun" contains strong elements of the fable; and a fable is a short tale that teaches a moral. As a morality tale, the narrative is the tip of the iceberg. The collective unconscious that Lawrence omits, and that he wishes to communicate, lies below the surface. Embedded there are the ideas he writes about in his essays. Nonetheless, even without the essays, "Sun" exemplifies many of Hemingway's iceberg tenets, and the reader feels Juliet's transformation under the erotic rays of the Sicilian sun. Lawrence's descriptions of the earth, the flowers, the lemons, the snake, and the vitality of the cypress tree communicate Juliet's flowering. Lying naked, she feels the sun penetrating her body, her emotions, and her thoughts and, sun-dazed, she feels rich beyond measure; and her warm half-consciousness is like wealth, not her husband's wealth, but a new cosmic well-being, a sense that she is vitally alive and that the whole world belongs to her. In *Reflections on the Death of a Porcupine* Lawrence puts it this way: "No creature is fully itself till it is, like the dandelion, opened in the bloom of pure relationship to the sun, the entire living cosmos" (Lawrence 1988b, 359).

The snake episode demonstrates that non-human creatures in Lawrence's world also have a right to exist and go their own way, and Lawrence's indictment of city norms and modern civilization, even in the brief description of Maurice as sunless and inept, is strongly felt. We also sense this negative potentiality for the child, until he is transformed. Lawrence's use of the word "unsunned" speaks volumes, as does the contrasting haptic language in descriptions of the sun: "Pulsing with marvelous blue, and alive, and streaming white fire from his edges, the sun!" (Lawrence 1988b, 21). Although Lawrence's essays situate his fiction in the context of cosmic consciousness in opposition to mercantile disillusionment, the story itself provides the erotic impact of this consciousness upon Juliet's distress and, although more background information helps, we need know no more in order to appreciate her "resurrection." When we apply both parts of Hemingway's iceberg theory—the tip and the underneath mass—to Lawrence's story, it becomes clear that "Sun" is permeated, buoyed up, and supported by many passages in his non-fiction. It is therefore difficult to agree with Graham Hough's reductive assessment in *The Dark Sun: A Study of D.H. Lawrence* that "Sun" is a dreary tale about an unfulfilled woman who sunbathes all the time (Hough 1956, 188). It is also difficult to agree with Fiona Becket's reductive assessment of "Sun" as "a curious fable about a woman's sexual transformation as she takes the sun for a lover" (Becket 2002, 96).

Juliet's transformation exemplifies the morality Lawrence would have us adopt if we are to resist "the vast cold apparatus of civilization" (Lawrence 1995b, 27)—the mad engine that would have shattered her had she not distanced herself from it (Lawrence 1995b, 19). Hemingway would not have inserted these two statements (and many others like them) into the narrative because they represent authorial intrusion. Lawrence, however, had no such qualms, and "Sun" is therefore not exactly iceberg. Nonetheless, it can be related in some ways to this tradition whenever he refrains from discussing ideas that find intuitive expression as *feeling* in the narrative of Juliet's rebirth. We don't need the essays to feel her joy. What the essays do give us is her relationship to the wider body of reference that supports the visible tip.

Philip Rieff points out that the prophetic intention of Lawrence's art is to re-awaken "the 'half-forgotten' knowledge, buried as emotion in the unconscious" (Rieff 1968, 226). This unconscious resides below the surface of Lawrence's narrative, wherein lies everything he knows and chooses to omit.

As the dark sun of Juliet's inner self meets the radiant Italian sun she experiences the fulfillment of the Lacanian/Freudian dictum: *"Wo Es war, soll Ich werden"* ("Where It was, there I must be"). It and I come together, find the sun at the inner core, and restore the balance of the self (*Écrits* 1977a, 136). Lacan's dictum is akin to Lawrence's "fourth dimension"—the dimension that Juliet experiences—the ultimate stage of psychosomatic integration. T.R. Whitaker phrases it nicely in Freudian terms:

> The ego must descend to meet and accept what seems darkly inferior and destructive but is really its own unconscious life-source—projected upon a man, an animal, a people, or a landscape. If that acceptance occurs, if the marriage with the "other" or the "unconscious" is consummated, the closed and defensive ego may be transcended. A new self may step free, open to the creative flux beyond and within. Then only is true meeting possible. (Whitaker 1961, 221)

Juliet meets the sun and herself in a "cosmorgasmic" dénouement that restores her physical and psychic self.[9] To understand how it happened, we need to read below the surface. To get there we bring the invisible and the visible together, as Juliet did in her *jouissance*, and we feel "the pleasure of the text." I hear, *J'ouis,* says Lacan, punning and *coming* on the words "hear" and *jouissance*—the orgasmic word for pleasure and insight (Barthes 1975b, 319).[10] If I hear the answer to the riddle in the metaphorical discourse of fiction I can also feel the bliss of the consummated unconscious and, like Juliet and the man who died, come to the sun. Roland Barthes asserts that the pleasure of the text, in a context of bliss, searches for a "language lined with flesh, a text where we can hear [. . .] the patina of consonants, the voluptuousness of vowels, a whole carnal stereophony" (Barthes 1975b, 66). Value shifts to "the sumptuous rank of the signifier" (Barthes 1975b, 65); and the signifier for Lawrence is the sun. It generates his voluptuous language, Juliet's orgasmic experience, and the phallic connotations, that is., the signified, embedded below the surface of consciousness. When the sun penetrates Juliet's lotus flower, her *jouissance* slides into the sumptuous enjoyment of the moment. The reader feels all this, even without the essays.

Juliet experiences the dark sun of the unconscious through the blood-sense of the ancients. Contact with it (as Lawrence's essays demonstrate) makes a return to an intuitive, pre-intellectual state possible. Accordingly, the future of the world, he says, must include a vision that breaks through the moneyed wall of industry. To get there, art must prepare the public for the necessary changes to come. In writing *The Plumed Serpent,* the idealist in Lawrence creates characters that turn their backs, as Kate Leslie puts it, "on the world's cog-wheels" (Lawrence 1987b, 109). Juliet embodies that change, and she turns her back on a flawed marriage, on the money-machine, on automatism itself (involuntary actions conditioned by technology and loss of contact with the primal self) and, in doing so, she finds selfhood and the regenerating potential of genital power linked to cosmic oneness and the potential rebirth of the world. A rebirth of the world is necessary if we are to combat the destructive practices endemic in the Anthropocene.

In addition to genital power and cosmic oneness, the following chapter will focus on Lawrence's essays and on *The Woman Who Rode Away,* a novella whose subtext hints at the destructive madness of an industrialized society. The essays, among other things, examine the noxious practices of the money-machine. They are an essential part of Lawrence's philosophical system because they unveil the unseen world of his fiction—the seven-eighths of the iceberg below the surface—the portion that underpins the behavior of his protagonists.

Chapter Two

The Woman Who Rode Away
Madness and Cosmic Sanity

One day in 1925, on D.H. Lawrence's ranch in Taos, New Mexico, a porcupine stuck quills into the snout of a neighbor's dog. Lawrence describes that encounter in *Reflections on the Death of a Porcupine* (Lawrence 1988b, 349–363). Afterwards, despite his efforts to remove the quills from the dog's nose, the dog ran away in pain with some of them still embedded in its chin.

Subsequently Lawrence killed the porcupine and transformed the episode into a universal metaphor symbolizing the vast, sluggish, greedy, lumbering mass of humanity, capitalist and proletariat alike, whose loss of vitality is responsible for cultural dysfunction and death of the soul: "mankind, the porcupine out-pigging the porcupine, can stick quills into the face of the sun" (Lawrence 1988b, 376). The dog's face became the face of the sun and the quills became mankind. During the last five years of Lawrence's life, these two images formed a palimpsest from which he drew fictional narratives and culturally engaged writings. With the sun's illuminating power in mind, I will refocus briefly on "Sun," while examining in detail *The Woman Who Rode Away*—two works that depict the efforts of two women to escape from the porcupine, e.g., the money-machine of an industrialized society. In their quest for identity both women find the sun and the cosmic consciousness of the ancients, even as each narrative dramatizes the dangers of the porcupine—the cause of mankind's alienation from selfhood—and the sanity of the sun—the illuminating warmth that leads toward selfhood. Philip Rieff, in his introduction to *Psychoanalysis and the Unconscious & Fantasia of the Unconscious* (Rieff 1968, xvi), paraphrasing Lawrence, says that in life, "fullness of being" should be every individual's goal. What are Lawrence's arguments and what does he propose?

Lawrence hates the greed of the very rich yet he mistrusts the behavior of the proletariat. He admires Jesus for the "The sermon on the mount" (Matthew, 5: 1–26) and also for His love of mankind but he rejects Christ's teachings concerning the renunciation of the flesh. Lawrence dislikes those elements in Christianity that he believes are repressive and life denying. He views modern Christianity as a paralyzing force because the Church has become the instrument of propaganda and self-congratulation which, according to James C. Cowan in *D.H. Lawrence's American Journey,* instead of coordinating spirit and flesh, the conscious and unconscious into an integrated self, it only satisfies "the chauvinistic requirement for a Sunday pantomime of weekday patriotism and business ethics" (Cowan 1970, 35). In *D.H. Lawrence and the Experience of Italy* Jeffrey Meyers says that Lawrence wanted to lead society back to the values of a pre-Christian and pagan awareness of vital possibilities (Meyers 1982, 150). In this regard, and on a personal level, Lawrence's *The Escaped Cock* is the novella in which the risen Christ discovers phallic love and the life-restoring power of the sun. On the political level Lawrence emphasizes the need for a strong, intelligent, and charismatic leader capable of harnessing the allegiance of the masses, yet he is critical of democracy because he mistrusts the proletariat. Nor does he believe that a state can be run on democratic principles. He thinks people need to be lead; that they should submit to the know-how of a forceful leader. Despite Lawrence's early drift toward fascism and political systems with strong centralized power, in his later writings he criticizes Mussolini's excesses and his aggressive nationalism. In 1927, Lawrence denounced the brute force of Italy's fascists, and he compared them to the Imperial Romans who destroyed the Etruscan civilization that, according to Lawrence, had the sensibilities of the ancients and a true sense of selfhood. As for relationships between men and women, Lawrence believes that women need to submit to the phallic power of men because the symbolic phallus—love—represents the deepest layer of spiritual and physical potency governing the relationship between the sexes and, ultimately, the cosmos.

All of these precepts are developed in great detail in *Reflections on the Death of a Porcupine and Other Essays, Sketches of Etruscan Places,* and *Apocalypse*—the essays Lawrence wrote toward the end of his life, from 1925 to 1930, the year he died.[1] Furthermore, in *The Plumed Serpent* and in *Women in Love* Lawrence advocates a deep blood relationship not only between a man and a woman but also between men. He fictionalizes these ideas in *Aaron's Rod, Kangaroo,* and *Lady Chatterley's Lover*; and they form the background from which and against which he wrote the short story "Sun" and the novella, *The Woman Who Rode Away.* These two fictions explore the alienation from selfhood of two women who distance themselves from the mercantilism of grey, sunless husbands. In doing so, the women also distance themselves from the exploitative madness of the industrialized world in which their husbands do business. Lawrence defines this madness and the remedies for it in the essays and the fictions he wrote during his final years

by advancing the proposition that the modern world is spiritually and morally bankrupt, and that it is slowly grinding itself into extinction. He sees this
self-destruction as a collective insanity; the remedy for the deadness gripping
mankind, says Lawrence, is to rekindle the sensual awareness of the cosmos
and the sense-knowledge of the ancients. Modern man is going mad because
he is no longer "in touch." We have seen how Juliet in "Sun" rekindles this
awareness of selfhood. We shall next see how the nameless woman in *The
Woman Who Rode Away* also rekindles this awareness.

As I noted earlier, in *Apocalypse* Lawrence tells us that the ancients' connection with the cosmos was emotional, as opposed to the Mind-logic of
modern man, who, says Lawrence, no longer feels the cosmic connection. For
ancient people life was full of mystery (Lawrence 1979, 130), and it was alive
with a cosmic power that Lawrence equates with the phallus, blood-sense,
love, and potency (Lawrence 1979, 171). For Lawrence the power of love
is the Holy Ghost—the symbol of redemption. As Jack Stewart points out,
Lawrence's Holy Ghost is the energy that fuses opposites in a vital equilibrium of incarnate Being (Stewart 2003, 49). We may not agree with all of
Lawrence's ideas, especially the submission of women to phallic power, but
considering current encroachments of human activity on the natural world—
the loss of habitat, the threatened extinction of thousands of animal species,
pollution of air and water, toxic chemicals in foods, the increased levels of
carbon dioxide in the atmosphere and the oceans, global warming, the rise
in sea levels, wars, terrorism, disease, and famine—it is difficult not to agree
with Lawrence when he says that mankind today has lost contact with the
Cosmos and that our values have gone awry. In *The Apocalyptic World of
D.H. Lawrence* Peter Fjägesund (Fjägesund 1991, 5–6) says that Lawrence
placed himself and his generation at the center of apocalyptic upheaval
because he was convinced that the world order was on the verge of collapse.
Had Lawrence been witness to the Anthropocene, that is, all those events of
the twenty-first century, not only the natural degradation of the environment
but also the social and political events, his warnings about global insanity
would have been even stronger.

World War I was for Lawrence a symptom of social and spiritual disintegration, a collective madness that presaged the collapse of civilization (we
can only imagine what he might have said about the insanity of World War
II, the loss of life, the Holocaust, the gulags, and "the great leap forward").
In *Fantasia of the Unconscious,* in reaction to the carnage of World War I,
Lawrence says: "the period of actual death and race-extermination is not far
off. [. . .] Our leaders have not loved men: they have loved ideas, and have
been willing to sacrifice passionate men on the altars of the blood-drinking
ever-ash-thirsty ideal" (Lawrence 2004, 141). In the first version of *Lady
Chatterley's Lover* the voluble narrator keeps insisting that all of society is

insane, and that if you do not have the disease you are somehow abnormal. In the second version of *Lady Chatterley's Lover*, in the wake of World War I, the narrator states that the world is insane and that the cure is death; and in the third version Connie notes that the air is soft and dead as though the world was dying (Lawrence 1999, 68). Also in the third version of *Lady Chatterley's Lover,* Sir Clifford, the crippled representative of his class, concludes that he too is an agent of modern madness because he has facilitated the destruction of the world by abetting the bitch Goddess of success whose appetite for flattery and adulation feeds on the meat and bones provided by men who make money in industry. Nevertheless, according to Fjägesund (Fjägesund 1991, 28), Lawrence never abandoned his vision of setting the wheel of creation in motion once again. Edmund Wilson concurs and, in *The Shores of Light,* he says that Lawrence's theme is indeed a high one, emphasizing "the self-affirmation and triumph of life in the teeth of all the sterilizing and demoralizing forces—industrialism, physical depletion, dissipation, careerism and cynicism—of modern English society" (Wilson 1952, 405); and, we might add, global industrialization, technology, and the fanaticism of terror.

Lawrence, as Fjägesund points out, had a profound sense of history, and he moved easily from one historical period to another (Fjägesund 1991, 7). In *Apocalypse,* in his analysis of mankind's historical evolution, Lawrence postulates three stages in the development of consciousness going from prehistoric times to the present: the cosmic-religious stage of primitive man, the god-religious stage of an evolving monotheism, and the philosophic-scientific stage of today (Lawrence 1979, 182). Cowan, paraphrasing Lawrence, adds a Christian dimension to these three stages saying that the second one belongs to the reign of the Father before the birth of Christ, the third one to that of the Son up to the present, and the fourth one, the stage yet to come, to the reign of the Holy Ghost which represents not only the love between a man and a woman but also the union of body and mind, and of flesh and spirit (Cowan 1970, 42). Lawrence himself attributes the symbolic "fall of man"—man's awareness of sex, sin, and fragmentariness—to the feeling of separation from oneness (selfhood)—a separation that coincides first with the god-religious stage and then with the philosophic-scientific stage, the stage we are in now. The Holy Ghost stage, sometimes also referred to as the "fourth dimension"—the stage in the making—would heal mankind's fragmentariness and alienation. It projects the vision of an ideal oneness into a utopian future. Lest we forget, Lawrence died in 1930, but his views of history and his criticism of our industrialized machine-age seem as valid for the twenty-first century as they were for the twentieth. Man, says Lawrence in *Apocalypse,* no longer feels a vital part of the cosmos and, instead, he wants to control it with reason and dominate it with *Mind* (Lawrence 1979, 181).

Modern man, says Lawrence, is all *Mind,* and he has lost contact with the primitive *blood-sense* of the ancients (Lawrence 1979, 91). As Seamus Perry points out, Lawrence was not unusual among modern writers in distrusting the conscious intellect (Perry 2021, 23): "My great religion," said Lawrence, "is a belief in the blood, the flesh, as being wiser than the intellect" (qtd. by Perry 2021, 23). Indeed, Lawrence believed in levels of consciousness— "blood consciousness"—working below the conscious mind, the ultimate goal being the full achievement of the self. Today's rejection of blood con- sciousness explains the deadness of modern man—a deadness from which both Juliet, the heroine of "Sun," and the woman in *The Woman Who Rode Away*, the other alienated heroine, try to escape. Juliet survives, and although the woman who rides away dies, her immolation represents a symbolic redemption of mankind. In an article in *Criticism* Thomas R. Whitaker notes, apropos Lawrence's discussion of Melville's primitivism, that although we cannot stride backward toward the ancients, we can nonetheless, "take a great curve in their direction," a healing curve toward redemption, that is, away from madness (Whitaker 1961, 219–21). The melding of *it* and *I* was to accomplish Lawrence's full achievement of the self.

With redemption in mind, in *The Plumed Serpent* Lawrence introduces "The Cult of Quetzalcoatl," a mythical political ideology designed to serve as an idealized vision of the culture of ancient Mexico (Lawrence 1987b, 127). It is a substitute for the religion of a past Golden Age and a model for the new millennium. According to Meyers the Quetzalcoatl movement hoped to restore the Aztec gods in order to reconnect Mexico with the mystery of the cosmos, thereby bringing about a revolution in consciousness. Lawrence was familiar with the politics of Mexico, and *The Plumed Serpent*, according to Meyers, is based on the political reality that its mythology was striving to transcend (Meyers 1982, 124). A principal feature of this novel, says Peter Scheckner in *Class Politics and the Individual,* is the hope that the vital, uncorrupted Mexican Indian will rekindle mankind, but the fear exists that, because, as a race, it is unconscious of itself, mankind will be swamped (Scheckner 1985, 128). Despite Kate Leslie's idealization of Indian mythol- ogy in *The Plumed Serpent*, Lawrence is critical of the failed Mexican revo- lution: "These old civilizations down here, they never get any higher than Quetzalcoatl. And he's just a sort of feathered snake. Who needed the smoke of a little heart's-blood now and then" (qtd. in Meyers 1982, 129). Although Lawrence criticizes bloodlust and the limitations of the cult of Quetzalcoatl, he presents the blood sacrifice of the white woman in *The Woman Who Rode Away* as a purification of the world—a much needed realignment of the cos- mic imbalance that prompted her departure from home in the first place. The contrast between *The Plumed Serpent* and *The Woman Who Rode Away* is striking and, according to Lawrence and the Indians who sacrifice her, it is the white man and his machine-technology that are responsible for the world's imbalance. As Scheckner points out in *Class, Politics, and the Individual*, Lawrence strives to reconcile opposing claims: on the one hand, pulling back from the dark, savage race of Indians and, on the other, declaring that only they can "save the white 'ruling' race from itself" (Scheckner 1985, 132).

Today, according to Lawrence, our culture views machine-technology as the necessary destiny of man (Lawrence 1979, 196–98). Indeed, men and women now seem to believe that only the "supreme Mind" can conquer the cosmos and, if that is true, Lawrence is not sanguine about the future of mankind (Lawrence 1979, 182). According to him, the only antidote to *Mind* is love, the erotic experience that repairs the damage done by abstract thought. Because the danger is immanent, he would have us restore our lost sense of wonder—a religious wonder of sense-impressions unconstrained by mind-control. Lawrence cites the red rose of love as a quintessential metaphor, and he believes that the tropes of his own writing will lead us toward selfhood, a selfhood that only a love-mind bond can achieve. For Lawrence madness is the pursuit of pure knowledge—a knowledge that has led to a loss of self (Lawrence 1979, 169). He laments this loss and the abstractions of mind-quest. He wants to re-establish the living organic connections with the cosmos, and, to get there, he would destroy all the false, inorganic connections, especially those related to money.

Modern man says Lawrence, has lost contact with the sun (Lawrence 1979, 76), and also with the moon. He is no longer in touch with their vital meaning and, consequently, out of touch with humanity. Modern man views the cosmos as an entity to be conquered, forgetting that it is "a vast living body" and that "we and the cosmos are one" (Lawrence 1979, 77).

Two of Lawrence's women feel unfulfilled: Juliet in "Sun," as we have already seen in Chapter One, and *The Woman Who Rode Away*. Not only does Lawrence foreground humanity's alienation from the self and the cosmos, he also dramatizes this state of affairs in his essays and in these two fictions. The women's husbands are good businessmen but financial success is not what the wives value. They feel alienated and unhappy. Juliet consults doctors in New York (none other than Lawrence's surrogates) and they prescribe the sun. The sun will be the metaphorical remedy for what ails her because Lawrence wants to free Juliet from "the tight little automatic 'universe'" in which she lives, and return her to "the great living cosmos of the 'unenlightened' pagans!" (Lawrence 1979, 76–77). Lawrence, the doctor, would return Juliet to her "naked sun self," that is, nature, and, once in Italy, as she communes with the sun and sheds her modern, nervous consciousness, her awakening is a symbolic prelude to the rejuvenation of mankind.

The woman who rides away in search of the Chilchuis, the descendants of Montezuma, knows, as Juliet had come to know, that something in her has died and that her life is beyond repair. She leaves the ranch in Mexico, her husband, and her two children, and rides off into the wilderness in search of she knows not what. At the climactic moment of the novella, after she has become the captive of the Chilchuis and has been given a hallucinogenic potion, she is sacrificed on the stone altar in a mountain cave at the exact moment when the setting sun of the winter solstice shines through a huge icicle at the mouth of the cave. That phallic moment is an epiphany: the woman and the reader apprehend the harmony of things, the movement of galaxies, and the dark spaces between the stars. The knife of the Indian cacique rips her heart out, and, according to Chilchui belief, when the sun and the moon converge, the cosmic balance will be restored.

In *Apocalypse,* Lawrence develops the idea that the killing of the mendacious porcupine and the emergence of a new blood consciousness will unite the symbolic sun in the sky with the inner sun of a person's *it.* Lawrence's *it* is a variant of Lacan's *ça* and Freud's *Id.* In her newly enlightened state of consciousness, the woman who rode away, like "the man who died" in the *The Escaped Cock,* will be "lifted up into heaven" (Lawrence 1988b, 259–63).

"Sun" is a fable, a short tale that teaches a moral, and *The Woman Who Rode Away* is also a fable, a story of Indian myths and extraordinary events. As a morality tale "Sun" is the tip of a narrative iceberg (Hemingway's metaphorical iceberg) because, for the most part, only one-eighth of what is going on is visible above the surface, whereas in *Woman* Lawrence reveals what lies below the surface, although not all of the remaining seven-eighths is exposed. Despite these narrative differences both women "kill" the symbolic porcupine, and both, in their different ways, experience the fulfillment of the Lacanian dictum: *"Wo Es war, soll Ich werden"* (Where *It* was, there *I* must be). They bring the Ego and the Id together, find the sun, and restore the balance of the self (Lacan 1966a, 136).

Lawrence's description of Juliet's life in the Italian countryside can be viewed as the visible one-eighth of Hemingway's iceberg, whereas the ideas contained in *Apocalypse, Reflections on the Death of a Porcupine,* and *Sketches of Etruscan Places* belong to the omitted seven-eighths of the story. They belong to the emotional level—the level of blood consciousness—the mass below the sea's surface. In his essays Lawrence writes about plum-blossoms, dandelions, vitality, the pursuit of wealth, the fourth dimension, the Kingdom of Heaven, and money—that "golden wall" [. . .] the "fatal wall" that keeps heaven out of our lives (Lawrence 1988b, 363). Juliet finds heaven in Sicily after she leaves New York, her husband, and the wall of the business machine.

In the lemon groves Juliet's body turns rosy and golden, and some mysterious power within her, deeper than consciousness, connects her with the sun. She soon feels like another being, and she wants her infant son also to absorb the sun and be transformed. So they frolic together, naked in the garden, and neither is afraid of the snakes that live there. In *Mornings in Mexico* Lawrence says that the snake represents the mysterious life-spirit because it lies in "the dark, lurking, intense sun at the centre of the earth" which is the source of potency (Lawrence 2009, 84). Juliet, and the child too, draw their strength from the potency of the inner sun within themselves, and this stream of life flows toward the sun in the sky, and the sun blazes back animating body and soul. The child with "burnt gold hair and red cheeks," is quick like a young [Etruscan] animal absorbed in life (Lawrence 1995b, 27). He turns the color of many Italians when they go naked in the sun; and they, like the Etruscans, have a profound acceptance of life (Lawrence 1992, 45–46). In Italy, Juliet and her son find what Lawrence calls the eternal quick of all things, and they are happy because they are in touch with the world and themselves.

It is interesting that Juliet's doctors recommend the sun. Who are these doctors, and why do they prescribe the sun? The story will tell us why, and so, off she goes to Italy, the land of the Etruscans who painted the murals that Lawrence admires so much; the Etruscans who were wiped out by Rome and whose lives and values Lawrence infers from the frescoes on the walls of their tombs, and which he describes in *Sketches of Etruscan Places*. He admires their vitality, their openness, and their "desire to preserve the natural humour of life" (Lawrence 1992, 32–33). In "Lawrence's Ontological Vision in *Etruscan Places, The Escaped Cock,* and *Apocalypse,*" Stewart notes that the Etruscans cultivated the fluid, ever-changing rhythms of the senses, as opposed to the rigid, mechanistic rhythms of Rome (Stewart 2003, 44); and Donald Gutierrez, in "DHL's Golden Age," says: "Etruscan society [. . .] symbolized a deeply realizable potential of enhanced being" (Gutierrez 1976, 406). No wonder Lawrence's doctors recommend that Juliet go to the land of the Etruscans whose elemental powers, liveliness, and natural sexuality will revivify her. "Sun" is a parable, and Juliet's transformation exemplifies the morality Lawrence would have us adopt if we are to resist the vast, cold apparatus of civilization—the mad engine that would have shattered her had she not distanced herself from it.

The woman who rides away, like Juliet, leaves her husband and the life he represents because she too feels alienated and unfulfilled. Desperate, she rides away from the ranch in Mexico, the silver mine, and the house in which she has been living. Silver (her husband's business) is a dead market, the Spanish town is thrice dead, the sun-dried church is dead, the covered marketplace is hopeless, and there is a dead dog lying between the meat-stalls and the vegetable array. "Deadness within deadness," says Lawrence, and he repeats the word "dead" six times in a seven-line paragraph (Lawrence 1995d, 39). After her marriage, the woman's conscious development has stopped, mysteriously, and, although her husband admires her, she feels morally ground down. He loves his work and, while running the silver mine, he was very successful, but the mines have closed and he is now a rancher raising pure-breed hogs. He views his marriage as an extension of his mining and ranching operations, and it provides "sentimental income." He hates the physical side of marriage, however, and, although he loves his wife, he keeps her in a state of "invincible slavery" (Lawrence 1995d, 40). Her name is her husband's patronymic, Lederman. Her very anonymity symbolizes the void in which she lives and the social expectations that have imprisoned her. As Shirley Bricout notes in "Le sacrifice du langage dans 'The Woman Who Rode Away,'" "Mrs. Lederman is dehumanized by the destructive mercantilism of her husband whose love is described in terms that connote obliteration: 'He admired his wife to extinction'" (Lawrence 1995d, 40; Bricout 2012, 39; my trans.).

Gone is the dazzling girl from Berkeley, California, who was once so full of promise; she now feels shattered because, like everything else in town, she has died. In a sense, she is Juliet's double, except that she lives in the wilds of the Sierra Madre, and there are no sun-doctors to counsel her. Unlike Juliet, who sails off toward Italy, the California girl gets on her horse and rides away toward the unknown. Whereas Juliet welcomes the dark sun at the core of her being, the nameless woman hears only the great "crash at the centre of herself, which was the crash of her own death" (Lawrence 1995d, 44). She is left with a semi-conscious romantic longing for the savage customs and religion of the Indians she has heard people speak about. One of her husband's mining engineers thinks that "something wonderful" lives in the hills, and another one says that there are wild Indians out there. So, the woman decides that something wild and wonderful in the mountains is better than a living death on her husband's ranch where everything is walled in.

The Chilchuis were said to be the sacred tribe of all the Indians, the descendants of Montezuma and the Aztec kings, with old priests still living among them, practicing their ancient religion, offering human sacrifices. These rituals appeal to the woman's girlish romanticism, and Lawrence crafts them into the wisdom of blood-sense and intuitive awareness of the world that his essays advocate. Even though the woman has a husband and two children, the call of the wild is too strong and the woman's despair overwhelming. That is why she rides away. Lawrence envelops her journey in a web of proleptic images that contribute to her disorientation and impending doom. Lawrence repeats words such as "dead, sacrifice, cavity, obsidian eyes, fangs of ice, slashes of snow, heart, died, and eternity." They prefigure the moment when the knife of the cacique will rip into her chest.

As the Indians prepare to sacrifice her to the gods, the woman lives in
a state of mescal-induced torpor during which she develops a heightened
awareness of the natural world that parallels the Indians' belief in cosmic
order. She learns that the sun and the moon are in misalliance and that the
white man is responsible for this imbalance. She learns that the Indian has
lost his power and that in the eternal cycle of birth and death the Indian will
prevail. These beliefs dovetail with Lawrence's conviction that humanity is
doomed because it has lost its sense of direction. He develops these same
beliefs in *Apocalypse* and *Reflections on the Death of a Porcupine* (Lawrence
1988b, 359–66). These ideas are also embedded in the seven-eighths of the
iceberg below the surface of *The Woman Who Rode Away*. The symbolic porcupine, the fourth dimension, and the wall of money that blocks fulfillment,
all belong to the iceberg. Whereas Juliet experiences the illumination of the
sun's life-giving rays, the woman who rides away experiences the illumination of the dark sun of her unconscious. In his introduction to *Psychoanalysis
and the Unconscious* Philip Rieff points out that the prophetic intention of
Lawrence's art is to re-awaken the "half-forgotten' knowledge, buried as
emotion in the unconscious" (Rieff 1968, vii–xxiii). Accordingly, the *it,* that
is, the *Id* of the woman's repressed and unfulfilled self, with the help of the
Indians' potions, rises toward consciousness where it melds with the insights
of *Ego,* even as Lawrence narrates the woman's psychic integration in terms
of ritual, drumbeats, and dancing. The Chilchuis aim is to connect individual
being and social being with cosmic Being. In *Mornings in Mexico* Lawrence
describes the meaning of the dance and the drumbeat as that of tribal blood-
sense; the Indian's bloodstream is generic and non-individual, thus very different from European ballads that describe personal experience (Lawrence
2009, 80). The beating drums and the dancing prepare the way for cosmic
insemination, procreation, and renewal, symbolized by the erotic ray of the
sun going "into the cave of the moon" (Lawrence 1995d, 61). There the woman's death will become the world's rebirth; it will restore the cosmic balance
and the Indians' strength. No wonder Hough views this novella as Lawrence's
most complete artistic achievement and the most profound comment on the
world of his time (Hough 1956, 146). Had he acknowledged *Apocalypse* and
Sketches of Etruscan Places as the invisible part of the iceberg in "Sun," he
might have seen it too not as a dreary tale but as yet another high artistic
achievement.

Paradoxically, the prelude to the woman's physical death will be her
psychic awakening—the emergence of a cosmic awareness—even as the
novella explores the meaning of the Indian rituals that will enlighten her.
The Chilchuis are for her what the Etruscans are for Juliet, but with one
big difference. In "Sun" Lawrence never mentions the Etruscans, although
their presence is felt throughout the story, and this presence constitutes the

invisible part of the iceberg, whereas in *Woman* Lawrence describes the meaning of the Chilchuis' rituals. That part of the iceberg is visible. The ideas expressed in *Apocalypse, Mornings in Mexico,* and *Reflections on the Death of a Porcupine,* however, are not; also not visible is the layered background of ancient solar rituals that required sacrificial victims for the rebirth of the sun and the salvation of the world. According to Cowan, in *D.H. Lawrence's American Journey,* Lawrence was not unfamiliar with the primitive concept of human sacrifice that is needed in order to replenish the source of life (Cowan 1970, 76). "The religious ritual of the Dying and Reviving God, the world over, re-enacts the natural ritual of the annual death and rebirth of the sun" (Cowan 1970, 74). As Cowan points out, the woman must be identified with the traditional sacrificial victims of solar rituals, and he notes that Lawrence relates her to "the traditional *pharmakos* of fertility rites by associating her with vegetation" of all kinds both during her voyage to the valley of the Chilchuis and after her arrival there (Cowan 1970, 76). Cowan cites the works of Robert Graves, William Tyler Olcott, Alan W. Watts, Sir James George Frazer, Victor W. von Hagen, Alfonso Caso, and Laurette Séjourné, all of them authorities on world myths and the rites of ancient peoples, and he notes that Lawrence, in addition to using world myth, also integrates the rituals and values of the Nahuatl religion of Mexico with the descriptions of the woman's sacrifice by the Chilchuis (Cowan 1970, 74–75). Clearly, Lawrence has fused myth, ritual, and his own ideas into one single religious metaphor—the necessity of human sacrifice for the rejuvenation of the world. In *D.H. Lawrence: Novelist,* F.R. Leavis notes that *The Woman Who Rode Away* "imagines the old pagan Mexican religion as something real and living" (Leavis 1967, 343). The historical record of sacrificial offerings throughout the millennia—the record that Lawrence has omitted because he does not describe it—lies embedded in that part of his iceberg below the surface.

Strict adherence to the iceberg theory of writing omits authorial intervention but Lawrence ignores the convention by describing the woman's stream of consciousness and the world of Chilchui mystery.[1] In "Sun" Etruscan mythology and porcupine symbolism are not described, whereas in *Woman* Aztec mythology and the blood-sense of the ancients are described; and the Indians are gleeful that the woman has consented to "give her heart" to their gods. She speaks figuratively while they interpret her words literally. The Indians explain to her that when a white woman gives herself to their gods, the "gods will begin to make the world again, and the white man's gods will fall to pieces" (Lawrence 1995d, 61). They explain that the white man has stolen the sun because the Indian was weak, that the white man is not using it wisely, and that the sun is angry; they say that the moon is also angry.[2] In anticipation of the sacrifice, they give her potions of mescal that "release her

senses into a sort of heightened mystic acuteness" and she diffuses "out deli-
ciously into the harmony of things" (Lawrence 1995d, 62). She hears the stars
in heaven, and also the snow twittering in the sky; she smells the peace of the
sun mingling with the peace of the moon; and she feels two great currents, one
golden ascending toward the sun, the other silvery, like rain, descending the
ladders of space toward the clouds on the mountain. In between she feels "the
blue wind, the go-between, the invisible ghost" that belongs to both worlds,
and it plays upon the ascending and descending chords of the rain (Lawrence
1995d, 64). The poetry of cosmic harmony has become visual, sensual, musical, and metaphysical. The woman is clad in blue, the color of the wind, and
"it is the colour of what goes away and is never coming back, but which is
always here, waiting like death among us" (Lawrence 1995d, 63). Earlier,
the woman felt an "icy pang of fear and certainty [in] her heart," a fear that
adumbrates the *fang of ice* at the mouth of the cave and the flint knife that
rips her heart out (Lawrence 1995d, 61). The Indians tell her that she must die
and go like the wind to the sun and tell him that they will open the gate to the
sun who will then leap over the white men and come back to them (Lawrence
1995d, 65). Lawrence's poetic passages communicate the blood-sense of an
intuitive cosmic presence he would have us feel, a necessary trope for the
harmony of things that he wants us to recapture and weave into our sensibilities. In keeping with these sensibilities, in "Lawrence's Ontological Vision
in *Etruscan Places*," Stewart notes that Lawrence is advocating a pre-logical
intuitive way of knowing the world, positing a Creative Power that can only
be grasped in pervasive immanence (Stewart 2003, 46–47).

The Indians see Mrs. Lederman as a white woman from a white culture but
she herself no longer shares the values of the people she has left behind. She
rode away from a dead marriage and a mercantile society that had imprisoned
her, and, ironically, she is now the prisoner of a race of people determined to
kill her in order to rebalance the cosmos. Bricout argues that if the sun and the
moon are to be realigned, the woman's immolation by the Chilchui becomes
a necessary, even voluntary, sacrifice (Bricout 2012, 40), and, as René Girard
notes, her sacrifice becomes a "ritual murder." She is the sacrificial lamb,
and her death will restore the cosmic order that has been missing (Girard,
1977, 137).

In their ceremonial garb the Indians are "golden-red, almost naked" (like
the Etruscans), and their drumbeat and chanting are "like an obsession"
(Lawrence 1995d, 68). They ascend the steep trail toward the sacred cave
where a "fang-like spoke of ice" hangs down in front of the opening. The
woman sees "the leopard-like figures of priests climbing the hollow cliff
face, to the cave that like a dark socket bored a cavity, an orifice, half-way up
the crag" (Lawrence 1995d, 69). Once inside, the priests lay her naked on a
large flat stone, and, knife in hand, the "darkly and powerfully male" cacique

watches the sun intently. The woman too experiences the power of her own womanhood but it is a womanhood that will soon be obliterated forever (Lawrence 1995d, 58–60). Nonetheless a phallic power streams between the man and the woman. It is the winter solstice, and the sun is sloping down the afternoon sky. Its rays are creeping round slowly. As they grow ruddier, they penetrate further and, as the red sun is about to sink, it shines "full through the shaft of ice deep into the hollow of the cave, to the innermost" (Lawrence 1995d, 70). At that exact moment the man strikes home, accomplishing the sacrifice and achieving the power (Lawrence 1995d, 71). The sexual imagery of the male-female tropes animates the sequence: the red sun, the phallic icicle, the hollow cave, the womb that belongs to the moon, penetration, the power of insemination, rebirth, and a mastery "that passes from race to race" (Lawrence 1995d, 71). The phallic connection between the powerful male and the heart of the woman confident in her womanhood is transferred to the cosmos where it will perform its magic.[1]

In the "Aristocracy" section of *Reflections on the Death of a Porcupine* (Lawrence 1988b, 365–76) Lawrence speaks of many things but also of the day and of the night, of man (the sun) and of woman (the moon), and of the moneyed wall of greed, and of the porcupine that sticks its quills into the face of the sun. The Indians who sacrifice the woman are killing the porcupine symbolically because the white man's money-machine and greed have stolen their power. As for Juliet, her decision to stay in Italy is a repudiation of the porcupine because she has found the sun. She has discovered the power within—a womanhood that is in touch—and she is lifted toward heaven, alive in the here and now. As for the woman who rode away, the blue wind carries her toward the sun so that the Indians may regain their lost power and glory. In death the woman loses her individuality and her womanhood but she and humanity will be rewarded with cosmic renewal.

Both Juliet and the woman who rode away discover the dark sun of the unconscious, the *it*. Access to *it* makes a return to a pre-intellectual state possible. Accordingly, toward the end of his life, in his essays and fiction, Lawrence advocates a more intuitive relationship of the self with the world, a rebirth designed to change the nightmare of an insane, industrialized society. The future of the world, according to Lawrence, must include a vision that breaks through the "wall" of the military-industrial complex; and the role of art is to prepare the public for the necessary changes to come: the advent of the Holy Ghost and the fourth dimension. They are the prelude to sanity. To this end, Lawrence, the idealist, creates characters that turn their backs to the world's madness. Juliet and the woman who rides away leave flawed marriages, the money-machine, automatism itself, and, in doing so, they find selfhood and the regenerating potential of genital power, Juliet in the sun, and the woman in a mystical and mythical cosmic oneness linked to the rebirth of the world.

Conventional wisdom will view the woman's departure as a form of madness. Why would she leave a successful husband, a comfortable home, two children, and ride away? Is she mad? If she is, it is a madness born of desperation—the need not only for self-preservation but also fulfillment. Lawrence paints her as the victim and symbol of an industrial civilization that has gone awry. She is immolated on the altar of the Chilchuis in order to repair the cosmic imbalance for which the Indians blame the white man.

In his essays and his fiction Lawrence dramatizes the plight of modern men and women enmeshed in cultural forces seemingly beyond their control—enmeshed in circumstances that have deadened their sensibilities. Lawrence wants us, as readers, to experience the destructive insanity of the modern world. He describes and rejects the dehumanizing legacy of reified greed thereby enabling us to transcend the historical circumstances that have fragmented selfhood. When men and women accept the healing powers of the sun and kill the porcupine, and when Lacan's *it* and *I* become one, then the selfhood of men and women will be restored.

Not all readers agree with this assessment. In *D.H. Lawrence* Becket notes that *The Woman Who Rode Away* has been central to the debates about Lawrence's misogyny, the voyeuristic pleasures of the text, and the description of the woman's immolation (Becket 2002, 97). As an addendum to my reading of the novella it will be useful, I think, to compare it with Kate Millet's feminist reading, a reading that is at such odds with Lawrence's work, and, for that matter, with Bricout's reading of it. It's as though the two women had read different stories, Millet's reading being a withering critique of it, and Bricout's one of high praise.

I noted in my introduction that Cowan, in his book, *D.H. Lawrence and the Trembling Balance,* argues that the way Lawrence presents ideas in his fiction invites the reader's collaboration, a collaboration in which the unconscious engages in "projective identification." This means that the reader's unresolved affective needs are projected onto the reality of the text. Every reader, says Cowan, needs to engage in a "psychic distancing" that moves beyond the projection of unresolved personal needs. I believe that Millet's essay is an example of the kind of reading that does not move beyond the negative projection of personal needs, and that, therefore, her "overidentifications" distort Lawrence's message and the meaning of his work. Here are some examples: Millet says that the death of the woman who rode away "is astounding in the sadism and malice with which it is conceived" (Millet 1969, 285). She describes the story as a "fraudulent myth" that represents "Lawrence's most impassioned statement of the doctrine of male supremacy and the penis as deity." It is also a "pornographic dream" (Millet 1969,

286–87), an "apotheosis of puritanical pornography," "a formula for sexual cannibalism," a "demented fantasy," "coitus as killing," and "the perversion of sexuality into slaughter" (Millet 1969, 290–93). Millet exaggerates, of course, but her critique is a sign of negative overidentification. With Carl Jung's theories of psyche in mind, Inez Martinez calls the anger they reflect "ego-readings." In "Ego Readings vs Reading for Psyche" she implies that Millet's ego-readings are false readings because their projective identification distorts the "reading for psyche" which, says Martinez, belongs to our collective unconscious, i.e., the collective unconscious that Jung talks about. Millet misrepresents the state of mind of a woman who escapes not only from a dead marriage but also from a world that is governed by money and the profit motive of business—worlds that Lawrence despises. Millet has also misinterpreted the motives of the Chilchuis. Their actions are the result of their own desperate need to restore balance to a planetary system that is off kilter, one that values lucre over life.

In "Writers and their Work" (1997) Linda Ruth Williams, using Freudian theory, addresses Lawrence's desire to "police the boundary between the sexes (Williams 1997, 67). In critiquing *The Woman Who Rode Away* she writes about the deferral of desire that is enacting a "foreplay of suspense," one that is also an "exercise in perversity" (Williams 1997, 106–07). Becket elaborates further by saying that the detailed preparations made for the woman's sacrifice invite and embrace "her spectacular destruction (which is masochism), or through the writer's delight at detailing her humiliation (which is sadism)" (Becket 2002, 147). In light of Lawrence's *Apocalypse* and *Sketches of Etruscan Places,* that is, his literary efforts to save the world from destruction, it is hard to agree with Williams's statement about perversity or Becket's emphasis on masochism and sadism.

Millet, before Becket or Williams, also slams Lawrence's story for its stock imagery and Hollywood clichés. It's interesting to note, however, that Romy Sutherland, in "From D.H. Lawrence to the Language of Cinema: Chaste Sacrifices in *The Woman Who Rode Away* and *Picnic at Hanging Rock,"* praises Lawrence's cinematic imagery which inspired Peter Weir's shooting of the film *Picnic at Hanging Rock* (Sutherland 2013, 241–51). "In both *Picnic at Hanging Rock* and *The Woman Who Rode Away,* colonial female protagonists respond in comparable ways to the indigenous world that surrounds their protective colonial enclaves" (Sutherland 2013, 241). Sheila Contreras says:

> The white man has metaphorically *stolen* the sun from the Chilchui, who must now reclaim it through the body of a white woman, the commodity of exchange between male cultures. The symbolic rape of a white woman reverses the white man's colonial rape of the Chilchui world. (Contreras 1993/94, 99)

Millet charges Lawrence with pornography despite the delicacy the Indians display when removing the woman's clothing. They are removing all vestments of white culture because the novella depicts a white culture in decline, as opposed to the life-asserting values of the Chilchuis. It is their point of view we as readers need to attend to, not, as Millet claims, that of the voyeur. The Chilchuis have higher things on their minds: nothing less than the cosmos itself; they want to restore the balance between the sun and the moon. Nor is the woman's immolation a rape; it is a sacred ceremony designed to overcome the inequity between two races. Only her sacrifice can restore the Indians' lost power, or so they believe. The ritual of human sacrifice was widely practiced by the Aztec, Inca, and Maya civilizations.

Sheila MacLeod views Millet's interpretation as especially controversial because it fails to account for the tale as "a modern fertility myth." MacLeod argues that the woman's journey is a "religious quest," and, that in "losing" herself she "finds" herself (MacLeod 1985, 141). This view defines the woman who rode away as a female Christ-figure, one that combines self-sacrifice with the concept of salvation. I would argue that her sacrifice corresponds not only to a rebirth of the self but that it is also the beginning of a cultural rebirth. Metaphorically speaking, it is a realignment of the sun and the moon, and, in Lawrencian terms, the passing of power from one race to another, from the white man to the Chilchui.

In addition to Cowan's, Martinez's, Sutherland's, MacLeod's, and Contreras's critiques, Marina S. Ragachewskaya praises Lawrence's craft and vision that turn "a moment into eternity" (Ragachewskaya 2017, 1). Lest I belabor the point, however, Becket does acknowledge that, recently, critics have been more charitable in assessing the novella's merits (Becket 2002, 97).

The culture that Lawrence admired the most was that of the Etruscans, and his book, *Sketches of Etruscan Places and Other Italian Essays* is ample proof of his approbation. When advocating a return to a simpler, more primitive culture, one capable of restoring sanity to a world that has gone mad, it was the Etruscans he had in mind: "There is a simplicity, combined with a most peculiar, free-breasted naturalness and spontaneity in the shapes and movements of the underworld walls and spaces, that at once reassures the spirit. The Greeks sought to make an impression, and Gothic still more seeks to impress the mind. The Etruscans, no. The things they breathing freely and pleasantly, with a certain fullness of life. Even the tombs. And that is the true Etruscan quality: ease, naturalness, and an abundance of life, no need to force the mind or the soul in any direction" (Lawrence 2002, 19). To the Etruscans, "the cosmos was alive, like a vast creature (Lawrence 2002, 57). Of course we cannot know what the Etruscans were really like, and Lawrence can only infer their free-breasted naturalness and spontaneity from the frescoes on the walls of their tombs and the bas-reliefs on each sarcophagus. Nonetheless, his inferences convey his deeply felt values and the kind of world he would like us to espouse.

We need to remember that Lawrence's final fictions were written toward the end of his life (as were the *Sketches of Etruscan Places,* published posthumously in 1932 by Martin Secker), and that Lawrence's fabulations differ from his earlier short stories. Gone is phallic dominance and the erotic submission of women. In "Sun" Juliet leaves her husband and asserts her independence. So does the woman who rode away. Ethel Cane, in "None of That," is a strong, willful woman. It is not her fault that she is raped. The boy's mother in "The Rocking-Horse Winner" is assertive in her desire for money and social standing. As for Cathcart, the man who loved islands, he is, ultimately, a failed human being. Carlotta, in "Glad Ghosts," is a woman whose behavior is ruled by the values and codes of the aristocracy. Morier's intervention leads to change, and, by the end of the story, she finds happiness in marriage and children. In *Ghosts*, members of the aristocracy, unlike Lawrence's customary view of them, do not possess the most life force. It is Mark Morier, the man who lives and works in sunny Africa, the man who shows the residents of the Lathkill estate how to overcome their hysterical behavior, who has the life force. His sanity, a sanity that mimes that of the Etruscans, rids the Riddings household of its death wish. And, finally, the mythical priestess of Isis, in her search for the lost phallus of Osiris, rescues the man who died. She shows him how to love and live. These are radical departures from what has generally been written about Lawrence's values, his men and his women, and their relationships.

Chapter Three

"None of That"

Lawrence and Hemingway at the Bullfights with Ethel and Brett

After analyzing the narrative levels in "Sun," and the sun's role in countering the "porcupine," I will use bullfighting not only to compare Lawrence's craft in "None of That!" with Hemingway's craft in *The Sun Also Rises,* but also to examine their treatment of love. Ethel Cane, Lawrence's heroine, falls for Cuesta, a Mexican bullfighter, and Brett Ashley, Hemingway's heroine, falls for Romero, a Spaniard, who is also a bullfighter. Ethel strives to control her sexuality with *Mind*, and we know from Lawrence's "psychoanalytics" that whenever a character chooses *Mind* over body the consequences will be disastrous. Brett, for her part, has no sexual inhibitions, and her infatuation with Romero fits into a larger and a more complex set of relationships.

Although their personalities are different, both Brett and Ethel are independent, new women of the 1920s. Despite this similarity, however, Ethel (an American) tries to manage her sexual urges, whereas Brett (a Brit) has many lovers and makes no attempt to repress her libido. Lawrence describes bullfighting and Ethel's behavior through the prism of psychological depth and sexual repression, whereas Hemingway describes bullfighting and Brett's liberated behavior through the prism of his iceberg theory of writing. The women's conduct may be different, but both authors share an interest in how women react to the *corrida*,[1] to men, and to sex.

Hemingway loved the *corrida*, Lawrence seems to have tolerated it, and both men wrote about it with insight and precision: Hemingway in *The Sun Also Rises*, *Death in the Afternoon*, *The Dangerous Summer*, and several short stories, and Lawrence in Chapter One of *The Plumed Serpent* and the short story, "None of That!" Hemingway was an aficionado and Lawrence was not, but the *corrida*, nonetheless, informs both works.[2] Kate Leslie's reaction to the bullfight in *The Plumed Serpent* is decidedly negative, whereas Ethel's reaction to it in "None of That" is quite positive; Cuesta's skill as a matador is, without doubt, a performance that entrances her no end. In addition to their descriptions of bullfighting, Hemingway and Lawrence also dramatize the culturally significant roles of Brett and Ethel in a male, macho environment.

Wendy Martin points out that during the 1920s women were changing from passive, private individuals into persons in pursuit of new experiences. Post-Victorian women were claiming a new mobility and visibility, and their actions exposed them to a heightened vulnerability because public space was still defined as male. Whenever women overstepped conventional boundaries they were perceived as interlopers, "fair game" for male predation (Martin 1987, 67). Brett's bare shoulders offend Montoya and his patrons at the bar in Pamplona, and Ethel's willfulness offends Cuesta's sensibilities. The cultural codes in Spain and Mexico are decidedly male.

Brett Ashley is an emancipated and oversexed woman of the 1920s. She feels no social constraints, does what she wants, and frequents places that were previously off limits to women, thereby posing a radical challenge to traditional values and codes. Although ostensibly in love with Jake and engaged to Mike Campbell, she has had love affairs with other men and now, most notably, with Robert Cohn and Pedro Romero. She may go off with a man, but she always comes back to Jake, who is her anchor. After the Pamplona festival, when she leaves with Romero, the youthful bullfighter who wants to marry her, she sends Jake a telegram imploring him to take the Sud-Express to Madrid from San Sebastian. She is short on cash and needs to be rescued. Romero, it seems, is too young, he wants her to grow her hair long like that of a real woman, and become a traditional Spanish wife. Brett says that she will have none of that because she does not want "to be one of these bitches that ruins children" (Hemingway 1926, 243). It is obvious that despite her lust for Romero's lithe body, she could never accept the conventional role of a Spanish wife. She has her standards, after all.

Ethel Cane is a rich blonde in her thirties, and she too is an emancipated woman. Luis Colmenares, the narrator in "None of That!," says that he knew her around 1913–1914. Like Brett, she has been married before and she has had affairs. She is also a strong-willed woman who believes in the mastery of mind over body. Unlike Brett, however, who says she is a goner because she must have Romero, Ethel believes that she can defer pleasure and control desire. She insists not only in directing her feelings, but also in controlling men. Although fascinated by Cuesta, she wants to dominate him and herself by not responding to his advances. She is an exemplar of the mind-body dichotomy that Lawrence despises.

Colmenares, Ethel's escort in Mexico, describes her as "a dynamo, full of American energy [. . .] a locomotive engine stoked up inside and bursting with steam," a woman who hates "all active maleness in man," wanting only passive maleness, a woman capable of sending "out of her body a repelling energy, to compel people to submit to her will" (Lawrence 1995a, 215–17). This description of Ethel can be construed as the visible part of the "iceberg." In *Psychoanalysis and the Unconscious* Lawrence analyzes its submerged meaning by describing Ethel's unconscious as the collusion between mind and will; this union, he says, "has all the mechanical force of the non-vital universe. It is a great dynamo of super-mechanical force" (Lawrence 1995d, 42). When the will becomes an accomplice of the mind, it imposes "its machine-motions and automizations over the whole of life" (Lawrence 1995d, 42). Lawrence's story describes the injurious effects of her conduct. The fact that she hates all maleness in a man would not have endeared her to Cuesta, a fifty-year-old bullfighter, who is portrayed as a vain brute, but an excellent matador; someone capable of playing not only with bulls but also with women. He is a man who has yellow eyes, like those of a tiger; a man who is able to cast a spell over anyone. So, it would seem that Ethel and Cuesta are evenly matched but temperamentally opposed. Moreover, says Colmenares, Cuesta is cool, beautiful and contemptuous, capable of looking inside your courage and melting it. He drives women mad, yet he disdains all who pursue him, and many do. He is rich, independent, and he has a big hacienda. In due course the conflict between Ethel and Cuesta evolves into a battle of wills: the domineering woman who says she would rather kill herself than lose control of her feelings, and Cuesta, the man who dominates bulls in the ring and women wherever they may be. "None of That!" describes not only a clash of wills between a man and a woman, but also a clash between two cultures, Mexican and American. With this scenario in mind Lawrence orchestrates and dramatizes a battle royal of the sexes, a life and death struggle between Cuesta, the body and Ethel, the mind. Their clash highlights not only Lawrence's blood-Mind dichotomy—a principal theme in his work—it also contrasts the values and expectations of two cultures. For Ethel, Mexico is "a land of naughty little boys doing obscene little things" (Lawrence 1995a, 217). But these boys will grow up to be like Cuesta, the man who embodies Mexico's code of machismo, a code that defines men as dominant and women as subordinate. Ironically, Ethel ends up fighting three adversaries: herself, the matador, and the code. Unfortunately for Ethel the battle is rigged because she is the victim of *Mind*—a mind that controls and directs her life. Lawrence views mind without body as anathema because when you make mind the absolute ruler, it's "as good as making a Cook's tourist-interpreter a king and a god" (Lawrence 2004, 155).

In *The Sun Also Rises,* Hemingway's man-woman relationship is different. Although Jake and Brett cannot consummate their love physically (he is impotent), they do love each other, and the tension between them derives from their inability to make love; whereas for Cuesta and Ethel the tension unfolds as a clash of wills. Each wants the submission of the other. Will Cuesta triumph or will Ethel? It is a protracted dance for supremacy in which Cuesta, eventually, triumphs. There is no such victory in Hemingway's novel. Jake and Brett are doomed to live their lives separately, together, as she lusts after men, but always comes back to him. Unlike Jake, Cuesta is a carnivore and, like a lion, he has the strength and cunning of a predator. By contrast, Ethel is all *Mind*, and because she cannot reconcile her mind and her body—her will and her desire—she loses. Cuesta kills her symbolically, as he kills bulls literally whenever he enters the bullring.[3] After a protracted struggle, and having lost the battle with herself, Ethel acquiesces to Cuesta's invitation, agreeing to meet him late one evening at his hacienda. There, instead of welcoming her submission, he hands her over to the men of his bullfighting entourage. They rape her. Ethel has lost all three battles. In the end she is so humiliated and traumatized, that, after a nervous collapse, she poisons herself.

The ending of *The Sun Also Rises* is less tragic because only the bulls die. However, "the death of love" (Spilka 1962, 129) as Mark Spilka points out, is one of the novel's themes and, subsuming love, is death itself: eight million dead in World War I, and many more millions of maimed soldiers, all of whom, although not sexually impotent, like Jake, are socially dysfunctional. In *The Sun Also Rises* the members of "the lost generation" are brash, they drink too much, and they fight. Gertrude Stein's epigraph is apt. Unlike Lawrence, who delves deeply into the mind-body duality of his characters, Hemingway tracks the social and spiritual consequences of a failure of civilization and its devastating effects on the survivors of World War I. He paints with a broader brush, and the *corrida* in his novel, as Allen Josephs points out, acts as a compass, a "moral axis" of tradition and stability to the disorientation and erratic behavior of its characters (Josephs 1986, 91). In "None of That!," the *corrida* is not a paradigm for art, honor, and order. Instead, Lawrence uses it to highlight Cuesta's skill, Ethel's admiration of his performance, and her demise. Nonetheless, in the submerged portion of the story's iceberg lurks Lawrence's critique of Ethel, Cuesta, and their flawed behavior.

For Hemingway, the *toreo* is a mythic ritual of life and death, a ritual with mystic and artistic connotations. Hemingway compares the art of bullfighting to the music of Bach, the sculpture of Brancusi, slow-motion film, and writing (Hemingway 1959, 130). For Lawrence, the *toreo* is less exalted, although it does connote power, love, and death. Despite these mixed connotations, the description of the bullfight in *The Plumed Serpent* is essentially negative, and it reflects Kate Leslie's point of view, namely shock at the sight of the bull's blood, the horse's entrails after it has been gored, and the pervasive violence of the spectacle (Lawrence 1987b, 14–16). In contrast to the relatively benign description of bullfighting in *The Plumed Serpent*, in "None of That!" it is viewed more positively. Both descriptions reflect the point of view of women.

Ethel Cane, however, unlike Kate Leslie, who calls bullfighting a silly ritual, is not repulsed by the suffering of the animals.

In counterpoint to Kate Leslie's distress, Hemingway, in *Death in the Afternoon,* addresses and dismisses Anglo-Saxon revulsion toward bullfighting, a revulsion that he thinks is no more than an expression of ignorance and prudishness. "The bullfight," he says, "is a Spanish institution; it has not existed because of the foreigners and tourists, but always in spite of them" (Hemingway 1932, 8). Furthermore, the *corrida* almost always ends with the death of the animal, sometimes even the matador. The event, he says, is a quintessentially Spanish performance, and he describes it as tragedy, not sport (Hemingway 1932, 16); death unites man and bull "in the emotional, aesthetic and artistic climax of the fight" (Hemingway 1932, 247).[4] Edward F. Stanton notes that Hemingway learned from the *toreo* how to make writing a performative art (Stanton 1989, 29–30), stressing the fact that his "prose of ecstasy" has the "pure classic beauty" of a "brilliant *faena*" (Hemingway 1932, 206–07).[5] At the climactic moment when death unites man and bull, the tragedy in the arena and on the page generates currents of emotional and spiritual intensity. In *The Sun Also Rises* Hemingway describes Romero's performance as giving "real emotion [to the spectators] because he kept the absolute purity of line in his movements [. . .] through the maximum of exposure" (Hemingway 1926, 168).

Lawrence's interests lie elsewhere. The detail that Hemingway lavishes on his descriptions of bullfighting as an art form and mystic ritual is, for the most part, absent in Lawrence's writing. Instead, he focuses mainly on Ethel's battle with herself and with Cuesta. Lawrence's mortal combat is not so much in the arena as it is in the psychological realm of will power, where Cuesta's animal strength and cunning are pitted against Ethel's steely determination to control the desires of the body. In contrast to Hemingway, Lawrence views the *corrida* primarily as a performance allowing the matador to display his competence. In "None of That!" Lawrence focuses less on the *corrida* as art and more on Cuesta's skill as a matador, although Cuesta's skill would necessarily and inevitably evoke the emotional response in the spectators that Hemingway refers to. Ethel Cane does, in fact, respond to his brilliance, and it is that brilliance that generates the beginning of their relationship. Lawrence describes it as follows: Cuesta's "fourth bull was a beauty, full of life, curling and prancing like a narcissus flower in January" (Lawrence 1995a, 221). Cuesta works the bull, playing "with death in the ring as if it had all kinds of gay little wings to spin him with the quickest, tiniest, most beautiful little movements" (Lawrence 1995a, 221).

Hemingway would never compare a bull to a flower, nor would he insert gay little wings into the struggle between man and bull. Nonetheless, these differences emphasize how the two writers view bullfighting. For Hemingway, the spectacle is a life-and-and death struggle, whereas for Lawrence it is almost frivolous, comparable to the silliness that Kate Leslie attributes to it in *The Plumed Serpent*. Although Hemingway does not portray the *corrida* as a cruel event, both he and Lawrence, in the best Mithraic tradition, refer to the killing of the bull as an act of love.[6] Ethel, like all the women under Cuesta's spell, responds emotionally.

> Cuesta opened his arms to the bull with a little smile, but endearing, lovingly endearing, as a man might open his arms to a little maiden he really loves, but really, for her to come to his body, his warm, open body, to come softly. So he held his arms out to the bull, with love. And that was what fascinated the women. They screamed and they fainted, longing to go into the arms of Cuesta. (Lawrence 1995a, 221–22)

Ethel shouts "Bravo!" because she is so moved, and her second "Bravo!" catches Cuesta's attention. He sees "her short, thick hair hanging like yellow metal, and her face dead-white, and her eyes glaring into his, like a challenge" (Lawrence 1995a, 222). He accepts the challenge and when at last, he kills the bull, it is as a man taking his mistress "because he is almost tired of playing with her" (Lawrence 1995a, 222). And the mortal love dance between Ethel and Cuesta begins.

None of this high drama is present in *The Sun Also Rises*. Jake explains bullfighting as an art form, and Brett is grateful for his knowledge and insights, but she only succeeds in catching Romero's attention when Jake introduces her to him. As with Ethel, the bond between the woman and the matador is immediate. Brett even reads the palm of Romero's hand, telling him that he will have a long life, and kill a thousand bulls (Hemingway 1926, 185–86). Later, after Romero kills the bull, he gives the ear to Brett (Hemingway 1926, 220). Despite their age difference, or perhaps because of it (Romero is 19 and Brett is in her 30s), Brett is smitten: "I'm a goner," she says. "It's tearing me all up inside" (Hemingway 1926, 183). Ethel is also a goner, although she does not know it yet, and for different reasons. When they meet, Cuesta, with his yellow eyes, looks at the little place in Ethel's body where she keeps her courage, and he tries to melt it, while she tries to catch his look on her imagination, "not on her naked inside body." For the time being neither manages to catch the other. Each one deflects the efforts of the other, and it is a standoff (Lawrence 1995a, 222).

Colmenares describes Cuesta as a rattlesnake and a scorpion, as an animal looking at Ethel with "rhapsodic hate" (Lawrence 1995a, 223–24). Meanwhile, Ethel, like Brett, is in a state of tension, but unlike Brett, who knows what to do with her body, Ethel cries out repeatedly that she does not know what to do with it (Lawrence 1995a, 225). Colmenares compares her pent-up desire to a dormant Popocatepetel on the verge of erupting, even as she continues to argue that the body and the imagination are two different things. She says, "If the imagination has the body under control, you can do anything" (Lawrence 1995a, 226). She even admits that her body has fallen for Cuesta, and she laments this abject condition of hers, seemingly unaware that she is the one who is keeping the two apart. Had she listened to the voice of her "blood-consciousness," and worked through the tangle of her feelings, she would have understood the futility of her efforts and perhaps even acted in time to save herself. The zeal of pure thought turns out to be lethal when it exiles the call of the body, as Lawrence's *The Man Who Died* discovers, after his "resurrection." *The Escaped Cock*, Lawrence's preferred title, is a cautionary tale for men and women who do not listen to the call of their bodies. Ethel was not unaware of sex, but she wanted her mind to control it, instead of allowing desire to meld with her will in order to become an integrated oneness. As Lawrence's *Escaped Cock* demonstrates, neglecting the phallus (desire) can lead to a dead end, in this case, a crucifixion. This novella demonstrates that "resurrection" and a new life are achievable if you cut through the knot that stifles desire. Ethel wanted none of that, and she paid for it dearly. Colmenares's descriptions of her behavior allow us to intuit its causes. His descriptions are the visible tip of the narrative iceberg. The implications of Ethel's mind-body split—the seven-eighths that are not narrated—are where the invisible portion of the iceberg resides. The narrated portion allows us to figure that which is veiled.

Hemingway's *Death in the Afternoon* and *The Dangerous Summer* reveal his expertise on the subject of bullfighting and his vast knowledge of its practices and traditions. Lawrence's books on psychoanalysis—*Fantasia of the Unconscious* and *Psychoanalysis and the Unconscious* are their equivalent. If the *corrida* is Hemingway's metaphor for life and death, courage, skill, and grace under pressure, then Lawrence's fiction, as an exploration of conscious and unconscious levels of being, dramatizes the psychology of self and demonstrates his psychoanalytic insights and artistic genius.

With the psychology of character in mind, Hemingway's fiction is all surface, although depths of feeling are implied everywhere. Descriptive passages of nature, places, events, and things, in keeping with his iceberg theory of writing that emphasizes omission and compression, act as objective correlatives for emotion and states of mind.[7] By contrast, Lawrence's writing moves freely from description to introspection, and his characters, unlike Hemingway's, describe their feelings and analyze themselves. Lawrence's sentences mime the mind's circular, sometimes convoluted search for meaning as it grapples with difficult situations, unusual relationships, and the tangle of the unconscious. Unlike Hemingway, both Lawrence and Colmenares, as narrators, comment freely on character motivation and feeling. Thus Ethel

Cane's obsessive need for control and lack of insight into herself or her sexuality, when paired with Cuesta's skill in the bullring, his social cunning, his appeal to women, and his male ego dramatize the clash of wills and Ethel's fatal flaw—the flaw that leads to her demise. It is the same control pattern and exclusion that, in *The Escaped Cock*, led to the man's crucifixion, the novella that is Lawrence's commentary on and rejection of repressed sexuality.[8]

In his *Studies on Hysteria* Freud concluded that sexuality was being excluded from the case histories he was recording, and, in this regard, Lawrence's *Psychoanalysis and the Unconscious and Fantasia of the Unconscious* inform us of what F.R. Leavis calls Lawrence's "diagnostic insight" (Leavis 1955, 9), an insight that is congruent with Freud's and Lacan's writings. If psychoanalysis, as theory, is the mind at work, then literature can be construed as the body. Lawrence's fiction—the body of his texts—is the kind of narrative that Freud valued (not necessarily Lawrence's, but all such narratives), due to the intimate link in Freud's mind between theory and the imagination. Freud says that when writing a psychiatric case history, he wants it to be judged as such but, dismayingly, it reads like a short story. Freud concludes that the short story as experience conveys information that is superior to psychoanalysis because theory must rely on the story in order to make itself heard (Freud 1953d, 160–61). Lawrence makes himself heard by combining theory and story and that is what makes works such as *The Escaped Cock* and "None of That!" so interesting and informative. These works and others reveal how "the psychoanalytic infuses Lawrence's work" (Williams 1997–98, 234) whenever sex and class, together—that which is excluded—become the story of "repression made flesh" (Williams 1997–98, 236).

In conclusion, Hemingway has a more extensive knowledge of bullfighting than Lawrence does, but Lawrence's psychology of self and the way he handles relationships between men and women is unmatched by Hemingway. Hemingway describes the social interactions of his characters in *The Sun Also Rises* with irony and humor, but his iceberg technique of writing precludes describing their inner lives or the psychology of their interactions.[9] We infer their states of mind from the realism of his descriptions, the objective correlatives, and the proleptic images.[10] Lawrence imposes no such limitations on his writing, and he is free to analyze his characters, describe motive, and delve into the inner recesses of their psyches. Hemingway avoids psychological analysis; he shifts this task onto the reader who must infer behavioral motives from the complex, linguistic machinery that he sets in motion. It is interesting and revealing that people and situations—in this case the emancipated women on the one hand, and bullfighting on the other—can result in two different, artistic renditions, both stylistically and thematically.

In Chapter Four we shall see how a boy's obsessive need to please his mother's mendacity and his compulsive rocking on the hobbyhorse lead to his demise. He lives in a house in which the walls repeatedly whisper "more money." It is not a happy house.

Chapter Four

"The Rocking-Horse Winner"

Pleasing the Mother

In the previous chapter we saw-how the "psychoanalytic," namely that which is excluded, becomes the story of "repression made flesh." Like "None of That!," "The Rocking-Horse Winner" also foregrounds the tragic consequences of a repetition-compulsion that kills. In order to understand what happens to Paul, the boy rocker, we need to frame the story within Freud's *Jokes and Their Relation to the Unconscious* and Lacan's "The agency of the letter in the unconscious or reason since Freud" (Lacan 1977b, 146). These two texts will explain the metaphorical slippages of language in relation to jokes and the metonymical desire of rocking in terms of the signifier. They will also highlight the deleterious effects of *Mind* and money-grubbing *doxa*.

"The Rocking-Horse Winner," one of a group of Lawrence's tales of the supernatural, appeared in October, 1926, in Cynthia Asquith's *The Ghost Book*.[1] It combines the mundane concerns of realistic fiction with the mystery of fantasy and fable and, like all good fairy tales, it also refers to social, familial, and psychological issues.[2] "On the social level, the tale reads as a satire on the equation of money, love, luck, and happiness" (Harris 1984, 225). On the familial level, the tale dramatizes the idea "that mothers shape their sons into the desirable opposite of their husbands" (Harris 1984, 225). Shaping the son, however, as Elizabeth M. Fox notes, can occur on the unconscious as well as the conscious level. She cites André Green's 1980 essay, "The Dead Mother," in order to analyze maternal loss within a psychoanalytic context, a loss that has profoundly shaped Paul, the boy in "The Rocking-Horse Winner" (Fox 2009, 151). Green's theory characterizes the impact of maternal loss due to psychic death, not physical death. Fox demonstrates how the boy's compulsive rocking to earn his mother's love is thwarted by her inability to love. Paul is the Freudian ego riding the id of his hobbyhorse. In trying "to get there" he rides but the *I* and the *it* never meld, and the two entities remain separate because his mother will not or cannot give him the love he needs.

73

Demetria DeLia, in "Bridled Rage: Preoedipal Theory and 'The Rocking-Horse Winner,'" echoes Fox's analysis of the story. However, instead of Green's theories about the causes of childhood rage, she focuses on Hymon Spotnitz's pre-oedipal theories (DeLia 2020, 219). DeLia also discusses the causes of Hester's mendacity and her inability to love Paul as the consequence of a generational gambling addiction (DeLia 2020, 222). From one generation to the next the family's dysfunction has played itself out on the narcissistic level as need, lack, rage, and compulsive behavior.

The psychological level is also the level that interests us here because the story uses the rocking-horse as a symbolic extension of the boy's need, the result of his mother's psychic death. According to W.D. Snodgrass, the sexual area is "the basic area in which begins the pattern of living which the rocking-horse symbolizes" (Snodgrass 1963, 121),[3] and, I would add, needy living. Its symbolic extensions are "the story's chief structural feature" (Snodgrass 1963, 117). As Snodgrass, Janice Hubbard Harris, Fox, and others have observed, Paul, the preadolescent boy, frequently retreats to his room where, in secrecy, he mounts his hobbyhorse and rides himself into a trance. Snodgrass maintains that even a brief reading of Lawrence's essay, "Pornography and Obscenity," in concert with "The Rocking-Horse Winner," should convince us that Paul's ecstasy is not only religious but also psychic and sexual. Insofar as riding a horse can symbolize the sex act, and "riding" was once the common verb for having sex, riding the rocking-horse can be construed as "the child's imitation of the sex act, for the riding which goes nowhere" (Snodgrass 1963, 122). Harris, like Snodgrass, believes that rocking and its results echo Lawrence's description of and objection to masturbation in "Pornography and Obscenity" (Harris 1984, 226).

In addition to Snodgrass's and Harris's equation of rocking with masturbation, W.S. Marks's essay on "The Psychology of the Uncanny" is a Freudian interpretation of "The Rocking-Horse Winner." Marks analyzes the tale in light of Freud's *Collected Papers,* and he alludes to "the kind of verbal ambiguity Freud delighted in exploring as a clue to the repressed life of his patients" (Marks 1965–66, 384).[4] Marks, however, makes no mention of the wordplay between *lucre* and *lucker,* Freud's analysis of *Jokes and Their Relation to the Unconscious,* or the *Fort!/Da!* episode in *Beyond the Pleasure Principle.* Nor has anyone analyzed rocking as a signifier without a signified. The essays of Snodgrass, Harris, and Marks point in the right direction, but we need to take rocking beyond onanism into the realm of the Symbolic where the signifier can act out its role on the scene of language.

If Paul rides his rocking-horse long enough and hard enough he can foretell the future. With uncanny insight the boy is able to predict the name of the next winning horse at the races. Paul wants to be lucky, desperately, and he succeeds, or so it seems, because, before he dies, and as a result of naming the winner, he earns 80,000 pounds. He wants to be lucky because his mother says that she and her husband, the boy's father, are "unlucky." Also, because the house whispers, "There must be more money! There must be more money!" The words come "whispering from the springs of the still-swaying rocking-horse" (Lawrence 1995d, 231). Although no one speaks it, the whispers are everywhere.

The house is haunted by this phrase, and all three children hear the whisper that springs continuously from every corner of every room. The horse, the dollhouse, and the puppy also hear the whispering as the story shifts from realism into the realm of the fantastic. If the story is to "get us there," the way rocking illumines Paul, the reader, like the boy, must believe in the horse's superior powers. But Paul's divination works only when he plays with his toy. Only his frenzied rocking gives him the names of the winning horses: Sansovino, Daffodil, Lively Spark, and Malabar.

The story's fantastic element derives in part from the strange collusion between the organic and the inorganic: the house has become a living, breathing, sentient entity that orchestrates a whispering campaign. "'Oh-h-h; there must be more money. Oh now, now-w! now-w-w—there *must* be more money!'—more than ever! More than ever!" (Lawrence 1995d, 239). The voices in the house come from "behind the sprays of mimosa and almond-blossoms, and from under the piles of iridescent cushions" in an orgasmic "ecstasy" that frightens the boy (Lawrence 1995d, 239).

Paul's goal is to stop the whispers. He also wants to prove to his mother that he is lucky. Although the rocking frenzy "gets him there" and gives him the luck he craves, this same rocking madness eventually kills him. Meanwhile, the horse rocks back-and-forth between the plausible and the uncanny, even as the boy slips in-and-out of his trances—trances during which God ostensibly communicates the name(s) of the winning horse(s). "It's as if he had it from heaven," says Bassett (Lawrence 1995d, 236).

One day Paul asks his mother if luck is money, and she says "no," luck is "what causes you to have money" (Lawrence 1995d, 231). Subsequently the boy rocks himself into the lucky kingdom of lucre in order to stop the house's whispering and to make his mother happy. Despite his mother's skepticism, he says that God told him that he was lucky. God is invoked again, ironically, at the end of the story when Uncle Oscar says to his sister, the boy's mother, "My God, Hester, you're eighty-odd thousand to the good, and a poor devil of a son to the bad" (Lawrence 1995d, 243). Although casually invoked, allusions to the supernatural give plausibility to an "impossible" story. Binary oppositions, such as God and the devil, or good and bad, reinforce the story's rhythm and emphasis on the acts of breathing in-and-out and rocking back-and-forth. It is perhaps inevitable that living and dying should also be part of the pattern. Although mounting and rocking are unlikely agents of luck, they are sexual metaphors that, when deciphered, transport us, or should I say rock the reader beyond the story's realism into the realm of the unconscious where Freud's analyses of jokes and Lacan's "agency of the letter" perform their magic.

Although the boy may play with his horse and adults may play the horses, there is also a semantic "free play" that activates the back-and-forth play of signifiers. In addition to child's play and the connotation of gambling, the word "play" also functions linguistically and psychoanalytically—linguistically with the continuous slippage of the floating signifiers, and psychoanalytically with the similarities between Paul's compulsive rocking and little Ernst's game of *Fort!/Da!*—a game that Freud describes in *Beyond the Pleasure Principle* (Freud 1953a, 15).

One day, after observing Ernst toss a spool over the crib and retrieve it by pulling on the string to which the spool was attached, Freud concluded that the boy's expression *Fort!* sends the mother away symbolically, and his *Da!* brings her back. The horse like the spool has become a substitute for the absent mother because rocking back-and-forth and throwing the spool across the crib are games of control that stem from the boys' desire to reduce the pain of loss and enhance the pleasure of presence. Little Ernst sends the mother away, symbolically, with each *Fort!,* and retrieves her with each *Da!*, a relatively innocent game compared to Paul's rocking and its highly charged erotic connotations. Little Ernst's game can be read as a paradigm of retrieval—the embodied presence of an absence and the substitution for it of the symbolic act and its object. Paul's rocking enables him to identify the winning horse, and, by betting on the winner, he earns money for his mother, proves that he is lucky, and earns her love. Because the world of words creates the world of things (Lacan 1977a, 87; Lacan 1966a, 183), symbolic language replaces absence, be it breast or mother, thereby generating contact with the body of one's mother tongue. The father may prohibit the language of incestuous longing and belonging, but the subject strives to circumvent his name (*nom/non*). Thus humor, jokes, puns, and slips of the tongue, act to circumvent the obstacle, even as paronomasia becomes the currency of intervocalic mirth. Paul becomes the "filthy lucker" conjured by his innocent question to his mother.

This "joke" plays with the difference and ambiguity of two words: *lucre* and *luck.* The conversation noted earlier between Paul and his mother illustrates the slippage when she tells her son that luck causes you to have money. "Oh!" said Paul vaguely. "I thought when Uncle Oscar said *filthy lucker* it meant money." "*Filthy lucre* does mean money," said the mother. "But it's lucre, not luck" (Lawrence 1995d, 231). This play on two words derives from the boy's misrecognition of his uncle's statement concerning *filthy lucre* and his transformation of it into *filthy lucker.* In this context, *filthy lucker* seems to imply that the lucky person derives his luck from some unsavory source. In any case, it is *money* that connects *lucre* and *luck.* Indeed, as a result of the conversation with his mother, Paul will associate luck with money and he will exercise his infantile power to amass it.

Despite the reader's amusement, Paul and his mother show no sign of mirth because the spelling, pronunciation, and mispronunciation of the word consist "in focusing our psychical attitude upon the *sound* of the word instead of upon its *meaning*—in making the (acoustic) word-presentation itself take the place of its significance as given by its relations to thing-presentations" (Harris 1984, 225).[5] Freud refers to children who are accustomed to treating the word as an object and who are inclined to find the same meaning in words of the same or of similar sounds. He has analyzed at some length what he calls "innocent jokes," jokes that "are likely to put the problem [. . .] before us in its purest form" (Freud 1953c, 94). Although the words *lucre* and *lucker* seem harmless, Lawrence places them on the tip of the narrative iceberg where they reveal the play of the signifier that is hidden within the sea of the unconscious.

The energizing sources are humor and slips of the tongue. Lacan, who is renowned for the elliptical nature of his writings, has characterized Freud's *Jokes and Their Relation to the Unconscious* as his most transparent text. Furthermore Lacan uses Freud's insights in his own writings, and he leaves no stone unturned in his efforts to uncover the hieroglyph written "in the sand of the flesh" (*"sur le sable de la chair"*; Lacan 1977a, 69; Lacan 1966a, 160). Because the unconscious is structured like a language, the father's rule is threatened whenever the subject plays with words, with tropes, and the combinatory power of language. This combinatory power may be conscious or unconscious. For example, Derrida's *Glas* is a voluntary gesture in which sound directs the play of meaning, whereas Freud's *Jokes and Their Relation to the Unconscious* argues in favor of the involuntary and unpremeditated display of linguistic comedy. Lacan says: "Through the word—already a presence made of absence—absence gives itself a name in that moment of origin whose perpetual recreation Freud's genius detected in the play of the child" ("Par le mot qui est déjà une présence faite d'absence, l'absence même vient à se nommer en un moment original don't le génie de Freud a saisi dans le jeu de l'enfant la recréation perpétuelle"; (Lacan 1977a;, 65; Lacan 1966a, 155).

Paul, his mother, and the reader focus on sound, but sense is by no means elided because this passage, and the story itself, will ultimately depend on meaning and the contamination of meaning by this preliminary wordplay. Although money and luck are not necessarily connected, they sometimes go together, despite the mother's allegation to the contrary. Lawrence's story does in fact exploit the lucre/lucker connection. Freud says that certain usages of language are able to produce a "good" joke or a "bad" one.

According to him a good joke, such as this one, depends on the exploitation of double meaning or on a slightly modified word in order to get from one idea to another by means of a "short cut," in this case *luck* and *money* (Freud 1953c, 121).

In the real world a currency's value is measured against the false, but in the realm of the Symbolic, the displacement, compression, condensation, and dramatization of the neologism override any prosaic denotation. Freud's "alcoholidays" derives its linguistic sparkle from the compression of two words: alcohol and holidays, and also from the three letters "hol," which they share. The ending of one word is the beginning of the other. The meaning of one word has been displaced, and it coincides with our recognition that the practice of drinking during the holidays is a frequent cultural ritual. We smile knowingly at and with the complicity of the neologism (Freud 1953c, 22). Freud's additional examples are *Traduttore—Traditore* (translator—traitor), and *Amantes—Amentes* (lovers—lunatics). "The two disparate ideas which are here linked by an external association, are also united in a significant relation indicating an essential kinship between them. [. . .] A 'translator' is not only called by a similar name to 'traitor'; he actually *is* a kind of traitor and bears the name, as it were by right" (Freud 1953c, 121). The same is true of *Amantes—Amentes.* Not only do the words resemble each other, there is also an affinity between the words "love" and "lunacy," which, according to Freud, has been noted from time immemorial.

Luck and *lucre* display comparable associations of sound and meaning. The boy's rocking, like the above slippages of language, "gets him there" by the shortest route he knows: he names the winning horse, he proves that he is lucky, and he wins the money. The reader also gets there, and the story works due of the meaningful association of ideas. Although mother and son don't know it, the wordplay on lucre/lucker is a "good" joke. It would be a "bad" joke if there were only a play on sound. The boy's mispronunciation of the word sets the stage for the story's ending, when the meaning and irony come into focus. Only then, when the boy is dead and his uncle calls him a "poor devil," does the full linguistic range of associative play manifest itself. Only then do words such as "God," "money," "devil," "luck," and "poor" resonate with and illumine the conversation between Paul and his mother when she tells him that his father has no luck because they are "the poor members of the family." Paul's response is that he is lucky and that God told him so (Lawrence 1995d, 82–83). Roy Lamson, in "A Critical Analysis of 'The Rocking-Horse Winner,'" also refers to Hester's obsession with money, and the fact that Paul experiences luck but no mother-love, without, however, acknowledging the wordplay that is such an important element in the story (Lamson 1949, 546–47). Jeffrey Meyers, in "D.H. Lawrence's Children" (Meyers 2020, 217), also refers to the mother's upper-class financial anxiety and social pretensions that destroy the family because she values money above affection. Hester, says Meyers, symbolizes "modern man's mad mechanical gallop for wealth and material goods" (Meyers 2020, 217).

The associative wordplay of the words *luck* and *lucre* manifests itself on the socioeconomic level of the story as well as the verbal level. The greater the economy in words, says Freud, the more effective the joke. In wordplay less is more because economy and pleasure are related. In Lawrence's story, from the characters' point of view, economy (little money) and displeasure are related, and Paul will try to master this economic disproportion. Because the family is poor the mother must economize in order to make ends meet and keep up appearances. Paul's lucky money—the money he wins by predicting the winning horse—should have pleased her but, ironically, more is never enough. It's as though Lawrence had used Freud's "Mechanism of Pleasure and the Psychogenesis of Jokes" deliberately in order to structure his story around the economy of pleasure—the economy that determines what is or is not a good joke: "This yield of pleasure corresponds to the economy of psychical expenditure that is saved," says Freud (Freud 1953c, 118). Verbal jokes are a source of pleasure because they exploit double meanings in the ambiguities of words. This ambiguity invites the reader to collaborate in the creation of a parallel text to the one the writer has scripted, and, in doing so, the reader forms a tropic network using the holes, traces, words, repetitions, sentences, structures, paragraphs, and figural motifs. Underlying all of this is the voice of the Other caught in the folds of the text—a voice that the reader unfolds so that the body can be heard and seen and touched and felt almost intuitively in what Roland Barthes in *Le Plaisir du texte* (Barthes 1973, 105) describes as orgasmic bliss (*jouissance*).

Although pleasure begins with the wordplay of related meanings in the lucre/lucker sequence, pleasure and its opposite—discontent—run throughout the story on a parallel track. Paul thinks that money will please his mother but she is forever discontent. For her son, being lucky is a source of pleasure because it stems from his ability to name the winner. Her dissatisfaction, however, despite the son's winnings, prompts him to keep riding, even when his mother says that God does not predict winners (Lawrence 1995d, 83). The boy, however, knows better because, when he rocks, he "hears" the winner's name. The bliss or pleasure of hearing, according to the French play of words, *j'ouïs* (*jouis*), when translated as to hear and to enjoy, is what getting there means—naming the horse. The sexual connotations of rocking inevitably enhance the *jouissance*.[6] Says Freud, "The technical methods of joking [such as] condensation, displacement, and indirect representation possess the power of evoking a feeling of pleasure in the hearer" (Freud 1953c, 95).

The technique of jokes is therefore due to a special process that has "left behind in the wording of the joke a second trace—the formation of a

substitute" (Freud 1953c, 28). This process has a striking similarity to the
processes of condensation in dreams that also lead to abbreviations and
substitutive formation (Freud 1953c, 166). But since the dream-work, as we
know, is the language of the unconscious, for Lacan the similarities between
condensation in dreams and condensation in wit point toward the discourse
of the Other, that is, toward the material that has been repressed. The concrete
(conscious) discourse of Lawrence's story veils the discourse of the Other
that begins to poke through with the initial witticism. Condensation produces
economy and it is this tendency to economize that produces the joke: instead
of putting together a few new words, "it has to take the trouble to search out
the Word which covers the two thoughts" (Freud 1953c, 44). Accordingly, the
logic of Lawrence's story structures the following syllogism: a poor family
must economize; if Paul's family had money his mother would not have to
economize; and if they have no money, it is because they are not lucky. Paul
will become the *lucker* who rescues the family and his mother. But there is
more in the word *lucker* than the mispronunciation of *lucre*. Besides, what
is a *lucker?* The word does not exist in the dictionary, but its association
with luck (both acoustically and in its spelling) establishes an affinity with
money. A purposeful association of ideas is established in Paul's mind and in
the reader's.

However, because Paul and his mother do not laugh at the lucre/lucker witticism and derive no pleasure from it, a third person is needed to activate the
play of the signifiers. The reader's role is to pick up on the verbal play and
give it the comic resonance it deserves. The story then becomes a formulaic
account of unconscious activity, and the joke alerts us to the condensations
and displacements that are unveiled by Paul's compulsive rocking. The word
"lucky" denotes winning at the racetrack but it connotes winning the mother's
love, hence Lacan's S_1/S_2 algorithm in which S_1 denotes and S_2 connotes. This
is indeed a weighty affair, and its success will be measured in British pounds.

Although the family has no *filthy lucre* it may have a *filthy lucker*. The
humorous and derogatory sense of the first term spills over onto the second
one, which has no meaning except in the boy's mind and our associative
fancy. The boy creates a neologism and then goes about proving that lucre
and luck are related. Nonetheless, as the reader tries to make sense out of
nonsense, the word *filthy* sticks to *lucker,* the new word. The boy's association
authorizes the reader's association and consequent free play with the floating
signifiers. If, in light of Lacan's *jouissance* and Derrida's traces, the reader
has been playing the linguistic game, the *f*-trace of *filthy* slides over to replace
the *l* of *lucker,* thereby producing the word *fucker.* The erotic connotations of
rocking and riding also lend legitimacy to this verbal slippage. We now have a
new noun and a new verb, words that the reader might dismiss were it not for

the baggage of the Oedipal triangle, repression, desire, and the dissemination of verbal (psychic) traces. The term *little fucker* becomes more insistent and is consonant with the boy's compulsive rocking and frenzied playing with his toy. "Words are a plastic material with which one can do all kinds of things," says Freud (Freud 1953c, 34). Derrida's *traces* apply the same plasticity of letters of the alphabet, the letters with which we form words. In a context of desire it is the structure of Lawrence's story that transforms *filthy lucre* into *little fucker,* the latter being an anagram of the first with a slight shift in pronunciation.

The verb "to fuck" derives from the Latin *word futuere,* the old French *foutre,* and the German word *ficken.* It means to strike but in popular speech it means to copulate with. The word "fuck" thus combines the vocalism of *futuere* and the consonantism of *ficken* (Partridge 1958, 239). No wonder Paul is interested in his Latin studies. It is the humor in the shift from *lucre* to *lucker* that also authorizes the use of the letter *f* from the word *filthy.* The words *filthy lucker* and *filthy lucre* are used contiguously and we might ask what kind of sense the letter *f* and the word *lucker* produce, if not *fucker,* since fucking is precisely the content of the story that is repressed but which is, nonetheless, manifest in the symptom "little rocker." *Fucker* is the word that the story omits, and this omission points exactly to that which has been repressed. The shift from and association with *lucker* and *lucre* invite other transpositions based on phonetic and phonemic similarities: lucker/lucre/rocker/focker/fucker, all of which seem to generate the boy's brain fever and the reader's illumination through the dissemination of paronomastic traces.

Derrida's and Lacan's emphasis on the inherent instability of the signifier and the resultant dissemination of meaning in structuring a reader's response encourages the kind of semantic free play that underlies all jokes. In *L'Écriture et la différence, De la grammatologie,* and *La Dissémination* Derrida elaborates in detail on intervocalic slippages in paronomasia because these pulsive forces inscribe their passage on the reader's mind.[7] Derrida calls it *frayage,* whereas Freud's metaphor for such inscriptions is the magical writing pad. Although the pad's inscriptions may be erased, they do, nonetheless, leave a mark—a trace—that can be seen when the pad is examined at a certain angle and under certain lighting conditions (Freud 1953a, 25). In writing, intervocalic slippage also leaves conscious and unconscious trails in the reader's mind. They may be hidden or disguised or barely noticeable, but their presence can be felt, and it is the reader who apprehends them, consciously or not, organizing them into meaningful units. These units circulate within a text energizing the activity of writing and reading. They reinforce the tropes and the voice of the Other, they disrupt realism and representation, they form gaps, and, in collusion with the floating signifiers, they bar the way to the signified.

Derrida's *Glas* (the sound of a bell, or knell) illustrates the process because the French phoneme *gl* shares *Glas*'s resonance, reverberating throughout the text. In *Deconstructive Criticism: An Advanced Introduction* (Leitch 1983, 209), Vincent Leitch points out that the *gl* of *glas* mimes the sound tolled by the death knell (*glas*). It both separates (*glose*) and joins (*glu*). "As *glace*, it is icing on the cake and flaw in the gem, or a window. Like *gleet*, the *gl* makes up bodily discharges like phlegm and mucus (*glaire*)." Overall, it is the cry of an *écriture* (*glapir*). The effect of such paronomasia is to foreground the materiality of language by shifting the reader's attention away from its "transparency" to the "opacity" of the signifier. The interplay of signifiers and their traces, whether orchestrated by the author or the reader or both, stresses the text, the intertext, the context, and the subtext. The reader's role is to listen to the sound of signs and to entertain their diversity because the voice of the Other is always speaking.

Traces take on meaning through their differential opposition to and in combination with other traces. Lacan's readiness to play with sounds is legendary: the word *lettre* (letter) becomes *l'être* (being), language becomes *lalangue*, linguistics evolves into a pejorative *linguisterie*, and everything ends up as *litière* (litter). There is also the ostrich from which Lacan develops *la politique de l'autruiche*, the word "Austria" enriched by the denomination of one letter and the familiar head-in-the-sand proverb of the bird (Lacan 1988, 32 and 1966b, 24).

If we subscribe to the generative possibilities of linguistic dissemination and the subversion of the father that writing represents (the boy rocks in order to compensate for the fact that his father is not lucky), then the letters in *filthy lucre* may be rearranged to produce the anagram *Lucifer*. In this context, worldly pleasures are Lucifer's temptations, even as the reader is tempted to associate the word filthy with the activities of the "little fucker" who wants more lucre. The reader's riches and pleasures are in the story's joke and in its irony. Indeed, the uncle's allusion to his sister's "poor devil of a son to the bad" (Lawrence 1995d, 243) is consonant with these shifts and transpositions insofar as we are dealing with a text that mimes the unconscious—that realm where the free play of the signifier encourages these otherwise implausible and perhaps outrageous slippages of sound and meaning. In the reader's mind, the pretext for happiness is the game of writing, the play of reading, and the sweep of similitude. This free play gives the reader a leading role in rewriting the text, because in reading a trope, they must decipher (figure out) the semantic transposition from a sign that is present to one that is absent. The reader has to work from the macrotext of the plot to the microtext of the traces embedded in it. Somewhere between, around, over, and under these pulsive forces, the points of join between visible language and invisible *effect* come into play.

We must not forget that jokes and dreams survive only on displacement, condensation, and irony. Surely the ending of Lawrence's story is ironic in that, despite the son's unusual powers, he is now a poor and dead devil, whereas his mother is 80,000 pounds to the good. But what good are all the riches in the world if she loses her son? With regard to luck, she was right to say that God never tells, because God is love, not lucre, and the one thing that Hester was incapable of doing was loving her children (Lawrence 1995b, 31). Because money is what she wanted more than anything, her wish has been fulfilled. The uncle's "My God" resonates with appropriate irony as we grasp the significance of Hester's relationship with her son and the fact that she has unconsciously sold him to Lucifer for lucre—the money that is the object of her mendacity and the source of Christ's temptation in the desert. The word *whisper* has a homonymic resemblance to the mother's name *Hester,* which appears only once, at the end of the story, where it echoes the house's whispers of the opening pages. Hester's whispers are what the boy constantly hears and acts on. The house is Hester, both symbolically and psychoanalytically, and the "ecstatic" whispers are charged with a sexuality to which the boy responds (Lawrence 1995d, 92). He needs his mother's love but she is unable to give him the love he craves. If Paul could only give her enough money, since his mother wants someone who is lucky, she might be able to love him. He could then recapture the happiness that now eludes him—the green paradise of the pre-Oedipal phase when he and his mother were as one and not yet separated by the Law. Baudelaire calls it the green paradise of childhood.

Furthermore, Lucifer comes from the Latin word meaning "light-bearer." The word "light" is also related to "luster" because in Latin, *lūcēre* means "to shine"; and "light-bringing" comes from the word *lūx,* which is light. Even without the anagram, the word *lucifer* in Latin leads to *Lucifer* in both Latin and English. *Lūx* also evolves into *luna* (the moon), and *fānāticus,* that is, living in the moon, allows for lunatic, trances, madness, and epileptic seizures. These illuminating associations from the Latin *lūx* all apply to Paul in one way or another. The anagram only serves to confirm the demonic source of the money, rather than its God-given origin. If Paul is lucky, his lucre comes not from God but from the devil. We, like Paul, need to study our Greek and Latin in order to understand the connection.

Whenever Paul rocks his horse his eyes are described as "blue fire" or "blazing" or "having a canny cold fire" in them or "blazing with a sort of madness." To name the winner Paul must indeed be illumined. In fact, there is an unusual congruence of light and rocking during the climactic moment when he names Malabar—the winning horse at the Derby. Let us relive the setting: Paul is in his room plunging to and fro on his horse at one o'clock in the morning. His mother has just returned from a party in town and goes upstairs.

> She switched on the light, and saw her son, in his green pajamas, madly surging on the rocking-horse. The blaze of light suddenly lit him up, as he urged the wooden horse, and lit her up, as she stood, blonde, in her dress of pale green and crystal, in the doorway.
> "Paul!" she cried." "Whatever are you doing?"
> "It's Malabar!" he screamed in a powerful, strange voice. "It's Malabar!"
> His eyes blazed at her for one strange and senseless second, as he ceased urging his wooden horse. Then he fell with a crash to the ground. (Lawrence 1995d, 242)

The mother switches on "the light" and the "blaze" *illumines* her and the boy. She cries, "Paul," he screams, "Malabar," and his eyes also "blaze." In French, *un illuminé* refers to someone who is both a visionary and a fanatic, words that describe Paul's ability to predict the future and his obsession. But what is the meaning of Malabar?[8]

The word *Mal,* from Latin and Old French, signifies *bad* and is usually a prefix, as in the word *malfunction.* In French, the word *mal* means "evil," as in *le mal*; *Le Malin,* in French, is the devil. This is indeed a "bad (evil) joke" that resonates ironically with the "good joke" in the text and Freud's analysis of verbal play. The disseminated meaning of *mal* echoes the "poor devil to the bad," thus connoting the evil of possessions (lucre), since the mother's obsession with money is a form of possession (by the devil), as is the boy's compulsion to be lucky: "Oh, absolutely! Mother, did I ever tell you? I *am* lucky!" (Lawrence 1995d, 243). These are the last words Paul speaks before he dies. His eyes are now like two blue stones, his mother's heart has turned to stone, and his father's voice is stony. Happiness, if that is what luck and money might have brought them, has eluded them. Lucre is all they have. Is it a coincidence that the boy rocking in the dark names Malabar when the light shines on him? Is it a coincidence that Lucifer, the light-bearer, fell from grace, and that the boy falls from his horse? After his fall and before he dies, Paul is sick for three days with brain fever. It is sometimes said that high fever is the result of demonic possession and that spirit control is exercised from without. The spirit is said to have entered the person in order to foretell the future or to proclaim the will of a god. Paul does foretell the future, when he can "get there," but his trancelike rocking and the lucre/lucker connection seem more demonic than Godlike. However, if Lucifer's light shines on the 80,000 pounds, it does not necessarily illumine the unconscious play of the signifier. To do that we must shed linguistic and semiotic rays on those invisible and repressed parts of the story where the devil may or may not be present.

It will be useful to focus on Lacan's "agency of the letter in the unconscious or reason since Freud" (Lacan 1977a, 146–78), because, as a metaphor of the unconscious, "The Rocking-Horse Winner" highlights the play of the signifier and the role of the symptom that veils desire (Lacan 1966a, 249–89, my translation). Indeed, the veiled sexual activity of rocking has a triple function: getting there, naming the winner, and winning the money, which, in effect, is winning the mummy. Whereas the father is unlucky, the son, by winning and displacing the father, proves to himself and to his mother that he is lucky. The homonymic slippage between the words money and mummy is consonant with the mother's compulsive need for money, the house's repeated whispering, and intervocalic play.

"Words," says Lacan, "are trapped in all the corporeal images that captivate the subject." They "undergo symbolic lesions" and they "accomplish imaginary acts of which the patient is the subject" ("Les mots sont pris dans toutes les images corporelles qui captivent le sujet. [. . .] les mots peuvent eux-mêmes subir les lésions symboliques, accomplir les actes imaginaires dont le patient est le sujet"). Lacan cites Freud's example of *The Wolf Man* and the word *Wespe* (wasp) whose *W* is castrated in order to become the subject's initials, S.P. (Lacan 1977a, 87; Lacan 1966b, 183). Words in the Lacanian system are less stable than they are in the Saussurean (and even less so in the Derridian), so that the traces, erasures, and slippages that affect signifiers are the "symbolic lesions" that help the subject "accomplish imaginary acts." For example, Paul mounts his horse in the house of the mother. The difference between "horse" and house is in the letters *r* and *u*. If the house is the mother's displaced signifier (because the house, like Hester, the mother, wants money), and rocking is the symptom of desire, then mounting the horse and rocking it in the mother's house, or in the mother's name, in order to get there, that is, acquire money (mummy) is tantamount to mounting the mother. To be lucky is to get mummy (money) and that is what all the rocking is about. Rocking is a variant of the *Fort!Da!* game in which Paul is indeed the "lucky fucker." Rocking the horse may be onanistic, but Paul is also fucking the mother symbolically, hence the *filthy lucre/little fucker* transposition, and, his climactic win is the horse's name inscribed in his head—the name that wins the money but not the mummy, since she can never have enough. Money is power and power is potency, and money pleases the mother. Her *lack* is that she wants money, a classical Freudian case of penis envy that also inscribes itself on the boy's psyche. He wants the phallus because he is not yet a man and the mother wants the phallus because she is a woman, yet the *non/nom du père* and female biology deprive them both of what they desire.

The inscribed lack materializes the bond between mother and son. Death and desire are bound together, inextricably, as the boy rocks himself to death listening to the mother's lullaby. The maternal house (voice) whispers "more money," and the boy who cannot sleep because he doesn't have the answer, rocks endlessly in the darkness of his room in order to get there. In the final episode, when his mother switches on the light, the name Malabar inscribes itself on the boy's inflamed mind and he falls into a coma. Malabar wins, but winning his *Ma* is the *grand mal* that kills him—be it sin or the penalty for violating the Law.[9] Visually, the boy's green pajamas and the mother's green dress are the symbolic link between the two. The word "arrested" also links mother and son because Lawrence describes the "arrested prance of the horse" and Hester standing outside her son's room with "arrested muscles" (Lawrence 1995d, 94).[10] The word "arrested" and the color green connect the mother, the son, and the horse in one unmistakable triad that features arrested development.

The rocking process bridges the time gap between childhood and adulthood, between fantasy and reality. A biological time warp is impossible, yet getting there is what Paul achieves symbolically. This is perhaps the meaning of the brain fever that kills him. On the realistic level Paul's ability to predict the winner is impossible, but on the symbolic level his rocking materializes (wins) the letter of the unconscious. The "little fucker" nets his filthy lucre.

Lacan's "agency of the letter" designates the structure of language insofar as the subject is implicated in it. The *Mal* (evil) within the name Malabar comes from the substitution of language for the thing. Desire implicates the subject, but it is language that names him. The gap between the signifier and the signified is not only a function of the aporia of language, but also a function of substitution. It operates metonymically. Playing with the toy horse—the compulsive rocking that names the winner in order to win the money (mummy)—names a "real" horse in the adult world where money is potency—a world in which money and potency are important because Paul's parents are the poor members of the family, that is, they have been castrated of their wealth. Winning mummy in the boy's world is a form of metonymic potency, but once again it underscores the gap between the signifier and the signified, between the unconscious and the conscious worlds. "Rocking" (S_1) is a sign that denotes serious play whose purpose is to name, but it (S_2) connotes "mounting the mother" in an equally serious although unnamed game of retrieval. The letter of the unconscious thus designates the very structure of language, literally, from which, the subject (the boy) borrows the material support of his conscious and unconscious discourse. The brain fever that afflicts him before he dies may be construed as the impossibility of crossing the Saussurean bar (S/s), as in Mal/a/bar, or of ever reconciling the difference between the signifier and the signified. The difference is forever deferred in the play of the sign, in the compulsive rocking that names a symptom that is also forever displaced. The letter of the unconscious is the "material support that concrete discourse borrows from language" ("Nous désignons par lettre ce support matériel que le discours concret emprunte au langage"; Lacan 1977b, 147; Lacan 1966b, 251), concrete discourse being the act of rocking, the activity itself that names. The letter of the unconscious is the material support that sustains the rocking/mounting that is the Imaginary and the Real. The "real" letter, as in Edgar Allan Poe's story, "The Purloined Letter," is hidden, but in a place so evident that no one sees it. Indeed the letter has a certain materiality and it occupies a space but this "relation to place" is always an "out of place" (*un manque à sa place;* Lacan 1966b, 35), that is, a displacement, and the symptom (compulsive rocking) is the material sign of that displacement. The problem to be solved and the letter to be found consists in recognizing the symptom and the significance of its displacement. The letter of the unconscious is not where we think it is, although it is always in plain view and, as with Oedipus, when he finally "sees" who Jocasta really is—his mother—he blinds himself in order to atone for the fact that his eyes had failed to see what had for so long been staring him in the face.

We are back to Oedipus, which is what the letter of the unconscious is about—the message inscribed in the subject's unconscious, the voice of the Other that manifests itself in symptoms—the displacements and condensations of Symbolic language. The subject is installed by the Other on the rocking-horse of desire where the symptom is played out in the game of loss and retrieval, impotence and potency; where the loser (Paul dies) wins the Derby (money/mummy). This is yet another example of the anteriority of language in relation to the individual, of an inscription that accompanies the misrecognition (*méconnaissance*) of self during the "mirror phase," evidence of the inevitable aporia between the Imaginary and the Real. Language is the symptom and lesion of this primal inscription where desire rocks back-and-forth in the energized game of foretelling. This foreplay is a matter of life and death in which the message ostensibly comes from God—the absent transcendental signifier who "never tells." Nonetheless, desire confirms the presence of the Law and the name-of-the-father is Malabar. The evil (*mal*) of crossing the Saussurean "bar" is in naming the unnameable—the impossibility of the sign, and the failure of its unity. Although Lawrence had no knowledge of Saussure's *Course in General Linguistics,* Malabar is such a fortuitous and convenient word that it would be sinful, even demonic, not to exploit its potential and symbolic link between presence and absence, as well as the story's formulaic accuracy in defining the agency of the letter in the unconscious.

All evil (*mal*), says Lacan, stems from the conception of language in relation to the thing (Lacan 1977b, 149–50; Lacan 1966b, 253–54). According to

Jean-Luc Nancy and Philippe Lacoue-Labarthe, Lacan destroys the sign "in order to consolidate the science of the letter" in the unconscious (Nancy and Lacoue-Labarthe 1992, 39). The sign of rocking the horse is under erasure because it no longer signifies rocking. The rocking itself has been displaced in order to signify something else. The S/s algorithm is a sign (under erasure). It is not destroyed, but then again it is not functioning as it should. The signifier, signified, and signification are still there, but the system has been perverted. It is being asked to perform differently. Malabar accents the "evil" (*mal*) of the Saussurean "bar" because accenting the bar highlights the division in the sign. The burden of signification is displaced from the signified, that is, the denoted, to the signifier because what it connoted is what is "absent," and it is absent only because it is in the unconscious and inaccessible to the subject. In the place of the signified (rocking) another function (mounting the mother) is introduced that erases it, and, in terms of unconscious desire, replaces it. Rocking the horse goes nowhere, except symbolically, because of its signified denotation, but "getting there" has its function because the repetition of the *Fort!/Da!* foregrounds the role of the signifier. The signifier, not the signified, makes connotation possible, and that is why the lucker/lucre joke is so significant. The play of the signifier, according to François Raffoul and David Pettigrew, is "confirmed in its threefold determination: materiality/localization/symbolization" (Raffoul and Pettigrew 1992, 42). The connotation (mounting the mother) displaces the denotation (rocking), but what was immaterial, unlocalized, and non-symbolic suddenly assumes all three functions in a new and positive role of signification. We are dealing with the difference between the denoted and the connoted, but the reality of the symptom—the meaning that it displaces—is as real (perhaps more real) than the meaningless and impossible task of rocking a toy horse into a winning position.

The function of rocking is to overcome the Law (the incest taboo)—a Law that is temporarily under erasure, or at least as long as the rocking continues. The Law, among other things, emphasizes the difference between adults and children, but the rocking suspends the difference symbolically so that the boy can get there, name the winner, and, in naming the biggest winner of all (Malabar), the story inscribes the signifier over the signified. The "bar" is the slash (S/s), and the so-called evil (*mal*) is in elevating the role of the signifier and in downgrading the signified. The triumph of the signifier is already present in the title of the story in which the letter of the Law manifests itself as difference: lucker/lucre, money/mummy, filthy lucre/little fucker. The dissemination of letters and phonemes, the "litter" of the "letter" to which Lacan alludes (Lacan 1966a, 35), encourages the free play of the signifier which is not unmotivated because the slippage of meaning, as in the *Fort!/Da!,* is sustained by desire.

The concrete discourse may be little Ernst's game of tossing and retrieving the spool or Paul's equally compulsive rocking, but the symbolic discourse is in the signifier that displaces the spool or the rocking-horse in order to replace them with the mother. The boy, however, remains symbolically separated from signification by the rocking-horse and/or Malabar, so that the meaning of his act eludes him. Whether rocker or bar, the sign of difference is inscribed by the algorithm S/s that displaces the signified. The boy's green pajamas and the mother's green dress illuminated by the light connote symbolic union. The color green is an entry into the signified. It is the "go ahead" signal and it "gets us there." The signifier crosses the bar and it rocks the horse in order to produce meaning. This is a signifying operation based on structural conditions that Lacan calls *articulation:* "the structure of the signifier is, as is commonly said of language, to be articulated" ('la structure du signifiant est, comme on le dit communément du langage, qu'il soit articulé'; Lacan 1966b, 258)."

The signifier's dual function of denoting and connoting is also linked to what Lacan calls *signifiance,* which is the operation of the signifier when it has "passed over to the level of the signified," when it comes "to be charged with signification" ("Qu'il est passé à l'étage du *signifié* . . . autant à se charger de signification"; Lacan 1977b, 155; Lacan 1966b, 262). If *signifiance* is not, strictly speaking, the same as signification, it is, nonetheless, what makes signification possible. Signification is thus constituted as the presence of the signifier "in the subject"—hence the "agency" of the letter—a letter that articulates the entry of the signifier into the signified. The subject's concrete discourse (rocking the horse) signifies "*something quite other* than what it says" ("*tout autre chose* que ce qu'elle dit"; Lacan 1977b, 155; Lacan 1966b, 262). The example Lacan uses to illustrate the shift to something other than what it says is from Victor Hugo's poem "Booz endormi" in which the metaphorical spark illumines the fact that the sheaf of wheat that "was neither miserly nor spiteful" ("n'était pas avare ni haineuse") belongs to Boas (Lacan 1977b, 156; Lacan 1966b, 264). The word "sheaf" has displaced Boas in the signifying chain, and now occupies the place that would normally be his. If we compare this metaphor with displacement in Freud's analysis of dreams, the sheaf becomes the manifest content and Boas is its latent meaning. Phrased differently, the sheaf is the signifier and Boas is the signified. Boas does not signify "sheaf" but the sheaf, inevitably and necessarily, signifies "Boas."

In "The Rocking-Horse Winner" *significance*—the signifier that has become the signified—functions as a regulated generalization of connotation, thereby displacing the denoted meaning of rocking which is, nonetheless, essential if the subject is "to know the truth." The boy must rock furiously in order to "get there," in order to name the winner. He can, if he knows the truth (and he says he does) "make it heard in spite of all the *between-the-lines* censures" ("la faire entendre malgré toutes les censures *entre les lignes*"; Lacan 1977b, 155; Lacan 1966b, 262). The truth is *Malabar:* the name that connotes the agency of the letter in the unconscious as well as getting the money/mummy.

The subject has access to the denoted truth (rocking and Malabar) but the Lacanian subject is incapable of "knowing the truth" of connotation. As Nancy and Lacoue-Labarthe point out, "It is precisely this subject deprived of knowledge who can be the subject of a connotation which is *purely and simply detached or demarcated from denotation*" (Nancy and Lacoue-Labarthe 1992, 67). In one sense "truth" is the same as speech, since it "is founded by the fact that it speaks" ("puisque la vérité se fonde de ce qu'elle parle"; Lacan 1971a, 233, my translation), and *Malabar* as an utterance is sufficient unto itself. The boy, however, has no access to the metalanguage, that is, the *signifiance* that Malabar connotes.

For Saussure the reciprocity of the signifier-signified relationship was essential: each *signifier* referred to its particular *signified* in an arbitrary coupling based on linguistic convention. For Lacan, however, the line between the S/s relationship is a *bar* indicating that the signifier does not have access to the signified. The signifier slides in a sea of signifiers in search of its signified, but encountering only other signifiers in a continuous systemic indeterminacy. As François Raffoul and David Pettigrew point out, "signifiers can only *slide along* the bar in an indefinite deferral of meaning" (Raffoul and Pettigrew 1992, xii–xiii). According to Freud there is an unconscious purpose that "drags the preconscious thought down into the unconscious and there gives it a new shape" (Freud 1953c, 176). This is where the sliding indeterminacy of the signifier occurs: "For, as we have learnt from the dream-work, the connecting paths which start out from *words* are in the unconscious treated in the same way as connections between *things*." (Freud 1953c, 177).

Lacan's originality is to have combined linguistics and psychoanalysis into the "science of the letter" (Nancy and Lacoue-Labarthe 1992, 81), and in doing so he has reinterpreted metaphor and metonymy—the two main axes of language—in their relation to desire. Metonymy becomes the trope of desire while metaphor is the operation of substitution of one signifier for another. Paul's desire (metonymy) rides the horse toward luck and lucre (metaphor), the signifiers that keep sliding along the bar where lucker/fucker, money/mummy, house/horse rock each other back-and-forth in their ongoing and frenzied indeterminacy. Paul's desire is the lack (luck/lucre, money/mummy) that articulates the signifiers. This is the *truth* of his condition. Rocking the horse is the metaphor of this lack. Lacan articulates the truth of desire in the very letter that "materializes the agency of death" ("matérialize l'instance de la mort"; Lacan 1966a, 33). The signifier, the letter of the Law that kills Paul, is Malabar, the name of the winning horse for which he bought his "lucky" ticket. Ironically, St. Paul, his namesake says: "The letter killeth, but the spirit giveth life" (2 Corinthians 3:6); ("La lettre tue, dit-on, quand l'esprit vivifie"). A further irony is that Lacan's quotation from St. Paul should apply to Lawrence's story with such uncanny precision (Lacan 1966b, 267).

In the final analysis, we have a pleasure principle in the service of the death instinct: desire to please the mother on the conscious level and the desire to ride the mummy on the unconscious one. However, the brain fever is the frenzied symptom of a compulsion that kills. The agency of the letter and the materiality of words—the signifiers—play themselves out in the life and death of the boy. Having named Malabar, the horse Paul *knows* will win the race, the boy falls into a coma and dies three days later. He has, literally, been consumed by the truth—his desire to know, that is, to get there—but the truth remains censored because the *signifiance* of naming Malabar (the signifier) does not give Paul access to the signified—the truth from which desire springs and which remains repressed. The truth is inscribed in the signifier and lucre/lucker is the joke, the letter's agent that sets the rocking-horse in motion. The brain fever is the symptom of the letter—the letter that kills— that "innocent joke" that whispers, "Oh, now, now-w! Now-w-w—there *must* be more money!" (Lawrence 1995d, 92). The homonymic slippage to "more mummy, more mummy, now!" is the veiled truth for which the boy gives his life. Kearney believes that Lawrence, in this story as well as in his work generally, is incriminating "all of modern society for its misplaced values, its unnatural self-absorption, and its deathward direction," while also noting that the message of "The Rocking-Horse Winner" nudges "mankind in the direction of life" (Kearney 1998, xxxix). This story, like most if not all of Lawrence's fiction, underscores the madness of the world and the need for change.

Freud's truth, which is also Lacan's truth, is that the only "good" father is a "dead father" (Lacan 1977a, 310; Lacan 1971a, 173). Naming Malabar is the boy's biggest win, a win motivated by his desire to please the mother and displace the father. But the Law cannot be displaced. Rocking can name the truth but it cannot understand or overcome it.[11] The coma and the brain fever are the sign of its inaccessibility. The censor triumphs, the son is dead, the father and Uncle Oscar remain, and Hester is 80,000 pounds to the good.

Paul rides his hobbyhorse in order to name the winning horse at the races, make his mother rich, and earn her love. He dies, she lives, and, because the house is eighty thousand pounds to the good, it will no longer whisper, "There must be more money." In the next chapter, Cathcart, "The Man Who Loved Islands," unlike Hester, the mendacious mother, divests himself not only of money, but also of land, people, animals, love, and even language. Instead of accumulating worldly riches, he sheds them. Chapter five will tell us why.

Chapter Five

"The Man Who Loved Islands"

A Return to the Womb

The theme, structure, and language of "The Man Who Loved Islands" replicate psychoanalytic concepts of the Other, castration, desire, and *aphanasis* or the loss of sexual desire. Aspects of Saussurean linguistics and Freudian theory (the touchstones of Lacan's thought) are embedded in the title. To love "I-lands" is to dwell within the split self, a division that mimes the splitting (*Spaltung*) during Lacan's so-called "mirror stage" of the infant's development (Lacan 1977a, 1–8). D.H. Lawrence foregrounds not only the islander's fragmented identity but also his progressive misanthropy. In due course, his arrested desire and attitude repudiate all contact with men, his wife, his daughter, even life itself.[1]

In *Écrits,* Lacan, like Freud, shows that the operations of the unconscious, encompassing the extremes of pictographic and linguistic analyses, are themselves a linguistic process. Like the iconic nature of dreams, language and narration have a manifest and a latent content. In dreams, condensation and displacement disguise the content of the unconscious in the same way that metaphor and metonymy veil the pulsive forces of the subject's (author's) desire whenever they use language.

Lacan's theories enable us to unveil the presence of the unconscious in literary discourse because the blockage of desire, along with its corollary, repression, produce a neurosis whose narrative symptoms are metaphorical. In the production of narrative, unconscious content is condensed as metaphor and displaced as metonymy. These discoveries prompted Lacan to say that the unconscious is structured like a language. We as readers, in order to decipher unconscious discourse, need to determine how the manifest discourse hides its latent meaning, that is, how the signifiers resolve simultaneously into manifest signifieds (metaphor and metonymy) and latent referents (the repressed). Hence the formula S_1 over S_2 in which the signifier has two signifieds, one of which is present, and the other absent because it has been repressed. If the dream is the iconic, although masked mirror of the unconscious, fiction is its linguistic reflector, and this is why Lacan melds Freud and Saussure into his own discourse.

Lacan's theories also show how an unconscious and decentered discourse parallels conscious narration and imbues it with the voice of the Other. Indeed, a decentered and tropical discourse contains repressed material that structures a never-ending dialog with the Other—the Other being that fictitious self made up of the coming together, during the "mirror phase" of the child's development, of the Symbolic, the Imaginary, and the Real. The Symbolic is the Law, the restrictive role of the father, eventually all *doxa. Doxa,* as we have seen, is public opinion, the mind of the majority, the reliance on cliché and the ready-made, and the violence of prejudice. Cathcart experiences the effects of *doxa* on the first island and he rejects them. The Imaginary is that displaced self that has to come to terms with the postponement of satisfaction, the repression of desire, and the nurturing of discontent. The second island is the one on which Cathcart nurtures discontent. The Imaginary reinforces the individual's desire for union with the mother while enabling Cathcart to define himself in relation to others. He cannot define himself constructively in relation to others either on the first or on the second islands. On the third one he has given up, and the Real, in terms of discourse, is the individual's unconscious relationship with death. It is the Real that directs Cathcart's discourse on the third island.

The following synopsis will highlight certain details, which, like buoys, will help us navigate the channels of Lacanian analysis. The summary will also remind the reader of everything Cathcart objects to in the world of men and women, and also, in his single-minded quest, the natural world he leaves behind. Cathcart moves from one large island to a smaller one, and finally to a rocky outcropping in the North Sea where he dies entombed in the snow. His isolation echoes Lawrence's opening lines: "An island is a nest which holds one egg, and one only. This egg is the islander himself" (Lawrence 1995d, 151).[2] Indeed, the whiteness of the snow that covers him resembles the whiteness of an egg, an egg a seagull might have left behind before its migration south. In the end, the islander's death is the result of his longing to return to the nest where he, like Humpty Dumpty before the fall, can be whole again; not the cracked egg of misrecognition (*méconnaissance*). According to Lacan, the infant's misperception of self pursues it into adulthood where the voice of the Other (the unconscious), in this case the language of Lawrence's man who loved islands, dictates the reasons for returning to the mother—the egg-white entity of an impossible perfection.[3]

There were pleasures for the islander on the larger island, at least in the beginning, where he attempts to mold a perfect community of men. But his utopia sours, and he retreats to a smaller island where he enjoys writing his book. Nonetheless, mechanical sex with his caretaker and the birth of a daughter prompt him to flee, yet again, to the smallest of islands—as far away as he can from human contact. There, he no longer writes, he does not read, he dreads the sight of the mail boat, he banishes the sheep because he dislikes their baa, and he compulsively tears the nameplate from the stove in order to remove all sight of language.

In the three stages of the islander's retreat from the world, Lawrence describes the content of his dreams in which Cathcart's unconscious feelings mime the language of desire, or, in his case, the lack of it. *Jouissance*, when present, is an affirmation of life, and its gradual disappearance represents Cathcart's repudiation of it.[4] Lacan argues repeatedly that everything we do is at the behest of the Other, and his question: "What does he [the Other] want for me?" must, in the islander's case, be answered by the word "death" (Lacan 1977a, 312). Whenever the death instinct overrides the pleasure principle, it forces us to reexamine Lacan's "mirror stage," that is, the splitting of the self into I-lands and the child's accession to language—language that the islander, before he dies, strives to obliterate so that he can enter whole into the snowy womb/tomb.[5]

Initially, the large island contains the promise of perfection and, believing that man and nature are good, Cathcart, the islander, strives to create an insular paradise. He loves his island very much (Lawrence 1995d, 152), as much as he loves flowers, and he fills it "with his own gracious, blossom-like spirit" (Lawrence 1995d, 153). He renovates an old semi-feudal dwelling, and, in due course, he establishes a small community of men, women, and children. Soon, it becomes "[a] minute world of pure perfection" (Lawrence 1995d, 153), of which he is the master. He is wise, "a fount of knowledge about everything" [. . .] he loves white clothes (white is an important leitmotif in the story) [. . .] he is wonderful with children [. . .] and, according to one woman, he "made you think of Our Saviour Himself" (Lawrence 1995d, 155). Why then does everything go sour?[6]

Lawrence's story describes three conditions in which the worm of adversity gnaws at the rose of happiness. One is the Rousseauistic notion that, despite man's good intentions, society is inherently evil; the second derives from an existential angst embedded in man's collective unconscious, a Pascalian fear of the eternal silence of these infinite spaces (Pascal 1982, 152); and the third is the splitting of the self when the infant accedes to language. Although the island is lovely, the people on it are not contented (Lawrence 1995d, 159). They accuse each other of real and imagined transgressions. The mason and the farmhand decide to leave, the housekeeper and the butler swindle their master, the people no longer love him, the bills accumulate, and Cathcart is soon almost bankrupt. Despite good crops, revenues from the island are not cost-effective. The people manifest their discontents. The wonderful experiment has failed. It's as though the binary opposition between nature and culture is thwarting Cathcart's endeavors.

But it's not only the nature/culture divide that is the source of trouble; nature itself can sometimes be malevolent: a cow falls over a cliff and dies, a man breaks his leg, another is crippled with rheumatic fever, the pigs develop a strange disease, and a storm drives the yacht on a rock. The island itself seems endowed with malicious intent (Lawrence 1995d, 159).

Because the island suffers from natural and man-made calamities, the people are no longer able to live in harmony together. Clearly, money, or the lack of it is one root of their evil, but another is rooted deeply in Cathcart's and the island's unconscious. He experiences "[u]ncanny dreams, half-dreams, half-evocated yearnings" set "far back in the mysterious past" when the island had known blood and passion, and lust (Lawrence 1995d, 159). At night, our islander steps off into the "otherworld of undying time" (Lawrence 1995d, 152–53) when men of Gaul with big moustaches had been there, and priests with golden knives and mistletoe performed their rites, and other priests with crucifixes worshiped their God, and pirates murdered on the sea (Lawrence 1995d, 153). Cathcart suffers all "the terrors of infinite time" when "[t]he souls of all the dead are alive again" (Lawrence 1995d, 153).[7] He strives to create a perfect world that will keep these terrors at bay, but the strange and perverse nightmares contaminate the island's waking hours. Cathcart's would-be utopia collapses midst enmity, accusations, and mismanagement.

After five years of effort and failure, Cathcart sells his island and moves to another smaller one. But the new island also harbors seeds of discontent. On the first one, Cathcart was compiling a book of references to all the flowers mentioned in the Greek and Latin authors. He now resumes his study, and the rhythm of his writing harmonizes with the voices of the sea and the noises of the wind. Soon, however, Cathcart experiences a "strange stillness from all desire," and he wonders if this dreamlike and submerged watery state is happiness (Lawrence 1995d, 162–63). The marine flora and fauna of his unconscious world meld with the conscious activity of his writing which spins "softly from him as if it were drowsy gossamer"; moreover, it is only "the soft evanescence of gossamy things" that now seems to him permanent (Lawrence 1995d, 163). Our islander even contrasts the howl of the Cathedral's "temporary resistance" with the gossamer's "mist of eternity." And so, in time, the island's ephemeral flowers become more important to him than those immortalized by the Greek and Latin authors. He discards the idea of progress, and he no longer cares if the book gets published or not.

Cathcart's will, like gossamer, soon succumbs to the ardent will of his caretaker. They make love. But Cathcart chafes against the automatism of their sex and he experiences "a new stillness of desirelessness" (Lawrence 1995d, 164). Despite his misgivings about her, he succumbs again and afterwards feels "shattered" (Lawrence 1995d, 165). He feels that his island is now smirched and spoiled and that he has "lost his place in the rare, desireless levels of Time" (Lawrence 1995d, 165). When he learns that Flora is pregnant (an ironic name, in view of Cathcart's interest in nature and flowers), his desire dies with "nauseous finality" (Lawrence 1995d, 166).[8] He gives the best part of his property to Flora and the future child, buys "a few acres of rock far away in the north, on the outer fringe of the isles" (Lawrence 1995d, 165), abandons the second island, and settles for good on the third.

By this time, Cathcart has lost all interest in his book, people, trees, and shrubs. All he wants is a "bare, low-pitched island in the pale blue sea" (Lawrence 1995d, 167). He even finds the half-dozen resident sheep offensive, and their raucous baa, like the sound of his own voice, disrupts the silence of space. Contact with living things becomes repulsive to him (Lawrence 1995d, 169). He dreads talking to the men on the mail boat and he leaves his letters unopened in a small box. He detests the smell of the fishermen and the sheep because they are "an uncleanness on the fresh earth" (Lawrence 1995d, 169). When the mail boat comes he gets rid of the sheep; when the weather changes, his cat vanishes and the birds fly away.

Cathcart loses track of time and he no longer reads because print and printed letters, like the depravity of speech, are obscene. He wants "nothing human to bring its horror into contact with him" (Lawrence 1995d, 170). He tears the brass label from his stove and he obliterates any bit of lettering in his cabin (Lawrence 1995d, 170). The only satisfaction he derives is from being alone. Even the air and the wind are dead (Lawrence 1995d, 171). Then it begins to snow and the house becomes "a cell faintly illuminated with white light" (Lawrence 1995d, 171).

The white flowers and blackbirds of the first island have been replaced with the inanimate cold of snow and black rocks. The blackish sea churns and champs, seeming to bite at the snow, impotent. The snow resounds in the sea and the man and his boat are soon buried by it. After shoveling the white drifts with great effort and futility, Cathcart staggers back to the cabin; he revives himself with hot milk. But it is perhaps too late because he looks "stupidly over the whiteness of his foreign land, over the waste of the lifeless sea" (Lawrence 1995d, 173). White and black have come to connote some kind of fundamental moral and physical state of being.

What is going on? Why, despite everything does this man love islands? Why will his future child be a *millstone* around his neck? Why is speech depraved? Why does he put his unopened letters in a box? Why this *horror* of the human? Why is the sea *impotent*, why is it a *waste*, and why is the house a *cell*? Why, despite the fact that Cathcart has chosen it, is this land *foreign*?

The emphases are mine but they are also Lawrence's. What kind of trauma can explain the metaphorical language and Cathcart's behavior?

To begin with, there is the nature/culture opposition and the demise of an island paradise. Then there is the collective unconscious yoked to the geography of place, the Pascalian *angst,* and the images of the past where space becomes a river of time. But do these elements explain Cathcart's choices, his misanthropy, and death wish? Do they chart the course of his retreat from the world and his *aphanasis*? To some degree yes, of course. But there is an additional unconscious dimension in the text—the Lacanian voice of the Other—that structures the patterns we *encounter* and the metaphorical language of the story.

We are never told why Cathcart loves islands, and we accept this love as a condition of his being. Besides, the word "love," when applied to "islands," is not the same as the word "like." Moreover, on the first island, Cathcart recreates a primal happiness before the fall; when the egg in the nest (the generative cell) was whole; before the plunder of the psyche by History's symbolic fathers: the Gauls, the priests, and the pirates. The island's new symbolic father is the hotel company that turns it into a honeymoon-and-golf island for profit. Money talks, and the island's latest plunderers are the speculators.

In effect, by repudiating language, Cathcart is saying "no" to the name-of-the-father—to all the authority figures that are responsible for his feelings of alienation and distress. According to Lacan, the splitting of the self coincides with the child's accession to language. Language not only structures our perception of the world, it circulates freely and relentlessly from person to person within every culture. Like money, it can also be counterfeit; it's a commodity that regulates values, attitudes, and relationships between people. Indeed, Cathcart's disenchantment with nature and society is yoked to language, to the very words that paint the flowers, the sea, the birds, and the sky. He rejects people and colors in order to live in an ascetic environment of black and white. Snow cushions his final voyage into death where all desire ends.

Furthermore, according to Lacan, the infant's accession to language coincides with the splitting of the self, and it is this fragmentation that seems to haunt Lawrence's story. Not only are islands split from the mainland, but also when Cathcart's love affair with Flora fails, he feels "shattered," as shattered as an infant does when the Law severs it from the mother. The birth of his child will be the last straw—additional evidence of the fragmentation of self through reproduction. There is also the millstone around Cathcart's neck— the unconscious knowledge that the name-of-the-father and the incest taboo are the same. In addition to his rejection of his daughter and Flora, he repudiates the Law; the millstone around his "oxymoroneck" is the impotence of desire. He himself is this foreign land, and the waste of the sea is the symbolic castration and death that every infant experiences when the self is split and language begins.

The whiteness of the egg resonates throughout the text and it reverberates on the black rocks of death. White flowers contrast with blackbirds, and snow contrasts with and covers the black island that is Cathcart's final refuge and tomb. Interim colors such as his blue eyes (they match the color of the sea), the bluebells, the rose-red bells of the foxgloves, the golden saxifrage, and the pale-dusky gold feet of the seagull are manifestations of life and they temporarily arrest the islander's rejection of the world. However, he can't stand the men on the mail boat, because they speak and bring letters—the messages of life from which he is trying to escape.

It's not only the social messages of greed and lucre that so befuddle Cathcart, it's also the weight of Freud's and Lacan's "letter of the law" (the incest taboo). Very early in the infant's development, when it accedes to language, when it looks into the symbolic mirror of consciousness, and when it sees itself as Other, the "no" of the symbolic father weighs the subject down with devastating consequences. This metaphorical moment is experienced as a misrecognition (*méconnaissance*) of the self, and is suffered as failure. The father's *no* (*le nom/non du père*), the mother's complicity, and the child's feelings of impotence are the result of symbolic castration and the death of desire.

Because writing and narration are manifestations of desire, discourse is the umbilical language that connects us with the lost mother. For Lacan, the act of writing and the repetition of writing posit the enticement of textuality, thereby acknowledging, unconsciously, the child's "wound" and alienation. To produce a text, whatever its conscious modes and operations, is also to relive the process by which an affective charge—a cathexis—is released from its generating poles. The writer, and eventually the reader, directs this charge, imbuing it with the Reality that both produces and attracts it.

Fiction links the conscious and unconscious selves in both the writer and the reader. Like psychoanalysis, writing repeats the discontent of what never took place during that "time event" referred to as "the primal scene." The fantasy of desire, incest, castration, death, and repression reenact not what took place, but what did not. Nonetheless, it is this scene that is replayed on the stage of discourse as the metaphorical actors (Lawrence, Cathcart, and the reader) put on their masks and perform (repeat) the ritual. Because language unveils the presence of the mother tongue, all discourse is a language of desire through which the subject seeks to retrieve the lost object, be it breast or mother.

Lacan's essay on "The function and field of speech and language in psychoanalysis" describes what he calls the combinatory power of language that resonates in the communicating networks of discourse. For him, this metaphorical slippage of meaning is the mainspring of the unconscious (Lacan 1977a, 59). The mail boat becomes the *male* boat that he dreads. The sea is "impotent" and the wind is "dead." In due course Cathcart rejects all language: the sheep's baa, his own voice, letters, and the nameplate on the stove. Language has to be obliterated (earlier it was money and belongings) because language coincides with the primal cleavage, and it is the voice of this cleavage that regulates everything Cathcart does.

Lacan says that "the moment in which desire becomes human is also that in which the child is born into language" (Lacan 1977a, 103). But our adult islander is shedding language, perhaps because language structures our (mis)perception of reality and, for him, reality has become unbearable. Nonetheless, unconscious desire is indestructible, and when forbidden satisfaction, it can lead to the destruction of the organism itself. *Jouissance*, says Lacan, moves relentlessly forward on the rails of metonymy (Lacan 1977b, 167). Accordingly, the nameplate on the stove functions as a displaced metonymic signifier. Cathcart's compulsion is the symptom of metaphorical behavior. When he removes the sheep and the nameplate, and does not open his mail, he is moving on the rails of metonymy because the baa, the stove logo, and the letters are a part of the whole, namely language. The connection between language and the stove is nowhere but in the signifier (Lacan 1977b, 156).

If the stove symbolizes the failure of culture to warm the hearts of men, it is because as a signifier, it has replaced "the evils of society" in the signifying chain. By removing the plaque, the islander sweeps away these evils and hurls them "into the outer darkness where greed and spite harbour him in the hollow of their negation" (Lacan 1977b, 157). Having discarded the sheep, the plaque, the letters, and his own voice, the islander can subsist only in nature—the snow's white silence. He has rejected the signs of language, that is, the words and the sounds that bound him to the society of men. Discarding the metonymic signifiers for language is what produces the metaphor because by discarding language, Cathcart also metaphorically abolishes culture.

Lacan believes that the "ethnographic duality of nature and culture" has given way to a "ternary conception of the human condition—nature, society, and culture" (Lacan 1977b, 148). For Lacan, culture and language are synonymous and that is what distinguishes human society from natural societies. The signifier has become a new dimension of the human condition because not only does man speak, but "in man and through man *it* speaks (ça *parle*), that his nature is woven by effects in which is to be found the structure of language, of which he becomes the material" (*Écrits* 284). When Lacan says that "it speaks" he means that we respond to the voice of the unconscious. Because the unconscious is structured like a language we respond to it. Indeed,

Lawrence envelops Cathcart in symptoms and language and, together, they unveil the meaning of his dreams, his choices, and his compulsion.

By shedding language, Cathcart refuses the human. He is not unlike Freud's grandson, Ernst, playing the game of *Fort! Da!,* except that Cathcart is playing the *Fort!* without the *Da!* His desire has become the desire of another, "an alter ego who dominates him and whose object of desire is henceforth his own affliction" (Lacan 1977a, 104). The game manifests itself symbolically as the murder of the thing (Fort!) and this death guarantees the persistence of desire. On the first island the *Da!* was present, on the second one it was sporadic, and on the third it disappears because desire has been redirected as a death-wish. Instead of the thing being murdered, it is now the self. Like Empedocles throwing himself into Mount Etna, Cathcart leaves forever present in our memory the "symbolic act of his being-for-death" (Lacan 1977a, 104).

Although repression veils the memory of the primal event, it allows us to live in the world as though nothing has happened. Repression, however, gives rise to desire, and desire is the driving force of all relationships. It is thus ironic and symptomatic that, on the second island, Cathcart seeks to suppress all desire, but when he reaches a state of desirelessness, he calls it happiness. He may dislike the automatism of sex, but had he gone to the mainland he could have found someone with whom to have a meaningful relationship. However, because he loves I-lands more than anything else, it is inevitable that he not seek that alternative.

Cathcart's decision to abandon the second island in pursuit of total desire-lessness is symptomatic of his primal wound. Lacan says that symptomatic behavior is a metaphor, a "signifier of a signified" (Lacan 1977a, 69). And "the symptom is itself structured like a language" (Lacan 1977a, 59). What is signified here is the repressed, the voice of the unconscious that makes Cathcart act the way he does. The unconscious is by definition veiled and inaccessible, except when it manifests itself through metaphor, metonymy, humor, paronomasia, and the symbolic slippages of language and behavior. "Language is not immaterial. It is a subtle body, but body it is. Words are trapped in all the corporeal images that captivate the subject" (Lacan 1977a, 87). Our bodies also contain our psyche's history and the scars of the past (whatever freedom choice may manifest) define our essence. Cathcart's essence is that he loved islands and he never escapes from that predisposing condition. The splitting of the self is inscribed in the unconscious and the islands are his unconscious. His desire, despite his claims to desirelessness, is to recover the self in the cell (the little house on the third island)—the egg-in-the-nest to which he has inexorably returned.

Cathcart's behavior is the result of a historical scar and he manifests it hysterically. His compulsion is the symptom—the symbolic displacement that has been brought into play and which functions as a signifier (Lacan 1977a, 51–52). He epitomizes the fragmentation of the self that is exacerbated by society and civilization. One important aspect of civilization and human exchange (perhaps the most important), besides money and exchange, is language, and it is language that Cathcart strives to eradicate. He seems determined to reshape the self, to recover an identity before the cleavage, before language, before consciousness. In order to succeed in this quest he pursues a death wish from which there is no recourse. Even the warm milk of his last-ditch effort to survive is not enough to override it. That's why he concluded that the first island, although mysterious and fascinating, was also "your implacable enemy" (Lawrence 1995d, 160). Why? Because the islands are the voice of his unconscious that is nudging him toward death.

In *The Post Card* Derrida demonstrates that the death wish is nothing more than another disguise of the pleasure principle. Indeed, the force that propels Cathcart to return to the egg in the nest of his island tomb is so strong that it overcomes his desire to live. Desire remains but it is now directed toward death. That may be the desirelessness for life to which Lawrence alludes but it is not a desirelessness for death. We must assume that the pleasure to be derived from a recovery of a whole self, however misguided, is sufficient to explain Cathcart's choices and the metaphorical language with which Lawrence envelops him. As Derrida points out, Freud never gets beyond the pleasure principle (Derrida 1987c, 295). The only thing that changes is its direction. On the first island, Cathcart was oriented toward life; on the third island he is oriented toward death; and on the second island, he is in between. There is always desire but it has been redirected. Only in death will our islander return to the wholeness of the self before the split. No wonder he was fascinated by the seagull that was as round and "smooth and lovely as a pearl [. . .] he had a meaning" (Lawrence 1995d, 168). This precious pearl, like the egg, symbolizes the islander's quest. It is a wholeness that has been lost and that he wants to regain:

> He pretended to imagine he saw the wink of a sail. Because he knew too well there would never again be a sail on that stark sea. As he looked, the sky mysteriously darkened and chilled. From far off came the *mutter* of the *unsatisfied thunder,* and he knew it was the *signal* of the snow rolling over the sea. He turned, and felt its *breath* on him. (Lawrence 1995d, 173, my emphasis)

We need to remember that the sounds of words often connote more than they denote. And they thereby conjure the presence of floating signifiers that, although not present in the text are, nonetheless, there, under erasure so to speak. Their implied presence has much to do not only with the feeling of a passage but, ultimately its meaning. Accordingly, the metaphorical slippage and combinatory power of the language of the above quotation veils Lawrence's intent. The "mutter" (*mother/Other*) of the "unsatisfied thunder" (*hunger*) is the signal that the "breath" (*death*) of "the snow rolling over the sea" will reclaim Cathcart. He looks at the sky that is mysteriously darkened and chilled. He is the "waif" in the paragraph where the slippages of meaning confirm desire, that is, a return to the wholeness that was sundered into the three islands of the Oedipus complex: the father, the mother, and the child. The first island is the island of the symbolic fathers where Cathcart is also the master-father. The second island is Flora's, the mother, and the third is the nest that holds one egg and one only—the islander himself.

In conclusion, "The Man Who Loved Islands," especially the third island, illustrates the melding of language and the unconscious. The audible S_1 of "mutter" has become the absent and displaced S_2 of mother, and the audible S_1 of "thunder" slides into the absent S_2 of hunger. Finally, the sensory "breath" of the snow (S_1) adumbrates Cathcart's imminent death (S_2). Metaphor and metonymy meld as floating signifiers in Lawrence's discourse, even as Cathcart's body begins to meld with the elements.

We have come full circle and Cathcart has recycled himself. He has reclaimed the immobility of the egg in the nest of death. His rock-of-an-island now holds him and him only, and all desire is frozen. All language has been suppressed, consciousness is gone, and pain has been stilled. The breath of the north wind is on him and he is on the island. His death wish has been fulfilled.

In the next chapter, "Glad Ghosts"—the Cure: Cutting Through the Tangle," Lawrence moves away from death toward life. He cuts through the hysterical knot that has bound and immobilized everybody in the Lathkill estate except Morier. The glad ghosts in the tale are the voices of the unconscious; and their arrival—their dreamlike, nocturnal coming—is Lawrence's annunciation—the good news of salvation.

Chapter 6

"Glad Ghosts"
The Cure—Cutting Through the Tangle

"Glad Ghosts" was written toward the end of 1925 for Lady Cynthia Asquith's 1926 collection of the supernatural, *The Ghost-Book: Sixteen New Stories of the Uncanny.* When the story was rejected Lawrence wrote "The Rocking-Horse Winner" in its place. "Glad Ghosts" was published, eventually, in two parts in *Dial* magazine.

From its publication to the present "Glad Ghosts" has frequently been misread and sometimes relegated to the ghost pile of the uncanny. An anonymous person at the D.H. Lawrence website of the *Literature Resource Center* contrasts "Glad Ghosts," the *mythic tale,* with his *sardonic fables* such as "The Rocking-Horse Winner" and "The Man Who Loved Islands," opposing the brilliance of the latter to the shortcomings of the former, which is allegedly obfuscated by religious rhetoric, ghost story devices, and layers of mixed metaphors ("D.H. Lawrence" 2003, 29). In a *New York Times* book review of 1928, John R. Chamberlain corroborates this view when he says that "Glad Ghosts" is a "triumph of obfuscation" because the key to understanding it is missing (Chamberlain 1928).

The key may be missing but that is because Chamberlain and others did not know where to look for it or how to use it. The paucity of commentary after the publication of "Glad Ghosts" suggests perplexity, and it is perhaps not surprising that the idea of the supernatural imbued the story with an obfuscating aura. In 1951, in *The Life and Work of D.H. Lawrence,* Harry T. Moore called "Glad Ghosts" a sex story of the supernatural (Moore 1951, 253), and, in 1998, Linda Ruth Williams, echoing Moore, infused its "uncanny bodies" with sex (Williams 1997–98, 235).[1] Williams argues cogently that "Glad Ghosts" is a sex story that is also a ghost story, "but that it might be its ghostliness, not its sexiness, which requires the input of psychoanalysis" (Williams 1997–98, 235). And, with respect to sex, Judith Butler, in "Gender as Performance," (Butler 1994, 34) says: "Crafting a sexual position [. . .] always involves becoming *haunted* [my emphasis] by what's excluded." Furthermore, the *ghost* (my emphasis, Butler's word) becomes more threatening as the rigidity of the position increases. It is revealing that Butler, who is referring to sex, not to Lawrence's story, should be using words such as *haunted* and *ghost,* the same ones that Lawrence and Williams do.

In articulating this relationship "Glad Ghosts" reads less like a story of the supernatural, the occult, and the uncanny—those strange phenomena of the hereafter—and more like a tale about hysteria. Indeed, Mark Morier believes that Lord Lathkill is sane and that the others are mad, saying that what is happening is "on a par with hysteria" (Lawrence 1995d, 197). Hysteria—the manifestation of sexual or cultural repression—reveals itself in bodily symptoms, strange events, and social lesions.

Freud, in his *Studies on Hysteria,* concluded that sexuality was being excluded from the case histories he was recording and that this exclusion was about the choice of words; that the choice tended to exclude words denoting or connoting sex. Adam Phillips, in "Making the Case: Freud's Literary Engagements," commenting on Freud and Butler, says, "Any genre is ghostwritten by the genre it excludes" (Phillips 2003, 11). Indeed, the story of sex (although this is by no means the whole story) seems to be embedded in the story of ghosts, and how one tells a story is every writer's dilemma, and also the problem Freud was also wrestling with. In 1895, in *Studies on Hysteria,* in his discussion of the case of Fraulein Elisabeth von R., Freud says that a detailed description of mental processes embedded in the works of imaginative writers enabled him, "with the use of a few psychological formulas," to understand hysterical symptoms (Freud 1953d, 160–61).

With respect to Freud's *Studies on Hysteria,* Phillips notes that Freud wanted to write using the "serious stamp of science" (Phillips 2003, 12) and that his case histories were intended to read like psychiatric ones. Yet, says Freud, they "read like short stories" because the subject matter dictated the narrative (Freud 1953d, 160). Freud also asserts that psychiatric case histories "lead nowhere in the study of hysteria," unlike the works of imaginative writers, and he concludes that the patient's story of suffering is linked to the symptoms of the illness (Freud 1953d, 161). Phillips points out that "the symptom is itself a story, or a story kept at bay" (Phillips 2003, 11). His reading of Freud is both succinct and illuminating, and is worth quoting because it addresses the intimate link in Freud's mind, and also Lawrence's, between theory and the imagination.

> The psychoanalyst as scientist is always under threat of turning into an imaginative writer. A psychoanalyst, in other words, is someone who has found his literary engagements so alluringly unacceptable, such a disarmingly forbidden

and forbidding pleasure—threatening to deprive him of the serious stamp of science—that he must guard against them. But he also can't help but incorporate them, like it or not. This helplessness will be Freud's definition of the repressed: it is what you cannot help but include, even if, or especially if, you include it by warding it off. Freud discovers that there is a *ghostwriter* [my emphasis] in the machine. He wants to write one kind of thing, and it reads like something else. He is writing a psychiatric case history—and wants it to be judged as such—but it reads, in some ways dismayingly to him, like a short story. (Phillips 2003, 12)

The conclusion is that the short story—an experience that conveys information—is superior to psychoanalysis as theory because *theory* must rely on the story in order to make itself heard. In this case, Lawrence, the writer, makes himself heard by combining theory and story, and how he tells the story is what, in due course, we will be looking at as we sort through the *tangle* of ill luck that has bound and immobilized the various characters at the Lathkill estate.

Lawrence's *tangle* is synonymous with Lacan's *knot* and both are symptoms of repression. Repression occurs when desire is thwarted; the subject's consequent frustration influences behavior in unforeseen and unpredictable ways. Whenever desire remains unfulfilled, due either to the primary repression (the Oedipus complex) or cultural repression, or both, an emotional knot is formed; this knot (Lawrence's tangle) stands in the way of self-realization. Except for Morier, all of the characters in "Glad Ghosts" are unhappy and unfulfilled. Williams is thus not wrong to see "Glad Ghosts" as a "key moment for any investigation of how the psychoanalytic infuses Lawrence's work" (Williams 1997–98, 234) because sex and class together—that which is excluded—are the story of "repression made flesh." Yet Williams wonders what psychoanalysis has to do with a story that might already be engaged in its own "vulgar Freudian reading of itself" (Williams 1997–98, 236). Unlike Freud, she seems to place theory above story because Freud wants his case histories to read like theory but acknowledges that the specificity of each story overrides the generalizations that theory requires.

In order to be scientific, theory must contain information that makes an experience replicable by others. Therein lies the paradox. The greatest stories, such as Sophocles' *Oedipus Rex,* are both specific and general. The story of Oedipus' abandonment, swollen foot, and rescue is unique in and to itself but also general because we recognize elements of ourselves in it—elements that Freud used to craft the Oedipus complex as a universal human condition. All stories contain psychoanalytic elements because the writer's unconscious is embedded in the story and we, as readers, respond to the pulsive forces of the narrative's unconscious. When Williams argues that Lawrence's "Glad Ghosts" is "ticking off motifs from Freud's essay on 'The Uncanny'"

(Williams 1997–98, 241), she is replicating Freud's analytical procedure; that is, she finds the same "scientific" ingredients in Lawrence's story that Freud discovered in his case histories—the stories that he wished were more theoretical. As for Lawrence, he does not have to list the motifs because they are already contained in the story.

Lawrence's *Psychoanalysis and the Unconscious* and *Fantasia of the Unconscious* also inform us of what F.R. Leavis, in *D.H. Lawrence Novelist,* calls Lawrence's "diagnostic insight" (Leavis 1967, 9), an insight that is congruent with Freud's and Lacan's writings. If psychoanalysis, as theory, is the mind at work, then literature can be construed as the body. But "Glad Ghosts" moves beyond this rudimentary schema because Morier's narrative describes states of repression that are embedded in Lawrence's story. The story melds mind and body, analyst and analysand in order to effect a cure: the ghosts become flesh, the spirit becomes matter, and everybody is glad.[2]

Despite all the uncanny things that are going on at Riddings, the ghosts in the story are essentially metaphors, and the key to understanding their presence—the key that Chamberlain claimed was missing—is to accept the fact that Lawrence, in addition to metaphor and the conscious crafting of a story, is using the psychoanalytic concepts of the unconscious, the Id, Ego, Super-ego, repression, hysteria, the knot, the talking cure, analyst, and analysand. No cure is possible until the emotional knot is severed. Jeanne Granon-Lafont, in *La Topologie ordinaire de Jacques Lacan,* says that cutting the knot is analogous to psychoanalysis (Granon-Lafont 1985, 113). The characters in Lawrence's story talk to each other, endlessly; and this talking—the talking cure to which Lacan refers—is the metaphorical cut that sets the residents of Lathkill free. Morier's insights cut through the knots and tangles of repression that have immobilized his friends and acquaintances. They are in a knot because their emotional rigidity has exiled them into hard dichotomies of body and mind, flesh and spirit, life and death, hot and cold. These binary oppositions will fuse and the oppositions resolve only when the ghosts (that which is repressed) that haunt the Lathkill estate deign to make themselves felt and heard whenever there is drinking and dancing. Morier is the narrator analyst, practicing his talking cure on the Lathkills and the Hales—the analysands.[3]

Freud's and Lacan's theories help us track the ghosts of sex and received ideas (in this case it is the repressed eroticism in the aristocracy's ideology) because they both address the symptoms in dreams and hysteria as metaphors and metonyms that are inscribed on the body. Lacan's emphasis on the signifying chain is particularly useful because it enables us to unpack Lawrence's craft and the way he melds the aesthetic with the psychoanalytic. Lacan's theoretical writings, which are so metaphorical and therefore difficult to understand, represent his own inclusion of theory within the imaginative body of his text—the imaginative body that was missing in Freud's theoretical writings.[4] Received ideas and the ready-made can also generate hysteria, and when the two are combined, in this case sex and the aristocracy, they leave their indelible stamp on the denizens of Lathkill. Lawrence envelopes them in an artistic weave whose warp is the unconscious and whose woof is language. The figure in the carpet is the sexy ghost.

Lawrence has infused "Glad Ghosts" with tropes that unveil unconscious states of mind, and the tangles that haunt the characters are metaphorical knots of dysfunction. Furthermore, the knots and tangles, the fear and unhappiness to which Lacan and Lawrence refer, are not immaterial symptoms (Lacan 1977a, 87). The unconscious sometimes expresses itself through somatic lesions (Lacan 1977a, 59); and we have access to these symptoms, says Lacan, because the unconscious is structured like a language. Indeed, the body-mind of every individual is the scarred battlefield of unresolved conflicts. Luke describes the Colonel as having one foot in life and one in death. "To us it was like madness" (Lawrence 1995d, 202). The madness at Riddings is a form of hysteria (Lawrence 1995d, 197, 202), and its language of distress permeates the lives of the Lathkills and the Hales. Moreover, the unconscious—the discourse of the Other—speaks through metaphor (condensation) and metonymy (displacement), the same figurative language that Freud uses in his analysis of dreams. Not surprisingly Morier has a vivid dream of the she-ghost who visits him in the middle of the night.

A knot occurs when a tangle of string or rope can only be undone by cutting through it. The analogy between string and tightly knit emotional strands suggests that the talking cure is the therapeutic cut that will help subjects change their behavior. Morier, with the aid of Bacchus and Eros, facilitates Lord Lathkill's cure and he, in turn, helps the other characters find happiness. In the final analysis, Lawrence is the omniscient narrator/savior, the story brings "good news," and readers benefit if, that is, they have been listening to the tropic and therapeutic message. Luke and Carlotta Lathkill name their newborn son Gabriel, and Colonel and Dorothy Hale name their newborn daughter Gabrielle. Gabriel is the angel of the Annunciation and the herald of good news and comfort (Luke i, 26). It is appropriate that Lord Lathkill's first name be Luke.

Morier, the narrator, is the only character free of knots. Carlotta Fell, Lord Lathkill (Carlotta's future husband), Lady Lathkill (Luke's mother), and Colonel and Mrs. Hale (the house guests) are all in a tangle. Whereas Morier is in touch with the vital center of life or, as he calls it, "the quick body [. . .] within the dead" (Lawrence 1995d, 174), the others are members of another species, the living dead (Lawrence 1995d, 175). Unlike them, Morier is not bound by convention, social codes, and ready-made values—every culture's *doxa*—that Lawrence despises. Roland Barthes, as I noted early on, says that *doxology* is a manner of speaking that adapts to appearances, to public opinion, and practice (Barthes 1975a, 51). All is surface without depth, and Carlotta and Luke are *doxa's* adherents. *Doxa* encourages inert repetition, and its discourse belongs to no one in particular, except perhaps to the dead (Barthes 1975a, 75). This is, in part, why the characters in Lawrence's story are in a tangle, and why Lady Lathkill, the matriarch and personification of British aristocracy, is also an advocate of spiritualism, that is, the immaterial. She is a forceful purveyor of death-in-life.

One of *doxa's* memorable images highlights the fact that Carlotta "belonged finally, fatally, to her own class "even though she hated it." [. . .] "The coronet was wedged into her brow, like a ring of iron grown into a tree" (Lawrence 1995d, 175). And her voice rings in a flat monotone, like metal (Lawrence 1995d, 177). Indeed, Carlotta is bound by the social unconscious of her class and is unable to free herself from the values and expectations that are encoded in her psyche. However, this knot that has entangled Carlotta has its antidote, if, that is, she can *unwedge* the coronet and get at the *It* that exists deep within her, as it does in Morier. This *It* is the life force, the unconscious, the "quick body" below the surface of dead values (Lawrence 1995d, 175).

John Turner in his book *D.H. Lawrence and Psychoanalysis* discusses the influence of Otto Gross's ideas on Frieda and Lawrence. Gross believed that the historical mission of psychoanalysis was to "emancipate people from the external forms of patriarchal government" (qtd. in Turner 2020, 10). In *Glad Ghosts* it's the internalized repressive voice of the aristocracy that haunts the residents at Riddings. When Mark Morier advocates dancing, drinking, and the emancipation of a *sansculotte,* he is echoing Gross, who said: "The psychology of the unconscious is the philosophy of revolution" (qtd. in Turner 2020, 11). For Gross this revolution was a human, hygienic necessity—a neurological necessity; and it would clear the pathways of the brain that had been blocked. Once these pathways are reopened, the hysteria at Riddings disappears. Carlotta, her husband, and the other neurotic casualties of the day are, at last, able to find happiness.

For Lacan, *It,* or, as he calls it, *ça,* as it was for Gross, is a function of the unconscious; and he believes that the conscious mind, that is, the *I,* must strive to be where *It* was: "*Wo Es war, soll Ich werdern*" (Lacan 1977b, 171). This shift in consciousness "is one of reintegration and harmony, I could even say of reconciliation" (Lacan 1977b, 171).[5] It is precisely this reconciliation of the conscious self with the unconscious *It* that Lawrence's characters, at the end of the story, manage to achieve. It is also Gross's "hygienic necessity." The family ill luck, generated by money, *doxa,* mind, and spiritualism, is finally overcome by the characters' reintegration of desire and sexuality within the oneness of body-mind. The ghosts of the past are discarded for a new harmonious relationship between *It* and *I*—a reconciliation that Lawrence equates with rebirth, springtime, and the fragrant scent of plum-blossoms.

Luke, like Carlotta, is also bound by the codes of the aristocracy, and, initially, he sees himself as perfect. Morier compares him to "a tortoise in a glittering, polished tortoiseshell that mirrors eternity" (Lawrence 1995d, 176). The emeralds on Carlotta's snow-white skin also reflect this aristocratic polish. At the opera Morier compares her to a crystal gazer, and the auditorium, down into which she is gazing, to a crystal composed of little facets of faces and plastrons. The word "plastron" is one example among many of Lawrence's intricate linguistic weave and tropic resonance. According to Webster's, a plastron has five meanings, all of which reinforce Morier's idea of the aristocracy's social defenses and its imperviousness to change: 1) a metal breastplate worn under a coat of mail; 2) a leather breastplate worn over the chest of fencers: 3) a trimming, like a dickey, worn on the front of a woman's dress; 4) a starched shirt front; 5) the under-shell of a tortoise. This last definition relates it to Luke's tortoise shell, which, in turn, is reflected semantically in the faces and plastrons of the auditorium. This image of aristocratic glitter and unchanging values prompts Morier to say, "God help him [Luke] if circumstances ever went against him!" (Lawrence 1995d, 177). Circumstances do in fact go against him: he is wounded in the war, his three children die, and his marriage is not a happy one. After the war, when Morier sees him again at Riddings, the Lathkill ill luck has taken its toll. Luke is sallow, smaller, shrunken, and his eyes have "a hollow look, like gaps with nothing in them except a haggard, hollow fear" (Lawrence 1995d, 182). Despite his aristocratic standing, Luke's unreality, his surface values, and his ill luck have transformed him. He, too, is one of the living-dead.

"Glad Ghosts" unveils the baneful effects of *doxa* and the downward health spiral that affects people when *It* and *I* remain disconnected. The characters of the story are trapped in the language of *doxa*. They have been blocking *I*'s access to *It* where desire resides. Nonetheless, because unconscious desire is indestructible, when it is blocked or tangled the knot can lead to the breakdown, even destruction of the self. This is what is happening to Luke, Carlotta, and the Hales.[6] The knots of conflicting needs have deadened them, even as the repressed tropes of desire are a source of unhappiness and ill luck. While articulating these truths the narrative advances along the binary rails of contrast: life vs. death, reality vs. unreality, happiness vs. unhappiness, luck vs. ill luck, body vs. mind, peace vs. war, hot vs. cold. The story's structure is one of opposition, and the metaphors themselves are oxymorons of conflicting desire. Not until the end will Lawrence sever the knots and, as the talking and dreaming sequences of the story cut through the tangle, the contrasts are resolved and the characters find happiness.

The story's knotty contradictions can be found at every turn. Morier is poor whereas Carlotta is rich (Lawrence 1995d, 174–75). She is a beauty, but she paints beastly still-lives known in French as *natures mortes*. Morier is crude but real, whereas Lathkill is perfect but unreal (Lawrence 1995d, 177). Although the people at Riddings behave like the living dead, Luke says "it's awfully important to be flesh and blood" (Lawrence 1995d, 200). Morier urges Carlotta to choose life, not death (Lawrence 1995d, 197). He believes that she needs a living body (Eros) to restore her body and her warmth because she is "shut up and prickly, in the cold" (Lawrence 1995d, 198), like the cactuses she used to paint. Her body and her mind are at war and she is also at war with Lady Lathkill, her mother-in-law, the spiritualist, who believes in appeasing the wrath of the dead Lucy Hale. Lady Lathkill has persuaded the Colonel that Lucy wants the new Mrs. Hale to remain virginal, and the Colonel believes her. It is only after wine, music, song, and dancing (and Luke's exhortations) that Hale sends Lucy's ghost packing, much to Lady Lathkill's distress. The Colonel comes to believe that Lucy is unhappy because, as her husband, he had not loved her body. Williams aptly says that Hale is trapped "by an hysterical post-mortem fixation on the dead wife he failed to satisfy in life" (Williams 1997–98, 242). His living body has become his dead wife's crypt. "The widowed Colonel, possessed, thus *becomes* the living sign of his wife's unfulfillment. She inhabits him" (Williams 1997–98, 244). Lawrence says that she is a "still-wincing nerve" disguised as a ghost (Lawrence 1995d, 203). This is the beginning of the Colonel's transformation and he will, in due course, love Dorothy, his new and living wife, even as he banishes the ghost of the dead one.

Money is no cure. Despite the Lathkill lucre, Riddings is cold and dark, and Luke and Carlotta are unhappy, whereas Morier, who lives and works in sunny Africa, is happy. He is centered and they are decentered. The Lathkills live on the surface of life and are dead, whereas Morier is alive and in touch with his unconscious. Riddings reflects the "obscene triumph of dead matter" (Lawrence 1995d, 182), not the reality of warm places and happy bodies. Although the radiators are hot, the house is cold (Lawrence 1995d, 195). Morier feels its tomb-like chill and he exhorts the others to drink the "good warm burgundy" in order to stay alive (Lawrence 1995d, 187).

The contradictory forces of life and death, hot and cold, war and peace are at work in the Riddings household even as the story unfolds around World War I. Morier believes in peace whereas society erects war monuments to the dead. Luke and Carlotta's values are superficial, like the monuments for which they stand, and they live in a house where the spirits of the dead rule. But *in vino veritas,* and the spirit of Burgundy, with the help of Morier's French drinking songs, eventually prevails. Meanwhile, Carlotta's will is locked in mortal combat with Lady Lathkill's, despite Morier's admonitions that she cut the knot and stop the battle of wills. "Why don't you get out of this tangle?" says Morier. "Why don't you break it?" "How?" says Carlotta, and Morier answers, "Just side-step, on to another ground" (Lawrence 1995d, 198). Morier's insights reinforce the conscious/unconscious dichotomy that haunts Riddings—a dichotomy that he will eventually help reconcile.

All along, Lady Lathkill's spiritualism has been predatory. Morier says that she has the eyes of a hawk (Lawrence 1995d, 186). Carlotta's skin, we should not forget, is snow-white. Because Lady Lathkill devours the living, the flame of life at Riddings is being extinguished. Hale is described as a man-boy in decay who smells already (Lawrence 1995d, 189–91). Fortunately for them Morier's presence arrests the decomposition, even as Luke's unexpected behavior and insights into himself and the Colonel break his mother's iron grip and chilling presence. Luke helps Hale cut through his knot and, in due course, he, Hale, and Carlotta are reborn. They emerge from the tomb that Lady Lathkill is building around them. Morier compares Luke's and Carlotta's lives together to a crucifixion, and their rebirth has connotations of the Resurrection. The forlorn characters move from the remote snows of Everest (Lawrence 1995d, 186) to the fresh scent of plum-blossoms in the springtime. The whiteness of snow has been replaced by the whiteness of flowers and the chill of winter gives way to the warmth of a new season. Hale's breast becomes as "white as plum-blossom," and his face shines "smooth with the tender glow of compassionate life, that flowers again" (Lawrence 1995d, 206). Carlotta's transformation is equally dramatic:

> She was looking like a girl again, and as she used to look at the Thwaite, when she painted cactuses-in-a-pot. Only now, a certain rigidity of the will had left her so that she looked even younger than when I first knew her, having now a virginal, flower-like *stillness* which she had not had then. I had always believed that people could be born again: if they would only let themselves. (Lawrence 1995d, 204)

Whereas exile from the quick of life—the *It*—is a knot that freezes and kills, the reconciliation of mind and body, surface and depth, the conscious and the unconscious moves the *I* to where the *It* was. This is a momentous shift that leads the characters toward harmony and the happiness of a new sexual identity. Lawrence achieves all this on a semiological level in which conscious signifiers connote unconscious signifieds. For example, Morier's description of Carlotta's voice highlights the distance between the *I* and the *It*. She has a flat "plangent" voice, but the word "plangent" means to beat with a deep sound, like waves; it contradicts the word "flat" (Lawrence 1995d, 177). She also has sea-colored eyes that harmonize with plangent. The images of the sea moving within her, and of the ocean depths are metaphors of the unconscious and also important elements in Morier's dream: "Deep from him calls to deep. And according as deep answers deep, man glistens and surpasses himself" (Lawrence 1995d, 208). Before her marriage, Carlotta wanted to "coruscate" socially (Lawrence 1995d, 174), but she begins to glisten with happiness only after the ghost's visitation. Lawrence's metaphors resonate in Carlotta's voice, eyes, and general demeanor along with the contradictions that have her in a tangle. Her voice has a metallic *ring* that echoes the metaphorical *ring* in her brow, and its plangent quality adumbrates future contact with an inner self as her breasts begin to lift "on a heaving sea of rest" (Lawrence 1995d, 201), another intentional oxymoron that belies the accusation that Lawrence, the bad artist, is mixing his metaphors.

This heaving sea of rest is an image and example of the contrasts that Lawrence is working with. There is also the fact that Morier will be spending the night in the ghost room—the Lathkill "equivalent for a royal apartment" (Lawrence 1995d, 183). Morier, however, has been referring to himself as a *sansculotte,* and he says, "I should never be king till breeches are off" (Lawrence 1995d, 178). A *sansculotte* is a revolutionary. There is irony in the fact that Morier will be occupying the royal apartment, because the term was one of contempt applied by the aristocracy to the republicans of the poorly clad French Revolutionary army that substituted pantaloons for knee breeches. In order to sleep, Morier will indeed take his breeches off in the royal guestroom where the she-ghost will visit him in a profound and erotic dream. There is additional irony in that Morier, the poor roisterer of French songs, will bring good luck to his aristocratic friends and peace to Riddings. Moreover, the ghost is as rare as sovereignty and she restores the family fortune—not money but, as Carlotta says, "luck for two" (Lawrence 1995d, 172). The pun here is not so much on *luck* and *lucre,* as it was in "The Rocking-Horse Winner," although some of the verbal slippage does rub off, but on *ghost* and *guest,* a prelude to the mirth and irony of a *sansculotte* occupying royal chambers and changing the world-view of his hosts.

Lacan's essay on "The Function and Field of Speech and Language in Psychoanalysis" describes the power of language to meld different entities of the self whenever they resonate within the networks of discourse (Lacan 1977a, 55, 59). The ghost room as guest room is where the combinatory power of language works its magic because that is where *I* and *It* finally merge, not just for Morier, but also for the other dreamers. Their unconscious will flower, like the plum-blossoms, diffuse the scent of love, and communicate the silkiness of touch. But conscious contact with the unconscious is ephemeral and it occurs perhaps most frequently during sleep. Afterwards, "that knowledge of *it,* which was the marriage of the ghost and me, disappeared from me, in its rich weight of certainty, as the scent of the plum-blossom moved down the lanes of my consciousness, and my limbs stirred in a silkiness for which I have no comparison" (Lawrence 1995d, 209).

Lawrence's tropes unveil the unconscious *It* and in reading his tropes we assemble semantic transpositions from signs that are present to ones that are absent. In joining visible language and invisible effect we work through the different levels of the written text in order to reveal the network of associations. In *Écrits,* Lacan, like Freud, shows that the operations of the unconscious, encompassing both pictographic and linguistic analyses, are linguistic processes that have both manifest and latent content. In dreams, condensation and displacement disguise the content of the unconscious in the same way that metaphor and metonymy veil the pulsive forces of the subject's desire whenever a narrator/author uses language. The ghost that visits Morier and, presumably the others also, is, for Lawrence, the Holy Spirit of the unconscious that is capable of renewing life and resurrecting the dead. In this case it is the living dead who reside at Riddings. Morier is the messenger of rebirth, and the ghost is the savior. At the end of the story, Luke says, "I am in love with this house and its inmates, including the plum-blossom-scented one, she who visited you, in all the peace" (Lawrence 1995d, 210).

The metaphorical spark generated by the coming of the ghost not only allows the *I* and the *It* to merge in the deepest recesses of the unconscious night, it also illumines the conscious use of figurative language. The plum-blossom-scented one has replaced the ghost in the signifying chain and now occupies the place that would normally be hers. If we compare this metaphor with Freud's analysis of dreams, the plum-blossom-scented one becomes the manifest content, and "ghost" is her latent meaning. Lawrence's network of associations allows us to link the scent of plum-blossoms with springtime, crocuses, open flowers, stillness, readiness, rebirth, love, insemination and, finally, the births of Gabriel and Gabrielle. Scented flowers are the signifiers, and rebirth is the signified. There is an unmistakable relationship between rhetorical poetics and the dream work. In both, a substitute signifier veils the signified. The ghost does not signify plum-blossom, but plum-blossom, inevitably and necessarily, signifies the ghost. By working through the chain of substitutions and displacements (Freud's *durcharbeiten*) we craft meaningful connections between different parts of the whole.

As noted earlier, Lacan believes that there is a ternary relation to the different parts of the human condition, namely nature, society, and culture. Culture and language are synonymous, and society's *doxa* is encoded in language. Its ideology speaks us as much as we speak it, and the knot forms whenever the ideology, as lived by *I,* contradicts the unconscious desire of *It.* This is what distinguishes human societies from natural ones (Lacan 1977b, 148). For Morier, man as an entity of nature "is formed through countless ages, and at the center is the speck, or spark, upon which all his formation has taken place" (Lawrence 1995d, 208).

In the final essay in the *Mornings in Mexico* quartet, "Market Day," Lawrence acclaims "the spark of contact" and "exchange" that connects dualities (Lawrence 2009, 55), dualities that, as Virginia Hyde phrases it, "cannot come together, except by means of a mediator, the 'gleaming Ghost'" (Hyde 2004, 124). Insofar as the ghost signifies the melding of *I* and *It,* her coming, as arrival and orgasm, denotes a successful union of the two. Similarly, in "Indians and Entertainment" (Lawrence 2009, 61), Lawrence's intermediary "Ghost" connects us with the quick of life or, as Ramón in *The Plumed Serpent* calls it, "the Quick of all being" (Lawrence 1987b, 253), that blessed realm where *I* and *It* unite in order to effect the transfiguration of being.

During Morier's dream, Lawrence's emphasis is no longer on *doxa* but on "the heart of life" where the *It* resides—an *It* formed through countless ages. The ghost will come only to the *It,* with all its erotic connotations, because both reside deep within the ocean of the unconscious. Morier says: "And even with so slight a conscious registering, *it* seemed to disappear, like a whale that has sounded to the bottomless seas. That knowledge of *it,* which was the marriage of the ghost and me, disappeared from me, in its rich weight of certainty" (Lawrence 1995d, 209).

The ghost comes to Morier, "at the heart of the ocean of oblivion, which is also the heart of life" (Lawrence 1995d, 208). That he meets her and knows her emphasizes the orgasmic nature of their union. Lacan's *"Wo Es war, soll Ich werden"* has at last been realized or, as Phillips phrases it, "Where literature was, there science should be" (Phillips 2003, 19). Freud's dilemma has been resolved and his wish fulfilled. Lawrence's story demonstrates not only the melding of *I* with *It* but the melding of literature and psychoanalysis. Psychoanalysis as theory is thus analogous to the conscious *I,* and literature as body is analogous to the unconscious *It.*

For Lacan, the signifier has become a new dimension of the human condition because not only does man speak, but "in man and through man *it* speaks *(ça parle),* that his nature is woven by effects in which is to be found the structure of language, of which he becomes the material" (Lacan 1977a, 284). When Lacan says that *"it* speaks" he means that the *I* responds to the voice of the unconscious. Luke's admonitions to the Colonel, warmed by the burgundy, are that voice, and Morier's dream is couched in the language of the unconscious *it.*

While Morier and Dorothy Hale are dancing his clairvoyance allows him to see her hairy legs beneath her dress. If he can be so prescient then surely he can also connect with the meaning of dreams or even conjure dreams for the Lathkills and the Hales. This extraordinary power explains the uncanny ambiguity of Morier's waking narrative and the content of his dream: "I shall never know if it was a ghost, some sweet spirit from the innermost of the ever-deepening cosmos. Or a woman, a very woman, as the silkiness of my limbs seems to attest. Or a dream, a hallucination! I shall never know" (Lawrence 1995d, 209).

He says he does not know if it was a ghost, a woman, or a dream because the erotic spirit of the unconscious is the latent *It* of the manifest dream. In any case, his dream restores sanity to a house that had become hysterical. Morier, the healer, cures everybody's symptoms.[7] Hysteria—their distress— was the metaphor veiling the disconnect between the *I* and the *It.* The cure is to connect the two; and it happens when Morier shows his friends how to be happy. The Lathkill ill luck has not only been transformed into luck for two, that is, Luke and Carlotta, but also luck for the Hales and even Lady Lathkill who "doesn't look over the wall, to the other side, any more," pre- sumably toward death (Lacan 1977a, 210). Such is the power of *It*—the good *ghost* and friendly *guest.* The vocalic transposition of the vowels *o* and *e* in the two words is sufficient to substitute one signifier for the other. If we add the *t* in ghost and guest to the *I,* the reconciliation with *It* on the linguistic level is complete. God, the spirit and host, has spoken to Morier when he says: "Beyond all the pearly mufflings of consciousness, of age upon age of consciousness, deep calls yet to deep, and sometimes is answered. It is new-wakened God calling within the deep of man, and new God calling answer, from the other deep. And sometimes the other deep is woman, as it was with me, when my ghost came" (Lawrence 1995d, 208).

"Glad Ghosts" reveals the fact that Lawrence shares Lacan's ternary con- cept of the human condition. Because language and culture are synonymous, language encompasses information, *doxa*, and art. The language of art is subversive because it undercuts ideology and the "plastrons" with which ideology protects itself. That is why Morier is a *sansculotte* and Lawrence is an artist. In order to cut through the knot of *doxa,* which, by definition, is a false ideology, Lawrence and Lacan emphasize the enduring nature of desire. At the end of the story, the characters have been reborn because they have cut through the knots of *doxa* and the tangles of hysteria.

It is remarkable that Lawrence and Lacan use language and ideas in such similar ways, and, that in order to communicate, they write the tropes of the unconscious into the signifying chain. There, we, as readers, recognize the affinity between science, literature, and the unconscious. Freud would be happy because language (words) is the magnetic field that brings them all together. This story is thus an allegory that enables us to reconcile the *It* in ourselves with the *It* in "Glad Ghosts" which, I believe, is one of Lawrence's best stories, easily the equal of "The Rocking-Horse Winner" and "The Man Who Loved Islands."

Morier helps the men and women of the Lathkill estate cut through their tangles of hysteria. He is the agent of their rebirth. In the next chapter, *The Escaped Cock,* we shall see how a human Christ cuts the knot of overweening care—the knot that has hobbled him. The priestess of Isis will be the agent of redemption, and their union will be transformative. His erection becomes a resurrection. He is risen. He finds salvation in erotic love.

Chapter Seven

The Escaped Cock
Salvation

Ethel Cane, in "None of That!," Paul, in "The Rocking-Horse Winner," and Cathcart, in "The Man Who Loved Islands," all die, but ironically, "the man who died" survives. In *The Escaped Cock*—the novella's preferred title— Lawrence's Christ survives the crucifixion. He repudiates the law of the Father, and, in the process, Lawrence's tale of repressed sexuality reenacts many tenets of Lacanian theory. In the temple of Isis, at the height of his newfound sexual identity, as the phallus of an aroused man-Christ "rises" to the occasion, Lawrence paints a formulaic image of a mythical union worthy of an inverted Oedipus complex.[1] Instead of castration, the son recovers his manhood, and possesses the mother, symbolically. Golden rays of desire between Christ and the priestess of Isis illumine the encounter, enabling a redeemed Christ to ascend toward "the great rose of space" (Lawrence 2005b, 160).[2] As Jacqueline Gouirand notes, "the cosmos [. . .] has taken on the flower form of the goddess," and Christ can now enjoy the absolute fullness of touch (Gouirand 2000, 44).

Freudian readings of Lawrence's work tend to look for the author behind it, whereas Lacanian readings free the text from this umbilical cord.[3] The text becomes a free-floating construct in which metaphor, metonymy, synecdoche, homonymy, aporia, puns, indeed every combination possible, including verbal traces, contribute to the artistic space that defines the work. Lacan privileges the text over the artist's life because the text already contains everything we need to know. Indeed, Lacan wrote his "Seminar on 'The Purloined Letter'" in order to demonstrate that meaning—the letter as the signifier—is always displaced, circulating throughout the text whether or not we refer to Lawrence's biography. As a signifier, the letter is "the letter of the unconscious," and it is a paradigm that functions independently of the author's life.[4] It is axiomatic that every text contains repressed material that manifests an ongoing record of the Other's presence, that is, the unconscious.

It is the play of language, its gaps, puns, repetitions, metaphorical slippages, and homonyms—the spaces wherein desire lurks—that reveal the discourse of the Other. Traces, dissemination, and floating signifiers, as we saw in "The Rocking-Horse Winner," confirm the fact that no signifier ever refers only to itself. Because language is a system of signs distinguished from one another only by their mutual opposition, no element in a discourse can function as a sign without referring to another element that is absent. Moreover, in formulating a theory of reading I am borrowing from Cowan, Lacan, and Derrida. For them, language always manifests desire because, even in its earliest stages, desire was proscribed by the Law of the Father (Derrida 1987a, 443). During the infant's "mirror phase," when it accedes to language, the child misrecognizes itself as Other, seeing itself and the mother as one. According to Lacan, this misrecognition coincides with the infant's accession to language. It also coincides with the primal repression of desire because "the law of the Father" proscribes union with the mother. The displacement of desire lingers on, nonetheless, embedded in the subject and its language.[5]

For Lacan, the unconscious is embedded in language. Lawrence, however, sees the unconscious as the life force, the soul, the individual itself that was formed at the moment of conception, when the sperm penetrates the ovum. The unconscious, says Lawrence, is the "active spontaneity which rouses in each individual organism at the moment of fusion of parent nuclei, [. . .] bringing forth not only consciousness, but tissue and organs also" (Lawrence 2004, 15). The true unconscious "is the spontaneous life-motive in every organism" and it begins where life itself begins (Lawrence 2004, 15). For Lawrence, the concept of repression is a false unconscious, whereas for Lacan, repression and accession to language form the unconscious. Lawrence believes in a phenomenological and ontological sense of presence, whereas Lacan and Derrida, postulate a self that is constituted by words. The self is also fragmented and decentered, and, because of this decentering, Lacan says, playing with Descartes' *cogito:* "I think where I am not, therefore I am where I do not think" ("Je pense où je ne suis pas, donc je suis où je ne pense pas" Lacan 1977b, 166; Lacan 1966b, 277).

Despite their differences, Lawrence and Lacan are moving in the same direction. For Lacan, discourse is always unconscious. Lawrence, however, is a conscious craftsman, although his discourse will also, inevitably, contain unconscious elements. Both discourses, the conscious one and the unconscious one, replicate Freud's "*Wo Es war, soll Ich werden,*" dictum which Lacan translates as "*Là où fut ça, il me faut advenir,*" or "*Là ou c'était [. . .] c'est mon devoir que je vienne à être*" (and both are also part of Lawrence's agenda), (Lacan 1966b, 284; Lacan 1966a, 227; Lacan 1977b, 171; Lacan 1977a, 129).[6] The English version ("Where the id was, there the ego shall be"), according to Lacan, mistranslates the German, insofar as the German does not say *das Es* (the id) nor *das Ich* (the ego). It only says *Es* and *Ich, namely It* and *I*. Lacan substitutes the word *it* for *id*, and even more radically, the letter *S* (signifier) for *Es*—the unconscious—because, for the subject, every symptom is a signifier. In psychoanalytic terms, the only way to close the gap between the subject and the signifier is to strive for a melding of the two: "Where it was, I must be" (Lacan 1977a, 128–29; Lacan 1966a, 226–27). The *it* is not, strictly speaking, the id, nor is the *I* necessarily the ego.[7] "The Other is therefore the locus in which is constituted the I who speaks to him who hears, that which is said by the one being already the reply, the other deciding to hear it whether the one has or has not spoken" ("L'Autre est donc le lieu où se constitue le je qui parle avec celui qui entend, ce que l'un dit étant déjà la réponse et l'autre décidant à l'entendre si l'un a ou non parlé" [Lacan 1977a, 141; Lacan 1966a, 242]). Lawrence also writes the metaphorical discourse of fiction as the answer to what he has already heard; and to which he has been listening. The Other is always speaking, and we should listen to it, but what does the Other want for me (Lacan 1977a, 312; Lacan 1971a, 176)? Since the speaking I is already in the Other, the passage toward consciousness for Lacan, as with Lawrence, is from *it* to the conscious *me*. What does the unconscious want to say and what does it want for me? Lawrence's *Escaped Cock* may provide an answer.

"I tried to compel them to live, so they compelled me to die" (Lawrence 2005b, 137). These are the words of Lawrence's Christ—a man who survives his death because they took him down from the cross too soon; and, having survived the crucifixion, he repudiates his past life by saying that "the day of my interference is done. The teacher and savior are dead in me" (Lawrence 2005b, 132). The man who died rejects his previous message of salvation in favor of a new earth-centered philosophy, a philosophy of healing. "No man can save the earth from tillage," he says (Lawrence 2005b, 131), and he concludes that "virginity is a form of greed" (Lawrence 2005b, 135); preaching is a mistake, "for in the tomb he had slipped that noose, which we call care" (Lawrence 2005b, 137). In short, he had run to excess because he had given more than he had taken; such excess was also a form of death (Lawrence 2005b, 133). The man who died rejects a theological idealism—an idealism that is consonant with Lawrence's own repudiation of it. Having cast off the excesses of his previous existence, the man shifts toward a radically different direction: personal fulfillment. As Becket notes, "personal rebirth is established as the necessary prefiguration to cultural rebirth" (Becket 2002, 89). When the man who died finds it, it allows him to ascend to the Father (Lawrence 2005b, 1136*)*. After his encounter with the priestess of Isis, and, after his "resurrection," Lawrence embarks his character on a mystical, mythical, and religious quest that melds the Christian crucifixion and the myth of Isis and Osiris into a parable for modern-day man. John Worthen believes that *The Escaped Cock* is the most religious of Lawrence's fictions because he uses sex as "an example, an opportunity, a metaphor and a myth" (Worthen 1991, 119–20).

In writing the parable Lawrence employs many nouns and verbs of touch. The sound of a cock crowing "made him shiver as if electricity had touched him" (Lawrence 2005b, 126). As a metaphor for the phallus, the rooster also adumbrates the novella's climax. The priestess of Isis is watching the sleeping stranger, and his presence touches her with the same "flame-tip of life" (Lawrence 2005b, 147) that, earlier in the story, surged through the "rocking vibration of the bent bird" (Lawrence 2005b, 130). Before making love to the priestess, the man who died wonders if he dare "come into touch? [. . .] into this tender touch of life" (Lawrence 2005b, 150). Touching her "was like touching the sun" (Lawrence 2005b, 155). The stranger believes that if he is naked enough for this *contact* (my emphasis), he has "not died in vain" (Lawrence 2005b, 155). In due course the priestess chafes the scar on his hand with oil, and then anoints and rubs all the scars on his body with the ointment (Lawrence 2005b, 158–59). The man lays "his hand softly on her warm bright shoulder" and he sees "the white glow of her white-gold breasts. He touches them and he feels his life go molten. 'Father!' he said, 'why did you hide this from me?' And he touched her with the poignancy of wonder, and the marvelous piercing transcendence of desire. 'Lo!' he said, 'this is beyond prayer'" (Lawrence 2005b, 159–60). Then the priestess envelops him with her arms, and, after making love, and referring to his scars, he says: "They are suns! [. . .] They shine from your touch. They are my atonement with you" (Lawrence 2005b, 160). Satisfactions of the flesh have, at last, displaced prayer and spirituality. Afterwards, all around him, the dew touches the darkness of the starry sky that is like a rose. "The world is one flower of many-petalled darknesses, and [he] is in its perfume as in a touch" (Lawrence 2005b, 160). He sleeps in his cave "in the absolute stillness and fullness of touch" (Lawrence 2005b, 160), and when the dawn comes, he says: "This is the great atonement, the being in touch. [. . .] the invisible Isis and the unseen sun are all in touch, and at one" (Lawrence 2005b, 160–61). The potency of the priestess's sun reminds us of the carnal power of the Sicilian sun that puts Juliet in touch with her blood-consciousness. The sun restores her health as it will restore the health of the man who died.

Like Juliet's repressed sexuality, Christ's repressed sexuality embodies the need to connect with all living things. Not only will he strive for union with a woman, but also for contact with the phenomenal world—a conjunction that will heal the wound and soothe the scars of his crucifixion. Like Juliet, the man who died gets in touch with his unconscious *and* with the realm of living things. The sun makes all this possible. Indeed, Lawrence uses the word *sun* almost as frequently as he does the word *touch*. Both words illustrate how unconscious discourse manifests itself. In *Apocalypse*, as I noted early on, Lawrence says, "Start with the sun, and the rest will slowly, slowly happen" (Lawrence 1979, 149). And in *Psychoanalysis and the Unconscious* he says, "It is necessary for us to know the unconscious [. . .] just as it is necessary for us to know the sun' (Lawrence 2004, 17). He equates the *sun* with the *soul*, and he knows the sun by "watching his motions and feeling his changing power. The same is true for the unconscious" (Lawrence 2004, 169). When crafting *The Escaped Cock*, the hypothesis of a partially premeditated metaphorical discourse is reinforced by Lawrence's equation of the words *sun*, *soul*, and *unconscious*. A passage from the "Future Religion" confirms the process. The mind, the will, and the spirit are "touchless," says Lawrence, but after death and aloneness comes the pure "resurrection into touch" (Lawrence 1964, 611). Gouirand, paraphrasing Lawrence, says that the unconscious is the spontaneous life-motive in every organism, and it rises, like the sun. The priestess's love and the sun give life. They bring the man who died into touch (Gouirand 2000, 53).

"The Man Who Dies" is resurrected only after he gets in touch with his unconscious, that is, after contact with the inner sun ascending toward the Father. This contact with the priestess of Isis does, nonetheless, have incestuous connotations because, as Lawrence phrases it, she embraces the man the way a mother embraces her child. She also heals the man's howling wounds even as a mother might soothe her crying infant's hurt. Moreover, the word *sun*, as a homonym for *son*, considering the importance that both Freud and Lacan attribute to the play of language, reinforces the incest motif. These paronomastic associations help to unveil the latent discourse beneath Lawrence's conscious metaphorical structures.

The story opens with Lawrence saying that a force greater than death prompts the man to awaken "from a long sleep in which he was tied up" (Lawrence 2005b, 124). He is literally and figuratively bound and hobbled, like the cock, whose "body, soul and spirit were tied by that string" (Lawrence 2005b, 124). We have already seen that for Lacan, the repression of desire means that the emotions are tied into a knot. Indeed, as Jane Gallop points out, the slang word in French for penis is *noeud,* meaning "knot" (Gallop 1985, 156).[8] Moreover, the essential problem in psychoanalysis is how to cut through the knot that binds and inhibits change. In Lawrence's novella the cock denotes rooster, but it connotes phallus, and it is the life force of the cock that overrides death: "something had returned to him, like a returned letter" (Lawrence 2005b, 125), because, despite the cold, the nausea, and the forlornness, the man who has survived death pushes at the bandages on his face, his shoulders, and his legs. He unties himself, the linen swathing-bands fall away, and he leaves the cave, stepping "with wincing feet down the rocky slope, past the sleeping soldiers" (Lawrence 2005b, 126). Because *The Escaped Cock* reads like a case study in psychoanalysis, the sleeping soldiers guarding the tomb behave like Freud's metaphorical censors who are asleep on the job, thereby allowing the unconscious to act out its dream imagery. Indeed, the man who died is free to set forth on his mythical quest only because the guardians of the Law are derelict in their duty.

It is quite remarkable that Lawrence should use the analogy of the returned letter, the analogy that both Lacan and Derrida use in order to explain the meanderings of the unconscious. One of Lacan's essays in *Écrits* is entitled "The agency of the letter in the unconscious" and one of Derrida's essays in *The Post Card* is entitled "Le Facteur de la vérité," in which the word *facteur* means both factor and mailman (Derrida 1987a, 411–96). The truth, according to Derrida, being that a letter does not always necessarily reach its destination, whereas for Lacan it always does. Poe's "Purloined Letter" is the basis for the disagreement and exploration of the workings of the unconscious by both men. Despite their differences, the event in Lawrence's story that redirects the letter to its addressee is death, not real death, but the symbolic death of a man who consciously rejects the ideology for which he was crucified. He repudiates the Father's Law, that is, the teachings for which he was tried and which he now finds so objectionable. His insight frees him from the tangle that had bound him, and, in due course, he rises to the Father, resurrected, no longer subservient to His Law. The man who died concludes that the coercive nature of the Law is a form of death in life. He accepts and discards his past and the symbolic death of a man who no longer exists. He is now free to go forth in search of a new self based on "the flame-tip of life" that had for so long been repressed (Lawrence 2005b, 147).

Lawrence's novella provides the answer to Lacan's question: "What does the unconscious want for me?" The answer being that it wants me to live, and to live productively, and, as Derrida asserts, the desire to live overrides the death instinct that Freud formulated in *Beyond the Pleasure Principle*. Life overrides the compulsion to repeat, illustrated by the *Fort!/Da!* episode of little Ernst throwing the spool across the crib and pulling it back in order to recover the absent mother. An iterative subservience to the Law is death, whereas the need to "get in touch" with life, dramatizes the ongoing force of the pleasure principle. The decision of the man who died to repudiate the Law and go forth in search of fulfillment is the affirmation of Eros over Thanatos.

The Escaped Cock can be read as a metaphor of Lacanian theory in which the Law, in this case God's law, proscribes desire. Christ's "death" is a reenactment of the primal scene—a prohibition that is experienced as castration and as a death of the self. On the denotative level, Lawrence's story has the vivid immediacy of realism, but on a psychoanalytic level his "wound" connotes all the hurt of the primal repression. When Christ comes down from the cell on the rock in which he had been entombed, Lawrence says, "It meant full awakening," movement accompanied "with the caution of the bitterly wounded" (Lawrence 2005b, 125). And he thinks of his own mission and "how he had tried to lay the compulsion of love on all men" (Lawrence 2005b, 140), and for which he was crucified. In *Fantasia of the Unconscious* Lawrence had already asserted that because every Ideal was evil, no idea should be raised to a governing throne. For him, forcing a pure idea into practice is the death of life because "the more we force the ideal the more we rupture the true movement of the unconscious" (Lawrence 2004, 9). It should not surprise us, therefore, that when the man who died comes in contact with the cock, he sees "not the bird alone, but the short, sharp wave of life of which the bird was the crest"; and he hears "the voice of its life, crowing triumph and assertion, yet strangled by a cord of circumstance" (Lawrence 2005b, 130). It is the "cord" of the Law that hobbles—a circumstance that Lawrence weaves into the fabric of his story. In the end, Christ overcomes his "wound"—the Ideal that the Law had imposed on him and that was responsible for his symbolic death—retrieves the phallus, and makes love to the priestess of Isis. He is now literally and figuratively in touch with the goddess Isis, the Magna Mater. It is Isis who rewards the priestess's quest and Christ's quest, since they are both searching for the same thing—the lost phallus. Finally, the symbolic reunion of the son and the mother is possible only in the temple of Isis. The priestess dreams that the stranger is the lost Osiris (Lawrence 2005b, 149), and he, the son of God, connects at last with the sun/son within himself, a homonymic union that was sundered when *le nom/non du père* intervened to split the child from the mother. Before his crucifixion, Christ's ego is the will of God—the Father, the Superego, for Whom or for which he "dies"—but having died, and having freed himself, he sets out to discover himself as subject. The self had been decentered but now the *it*, namely the sun and the phallus—the life force—can assert itself. It is this displacement and acceptance of a repressed sexuality that transforms this novella into a specimen-story of Lacanian theory.

For Lacan, every symptom of aberrant behavior is a metaphor. According to Lawrence, the symptoms of Christ's ideology are virginity, excess, preaching, and the need to compel others to believe these "virtues." In structuring Christ's quest for a new life, Lawrence orients him and the reader toward the reenactment of a scene that dramatizes the child's repressed desire. Although the priestess is not the mother, Lawrence's discourse, imagery, and metaphors weave a web of enchantment that re-orients the man-child toward the maternal womb where he, the son, reestablishes contact with his inner self. Only then does he achieve fulfillment. Christ's erection and "resurrection" would not have been possible without this backward journey. Let us track the slippage of Lawrence's metaphors and pursue their traces.

In part two of The *Escaped Cock,* Lawrence anthropomorphizes nature and objects, imbuing them with the colors and symbolism of womanhood. Isis, nature, the priestess, and space become one maternal network contributing to the resurrection of the son. The temple of Isis stands on a "tongue of land between the two bays" (Lawrence 2005b, 141). A causeway of rock is "the neck of her temple peninsula" (Lawrence 2005b, 142). The peninsula is also "humped" (Lawrence 2005b, 146), pine-covered, and the light falls on it "triumphantly" (Lawrence 2005b, 148). Lawrence's tropological weave introduces a decidedly human pattern—a point of view that transforms the four wooden pillars of the temple into stems of "the swollen lotus bud of Egypt" (Lawrence 2005b, 143), a bud that reminds us of Juliet's opening herself to the sun like a lotus flower. The shadow of the afternoon "washes" over the pillar-bases (Lawrence 2005b, 143). The little world of the peninsula is "sacred"; the sunshine "pours"; it is also "royal," and "pure" (Lawrence 2005b, 152). A black-and-white pigeon flies over the "immaculate loneliness" of the sea "like a ghost" (Lawrence 2005b, 142). Objects are animated, shadows "wash," sunshine "pours," and the sea is "lonely."

These descriptions imbue nature with human attributes. A peninsula can only be sacred if a person describes it that way. This is also true of the adjective "royal," as in "royal sunshine"—another example of the way our use of language contaminates nature and objects. How can the sea be lonely? It knows nothing of its loneliness. These pathetic fallacies are disguised forms of perception that give us little real information about nature but say a great deal about the person who is speaking figuratively. The same anthropomorphism links the pink and white temple, which is "like a flower in the little clearing" (Lawrence 2005b, 143), to the priestess dressed in yellow and white—the exact colors of the "narcissus sparkling gaily in the rocks" (Lawrence 2005b, 148). Can flowers be gay? People, yes, but flowers? The gaiety of a flower emanates from one source only, a human source. The flowers animate the temple with qualities that belong to the priestess, thereby transforming the whole scene into one vast pagan evocation of the Holy Ghost over which Isis, the Egyptian goddess, presides. Thus, the adjectives "royal," "immaculate" and "pure," while used to denote the landscape, connote a sacred entity that is embedded in a non-Christian setting.[9] As Cowan phrases it, "in *The Escaped Cock,* Lawrence brings modern Christianity, which he finds to be overintellectualized and therefore sterile, into contact with the instinctual experience of flesh-and-blood sexuality through allusions to the Osiris-Isis myth" (Cowan 1990, 252).

The man who died was known formerly as the son of God, the Father, but he will soon become the son of Isis, the Mother, because Lawrence's descriptions of nature establish a metaphorical link with motherhood. The stranger spends the first night in a cave in a little gully where a rock basin fringed with *maidenhair* (my emphasis) contains a dripping mouthful of water. The man eats bread and he dips it into the water (not wine)—the new source of his life—the spring fringed with maidenhair. The word "maiden-hair" denotes the plant but connotes a woman's sex (Lawrence 2005b, 146). Every paragraph contains metaphorical associations and anthropomorphized images. The priestess is a virginal lotus bud, or a narcissus, or "the deep interfolded warmth, warmth living and penetrable, the woman, the heart of the rose!" (Lawrence 2005b, 160). The heart of the rose is "like the core of a flame" (Lawrence 2005b, 156), and the flame, as an earlier passage tells us, is life itself. In due course the world becomes "one flower of many-petalled darknesses" whose perfume brings the stranger and priestess together (Lawrence 2005b, 160). The world and everything in it is now alive, and the man who died experiences his resurrection as a universal oneness. Lawrence's metaphorical equations state, in essence, that woman is a flower, that a rose has the life force of fire, that woman is therefore life itself, and that space is female, fertile, enveloping, and maternal.

The metaphors that maternalize nature and space are a necessary prelude to the man's ascension. He, like the priestess, is still "in Search" (Lawrence 2005b, 150), and he seems hesitant, unable to fulfill himself without reliving the original mother/son union that was severed by the father. "Suns beyond suns had dipped her in mysterious fire, the mysterious fire of a potent woman, and to touch her was like touching the sun" (Lawrence 2005b, 155). Not only does the man feel the sun's warmth, but also, homonymically speaking, the child within himself. His face shines with the invisible light of "the violet-dark sun" (Lawrence 2005b, 145). He is ready for the climax, but still impotent, "faced by the demand of life, and burdened still by his death" (Lawrence 2005b, 157). The scar on the man's side "is the eye of the violet" (Lawrence 2005b, 157), and the wound is the source of the reborn man. The external wound has healed but the psychic wound has not. The man's sexual impotence cannot be healed until he unites symbolically with Isis. Only this union can soothe the inner cry by conjuring the lost mother and retrieving the absent breast. In *Psychoanalysis and the Unconscious* Lawrence speaks of birth, pain, and the child's desire to heal the wound. The child seeks the mother's breast in order to reinstate "the old organic continuum—a recovery of the pre-natal state" (Lawrence 2004, 21). Indeed, "the nipples of the breast are as fountains leaping into the universe, or as little lamps irradiating the contiguous world, to the soul in quest" (Lawrence 2004, 80). The man's wound is like a baby's mouth seeking to recover the warmth and comfort of the breast. Accordingly, the priestess puts "her breast against the wound in his left side, and her arms round him, folding over the wound in his right

side, and she pressed him to her, in a power of living warmth [. . .] And the
wailing died out altogether, and there was stillness and darkness in his soul,
unbroken dark stillness, wholeness" (Lawrence 2005b, 159). The breast and
the embrace heal the wound and the wailing, and the child's silent ongoing
and unconscious wailing is silenced only after this primal, maternal contact
has been reaffirmed.

We are witnessing the ascent, the rising of the unconscious—the *it/ça.* "In
the perfect darkness of his inner man," the man who died "felt the stir of
something coming: a dawn, a new sun. A new sun was coming up in him,
in the perfect inner darkness of himself" (Lawrence 2005b, 159). This rising
of the inner darkness is the unconscious. In Lacanian terms it is the voice of
the Other that has been repressed by the Law. The dark sun of the man who
died rises, at last, in the temple of Isis. Christ now feels the new man within
himself, and, again, homonymically speaking, there will also be a new son
who will be the seed of his union with the priestess of Isis. But this sun is
now the son of Isis in search. Truly, the man who died, echoing Freud, can
say, "The id and I are now one," or, as he prefers to say "'Now I am not
myself. I am something new'" (Lawrence 2005b, 159). The new man, no
longer impotent and now in touch with the primal Mother (Isis), says: "'I am
risen!' Magnificent, blazing indomitable in the depths of his loins, his own
sun dawned, and sent its fire running along his limbs, so that his face shone
unconsciously" (Lawrence 2005b, 159).

The union of the man with the priestess of Isis is, in Lacanian terms, a
metaphor for moving the contents of the unconscious into consciousness.
The role of the sun in its denotative and connotative forms is essential. The
mystery and power of the sun generate the "flaming buds of life" and "the
foaming crest of the wave"; the revivifying power of the goddess Isis in
contact with the sun god heals the stranger on the shores of Lebanon. This
is the message of the unconscious that is manifest in the puns, metaphors,
and slips of language that, like a letter, always has a destination (what does
the unconscious want for me?), even though sometimes it may not get there.
What had been silenced and repressed by ideology and the Law was the phallus. The man's erection is his resurrection—a retrieval of wholeness. The
child's wound has been healed, and the man who died is reborn. He is now
alive. Lawrence's novella relives with formulaic accuracy the events of the
so-called primal scene.

The Son, the Father, and the Holy Ghost are now one, insofar as the resurrected man incorporates all three: the unconscious, his I, and the displacement
of the Father by his own impending fatherhood. The man is now in touch
with the principle of life—universal motherhood—and free at last to pursue
the call of a new identity. Barthes would have called this inner radiance *jouissance.* Its incestuous connotations are the happiness of freedom, wholeness,

fulfillment, and absence of pain. The priestess is happy because she is "full of the risen Osiris" (Lawrence 2005b, 160)! The phallus, as Lacan points out, is a signifier and its function is to lift the veil from the Other so that the id may speak, rising to the occasion one might say, and becoming the subject, a subject who can at last assume his identity in the Father (Lacan 1977a, 285; Lacan 1971b, 108). *The Escaped Cock* demonstrates that Freud's "*Wo Es war, soll Ich werden*" (Lacan 1977a, 128; Lacan 1966a, 226), as it was in "Glad Ghosts," is not an incursion of the ego-ideal into the id, but its opposite, namely the illumination of the ego by the rising sun of the unconscious.

The new father retires to the cave where he sleeps, knowing that "this is the great atonement, the being in touch. The grey sea and the rain, the wet narcissus and the woman I wait for, the invisible Isis and the unseen sun, we are all in touch, and at one" (Lawrence 2005b, 160–61). Isis, the earth mother, watches over the man in the womblike cave with its spring and its maidenhair, and he sleeps in this protective enclosure as a child sleeps in its mother's womb. Lawrence's novella can thus be read as the discourse of a man in search of the mother, and of the son's primal contact with her. When he finds her and himself, the son of the father—and the sun that shines—ascend together as one heavenly body. The sexuality of the unconscious illumines the whole. But the man who died is now also the new father. He "rowed slowly on, with the current, and laughed to himself—I have sowed the seed of my life and my resurrection'" (Lawrence 2005b, 162). His departure leaves the priestess of Isis, the child's mother, to raise it.

In conclusion, *The Escaped* Cock suggests that the future mother and nature are now one, and that this new oneness is the "retrieval" that resurrects the son. Now that he is healed and whole, he will venture forth into "the great rose of space," and be "like a grain of its perfume" (Lawrence 2005b, 160). The man's desire is not to merge with a caretaker mother, although she is present everywhere, but to function as an individual within the maternal realm. In the final analysis, both Lawrence's message and his achievement, at least in *The Escaped Cock,* show that his mother fixation is not emotionally and artistically crippling, as some commentators allege, but ennobling. As a future father, the man who died has proved his manhood. He is now ready to assume his place in the world as a free, independent, and integrated person.

Conclusion

In his fiction and in his essays D.H. Lawrence advances the proposition that because men and women are no longer "in touch," the world is spiritually and morally bankrupt. As a result Lawrence believes that humanity is slowly grinding itself into extinction. He believes that this moral bankruptcy is a form of collective insanity, and that the remedy for the deadness gripping mankind is to rekindle the sense-knowledge of the ancients while also emphasizing a renewed contact with nature. The sun becomes a metaphor of renewal, and with renewal in mind, the future of the world must include a vision that breaks through *doxa,* the ready-made, and the "wall" of the military-industrial complex. In the third version of *Lady Chatterley's Lover,* Sir Clifford, the crippled representative of his class, concludes that he too is an agent of madness and destruction because, by making money in industry, he has abetted the bitch Goddess of success. In order to prevent such aberrations, Lawrence believes that art should not only expose but also criticize the cultural decline, a decline that began with the Industrial Revolution, and, ever since, has been accelerating. He believes that art should prepare the public for the necessary transition to "The Holy Ghost" stage of human interactions, a stage he also calls "the fourth dimension." If and when men and women achieve the fourth dimension, its wisdom will restore the blood-sense of the ancients, and, along with it, the world's sanity. With sanity in mind I have analyzed how three of Lawrence's characters—Juliet, Morier, and Christ—turn their backs on the world's madness. They survive because they have found and understand the metaphorical meaning of the sun. I have also analyzed why Ethel Cane, the boy rocker, and Cathcart—the man who loved islands—fail and die because they are out of touch with blood-consciousness.

We have seen that in the stories "Sun," "Glad Ghosts," and *The Escaped Cock*, the conscious mind and the unconscious body come together whenever *it* and *I* meld. We have also seen how Lawrence's art, an art designed to heal the divide between consciousness and the unconscious works its narrative magic. Juliet, Morier, and Christ live because they have heard the call of blood-consciousness, Lawrence's "lowing beasts" of the unconscious.

In "None of That!," "The Rocking-Horse Winner," and "The Man Who Loved Islands" *it* and *I* remain separate because the mind and the body are not in touch. Because of that no healing of the self occurs, and Ethel Cane, the boy Rocker, and Cathcart die, either because they were not listening to the voices of their unconscious or circumstances beyond their control prevented them from doing so.

Cathcart hears the lowing beasts but the "death drive" thwarts his quest for happiness. The death drive, in collusion with the pleasure principle, overrides the vital warmth of the sun, causing him to seek solace on a small, rocky island in the North Sea where he dies entombed in the womb-like whiteness of winter. "The man who loved islands" asks us to re-examine Lacan's definition of the infant's "mirror stage" when the infant identifies with the mother and perceives her and itself as one entity. In due course when the infant sees itself as Other, it splits into an "I-land" and accedes to language. At the end of his life, it is this very language that Cathcart strives to obliterate by removing the nameplate from the stove in his cabin. His behavior manifests the death wish but it is a death wish overridden by the pleasure of returning to the mother's womb where he can, once again, be the perfect replica of a pearly-white egg. As for the boy who rocks his rocking horse, he does not hear the lowing beasts because he is too busy playing the horses. Instead, he listens to what he thinks is God's message, naming Malabar. He wins big money but, in the process, dies a "poor loser." When, at last, after trying to control body with *Mind,* Ethel Cane hears the lowing, it is too late. Questa, the matador, has won. She dies.

As for "the woman who rode away," Lawrence highlights the need for cosmic renewal by having the Chilchui Indians immolate her. The novella dramatizes the plight of a desperately unhappy woman. She rides away, and her escape from a dead-end marriage coincides with Lawrence's own quest for a more intuitive relationship with the world. Although eventually the woman hears the voices of her unconscious and sees their colors—the harmonies of the rain and the blue color of the wind—it is too late. She dies, but her immolation realigns the cosmic imbalance. The Chilchui think that her death will indeed realign the sun and the moon..

The true function of Lawrence's art, as Cowan notes, is to help men and women get in touch with their feelings by listening to their inner beasts. Their lowing *is* the voice of the unconscious, a voice that Lacan also wants us to hear. When he asks, "What does the unconscious want for me?" the answer is, "heed its message so that *it* can illumine *I.*"

Because Lawrence is a British writer he uses the English language, and because Lacan is a Saussurean psychoanalyst he says that the unconscious is structured like a language. Lawrence weaves the language of his art into consciously crafted stories but his unconscious is, inevitably, embedded in their narrative tissues. When readers read his tales their own unconscious responds to the unconscious in the narrative subtext. In his *Study of Thomas Hardy and Other Essays* Lawrence says that listening to the voices of novels and short stories can have a healing effect, and be the beginning of a cure:

> Listening-in to the voices of the honorable beasts that call in the dark paths of the veins of our body, from the God in the heart. Listening inwards, inwards, not for words nor for inspiration, but to the lowing of the innermost beasts, the feelings that roam in the forest of the blood, from the feet of God within the red, dark heart. (Lawrence 1985, 205)

The doctors in the story, "Sun," are Lawrence's messengers, and they urge Juliet to go to Italy. They know that in Sicily she will find the sun and be illumined by the blue light that shines from its red, dark heart. In Sicily she opens herself like a lotus flower to the rays of the sun; she listens to the cosmic voices of the ancient Etruscans, and she feels renewal coursing through her veins. In Italy Juliet comes in contact not only with the shining orb in the sky but also with the dark sun deep within the earth, beneath the lemon grove. Her return to a pre-intellectual state is realized because she heeds the voices of the ancients while in contact with the two suns. Empowered by this "fourth dimension," she discards *doxa,* the moneyed wall of industry, and the abstractions of technology.

The story, "Glad Ghosts," also works eloquently toward the fourth dimension. The guests at the Lathkill estate are healed, the ghosts become flesh, spirit becomes matter, and everybody is "glad." The plum-blossom-scented-one comes to Morier in the middle of night, rising from the depths of his erotic dream. The next morning an enlightened Morier conveys the good news to his friends, and the message of life/love touches all the guests at Riddings, healing the hysteria of an entire household.

Morier and his ghost, in the context of Freud's dream-work and Lacan's rhetorical poetics, show us how Lawrence crafts figurative language on the conscious and unconscious levels. In essence, the story thinks. It tells us how to listen to the message that resonates in the communicating networks of discourse. The combinatory power of language transmits its magic. If we listen to the voices and welcome the message, something happens. We as readers come to understand that the goings on at Riddings, when *it* and *I* merge, can cure hysteria. Given the fact that lucre drives the money-machine, the union of *it* with *I* becomes a physical, spiritual, and semiological paradigm for well-being. It *rids* the guests at Riddings of *Mind,* the values of the aristocracy, the lure of lucre, and the ideology of death. It restores their souls.

In *The Escaped Cock* Lawrence brings together the Christian mystery of resurrection and the Egyptian myth of Isis and Osiris. The novella dramatizes

Lawrence's notion of blood-consciousness. It asks every reader to shed death-in-life habits, cast off an overintellectualized religion, and find an authentic self. It shows its readers how to restore the easy mind-set of the Etruscans. *The Escaped Cock* demonstrates that Freud's *"Wo Es war, soll Ich werden"* is not an incursion of the ego ideal into the id, but its opposite, the illumination of the ego by the rising sun of the unconscious.

For people to get in touch with each other, both Lawrence and Lacan implore us to listen to the lowing beasts so that we may get in touch with our unconscious. In *Sketches of Etruscan Places* and *John Thomas and Lady Jane* Lawrence suggests that life can be renewed through the medium of touch, and that the act of touching can be therapeutic. It can heal psychic wounds. Morier and Christ show us how. In a letter to Arthur McLeod, dated June 2, 1914, Lawrence wrote: "The only way for art and civilization to get a new life, a new start—by bringing themselves together, men and women—revealing themselves each to the other, gaining great blind knowledge and suffering and joy, which it will take a big further lapse of civilization to exploit and work out" (qtd. in Thornton 1993, 119). Juliet begins by getting in touch with the sun, and, after the ghost's nocturnal visitation, Morier gets in touch with the other guests at Riddings. The sexual union of Christ with the priestess of Isis is a resurrection. These are all acts of sacramental healing. The sun for Juliet, the plum-blossom-scented-ghost in Morier's dream, and the "escaped cock"—are all paradigms that, according to Lawrence, can put civilization back on track.

Getting back on track puts us in touch with the maternal "great rose of space." Lawrence also wants his fiction, like the dandelion, to draw sustenance from the earth's humus. Each yellow flower is a miniature sun, and Lawrence's stories, like the dandelion, open toward the orb in the sky, mature, and when the wind blows the metaphorical seeds to the four corners, they take root in the consciousness of men and women. Symbolically, the yellow flower is the sun, the puffball is the moon, and the dispersing seeds are the stars. The dandelion is the perfect floral metaphor for realigning our cosmic imbalance. To further that goal Lawrence uses not only botanical metaphors but also animal ones. A dog's snout becomes the sun, and a porcupine becomes mankind sticking its quills into the face of the sun.

Finally, the fictions Lawrence wrote during his fabulation period are parables designed to counter the dehumanizing legacy of the money-machine, war, and reified greed. Insofar as Lawrence's writings dovetail with Lacan's psychoanalytic theories, their appeal to readers of literature, as Juliet MacCannell has noted, derives from their emphasis on the cultural context of the inter-human situation (MacCannell 1986, 39). Today, the inter-human situation is omnipresent: nations are grappling with the effects of the Industrial Revolution and the technological innovations that are contributing to climate change—a change that, in great measure, is the consequence of cultural dysfunction. The wars in Korea, Vietnam, Iraq, Afghanistan, Syria, Ukraine, Yemen, and elsewhere manifest not only social conflict and political instability but also our inability to find a solution to global problems. In light of these disturbances, if nations reject the scientific evidence of climate change, and if they pursue self-serving economic and political policies, instead of engaging in policies of cooperation, the result will be ongoing suffering, injustice, and endless war. "Start with the sun, and the rest will slowly, slowly happen."

Notes

INTRODUCTION

1. See Jacques Lacan, *The Four Fundamental Concepts of Psycho-Analysis,* trans. Alan Sheridan. In addition to transference, Lacan discusses the three other fundamental concepts of psychoanalysis, namely the unconscious, repletion, and the drive.

CHAPTER 1

1. For more information on Hemingway's iceberg and its influence on Camus, see Stoltzfus 2009.

2. For an iceberg reading of *The Sun Also Rises,* see Stoneback 2007.

3. See Marina S. Ragachewskaya 2013, 89–99, and Izabel F. O. Brandão 2013, 123–40. After reviewing the early criticism of Lawrence's "Sun," Brandão concludes, as I do, that Juliet is ill, and that the remedy for her illness is to get in touch with nature and the sun (127–34).

4. See Jane Costin 2013, 260–70.

5. The short version of "Sun" appeared in *New Coterie* in Autumn 1926, and was included in the original *The Woman Who Rode Away and Other Stories* in 1928. The final version, written and published in 1928 (in a small volume *Sun* by the Black Sun Press, Paris) is now the standard and appeared a year later than Lawrence's review of Hemingway's *In Our Time.* See also Dieter Mehl and Christa Jansohn 1995, "Introduction," in *The Woman Who Rode Away and Other Stories*, xxx–xxxii.

6. When he touches Isis, the man who died, like the dead-alive Juliet, feels the power of the phallus—the inner and outer sun—and this new consciousness gives him access to a newly integrated self and an understanding of the oneness of the world around him.

7. For more information on Lawrence's "Fourth Dimension," see Young 1980, 30–44.

8.. This terminology derives from Balzacian criticism. It refers to the "realism" of Balzac's fiction in *Le Père Goriot*, the novel of rich descriptive detail, and to the "visionary" aspect of novels such as *Séraphita* that deal with speculative phantasy and metaphysics.

9. Freud coined the word "alcoholidays" to describe people's behavior during festive occasions, and we recognize a certain truth in the neologism. He would have appreciated the paranomasia (word play), that is, the fusion of the two words "cosmos" and "orgasm." See Freud 1953c.

10. *The Pleasure of the Text* is the title of Roland Barthes's work in which he highlights Lacan's *jouissance,* savors the texture of language, and hears the sensuous connotations of its matrix.

CHAPTER 2

1. As I noted earlier, Lawrence's essays, like Hemingway's *Death in the Afternoon* and Camus's *Myth of Sisyphus,* help to illuminate his fiction. They are the submerged portion of the iceberg. They buoy the fictive narrative above the surface. We must remember, however, that Hemingway's iceberg theory of writing was not Lawrence's strategy. If the short story "Sun" comes closest to illustrating it, his other short fictions and novellas make no effort to do so.

2. See D.H. Lawrence, *Fantasia of the Unconscious,* where he says that mankind lives "between the polarized circuit of sun and moon" [. . .] "between the two infinities all existence takes place." [. . .] Midway between them "lies the third, which is more than infinite. This is the Holy Ghost, Life, individual life" (Lawrence 2004, 170, 173); see also *Psychoanalysis and the Unconscious*: "The whole of life," says Lawrence, "is one long, blind effort at an established polarity with the outer universe, human and non-human; and the whole of modern life is a shrieking failure" (Lawrence 2004, 41).

CHAPTER 3

1. *Corrida* is the Spanish word for bullfight (Hemingway 1932, 398).

2. An aficionado is someone "who understands bullfights in general and in detail and still cares for them" (Hemingway 1932, 380).

3. In *Psychoanalysis and the Unconscious* Lawrence says, "The mind is the dead end of life. [. . .] It has all the mechanical force of the non-vital universe" (Lawrence 2004, 42).

4. "There are two things that are necessary for a country to love bullfights. One is that the bulls must be raised in that country and the other that the people must have an interest in death. The English and the French live for life" (Hemingway 1932, 265).

5. A *faena* is the work done by the matador with the *muleta*; and the *muleta* is the heart-shaped scarlet cloth that is used to defend the man and tire the bull as the matador performs a series of passes.

6. Mithras is a god mentioned in Sanskrit and ancient Persian documents. The cult of the bull was the foundation of Mithraism and its legacy has been passed down

through the ages, influencing the tragedy and spectacle of bullfighting in Spain. Mithraism and Christianity evolved simultaneously and they share common symbols: blood, wine, and the sun. In Catholicism, the Eucharistic wine represents the blood of Christ. The host recalls the solar circle. In Spain, all three symbols converge around the bull, which bled, was sacrificed, and worshiped as a god for millennia. See Swerdlow 1991; see also Stoltzfus 2010, chapter 4: "*Death in the Afternoon* and *The Dangerous Summer*: Bulls, Art, Mithras, and Montherlant*."

7. "If a writer of prose knows enough about what he is writing about he may omit things that he knows and the reader, if the writer is writing truly enough, will have a feeling of those things as strongly as though the writer had stated them" (Hemingway 1932, 192).

8. See Chapter Seven of this book, *The Escaped Cock*: Salvation.

9. In an interview with George Plimpton for the *Paris Review* Hemingway said that he always wrote on the principle of the iceberg. In practice, this means that Hemingway omitted inner monologue, stream of consciousness, and authorial commentary because he believed that description and dialog could do the work, and that such writing, if well crafted, would give the reader the true feeling of lived experience.

10. See Chapter 1, "*Madame Bovary* and Poetry," in Stoltzfus 2010, 21–38. Hemingway learned from Flaubert's *Madame Bovary* how to use proleptic images when structuring poetic resonance in his work. Both writers refer to fourth and fifth dimensions—poetic dimensions—that create network of interrelated tropes. Tropic weave and verbal play together generate nuance and coloration; they resonate throughout the fiction from beginning to end.

CHAPTER 4

1. See Marks 1965–66, 381.

2. See Freije 1989, 82.

3. See Martin F. Kearney for a comprehensive overview of "The Rocking-Horse Winner" scholarship: its publication history, circumstances of composition, sources, influences, critical studies, and the relationship of the story to other works by Lawrence.

4. Marks focuses on six essays in Freud's *Collected Papers:* "A Special Type of Object-Choice," "Obsessive Acts and Religious Practices," "The 'Uncanny,'" "From the Neurosis of Demoniacal Possession in the Seventeenth Century," "The History of an Infantile Neurosis," and "A Phobia in A Five Year Old Boy." Marks says, "Paul's ability to make lucky predictions by riding himself into a trance on his totemic hobbyhorse is principally suggested by Freud's paper on "The 'Uncanny,' where this phenomenon is defined as a product of narcissistic regression to a primitive belief in animism (Marks 1965–66, 384). [. . .] Paul's self-destructive act of rocking comes under the heading of Freud's *repetition-compulsion:* [. . .] 'a principle powerful enough to over-rule the pleasure principle, lending to certain aspects of the mind their daemonic character, and still very clearly expressed in the tendencies of small children' [IV 391]" (Marks 1965–66, 384).

5. Harris says that the mother has given her son a murderous education because she represents a society that runs on a money ethic: "The tale reads as a satire on the equation of money, love, luck, and happiness" (Harris 1984, 225).

6. "The Law," says Lacan, "appears to be giving the order, 'Jouis!,' to which the subject can only reply 'J'ouis' (I hear), the *jouissance* being no more than understood" ("La Loi en effect commanderait-elle: Jouis, que le subject ne pourrait y répondre que par un: J'ouis, où la jouissance ne serait que sous-entendue" (Lacan 1977a, 319; Lacan 1971a, 184).

7. Translated respectively as *Writing and Difference* by Alan Bass and *Of Grammatology* by Gayatri Chokravorty Spivak.

8. See Freije, who states that the *bar* of Malabar, according to the *OED,* "is a proper term for a part of a horse's mouth, a section of the hoof, and a piece of the bridle bit used in controlling the horse. [. . .] The psychoanalytic interpretations of the story (whether they discuss the Oedipal quest [. . .] or the rocking-horse as allegory of self-abuse) make it difficult to avoid seeing *bar* as a symbol of Paul's destructive sexuality" (Freije 1989, 82). In legal matters, again according to the *OED, bar* is a "hindrance to the achievement of a goal or a right." But Malabar is also interpreted as one of a series of names within a floral motif—the culmination of a sequence that began with Daffodil. Freije: "Sansovina suggested the garden deity as punisher of those who distort love. Mirza differentiated between virtue and corrupt striving, flowery paradise and shrouded hell. Blush of Dan and Lively Spark recalled the expulsion from the garden. Singhalese introduced the demonic intruder." Malabar is a toxic plant, a member of the nightshade family, and the poison's symptoms are characteristic of Paul's madness and fever (Freije 1989, 81–82). There is also an Oriental motif. Freije believes that Mirza can be interpreted in light of Eastern fantasy (Freije 1989, 78). Snodgrass mentions two British colonial regions named Singhalese and Malabar: "For years Malabar and Singhalese were winners for British stockholders and for the British people in general" (Snodgrass 1963, 121). The Singhalese (Cinglese in Frazer's *The Golden Bough*) are the largest group of people in Sri Lanka. Freije cites Frazer and the fact that the Cinglese believed their world to be populated by infinite numbers of demons (Freije 1989, 81).

9. See Marks who says that Paul "becomes a scapegoat who atones for the sins of his house—the material, social, and intellectual ambitions that corrupt normal affections, dislocate the proper authority of the father, and disintegrate the moral ties of the family, replacing them with the cash-nexus" (Marks 1965–66, 385).

10. See *Fantasia of the Unconscious.* Lawrence says: "In becoming the object of great emotional stress for her son, the mother also becomes an object of poignancy, of anguish, of arrest, to her son. She arrests him from finding his proper fulfillment on the sensual plane" (Lawrence 2004, 181). Hester's behavior reinforces the "devouring mother" syndrome, and Lawrence reinforces it with repeated use of the word "arrested." In French, "un arrêt de mort" is a death sentence, and Lawrence's sentence that describes Paul's arrested development and the impossibility of crossing the Saussurean "bar" is indeed the sentence that condemns him.

11. See Marks 1965–66, 383. "Fixated at a narcissistic stage of development, Paul's libido is precisely objectified in the rocking-horse. Lawrence's young hero gives a

first indication of his symptomatic preoccupation with riding (which later becomes obsessional) when he asks his mother 'Why don't we keep a car of our own? Why do we always use uncle's, or else a taxi?' Her reply, 'Because we're poor members of the family,' fatally impresses Paul with the association between money and the power to 'ride,' precipitating his short but sensational career as a gambler." It is worth remembering, as Snodgrass points out (Snodgrass 1963, 122), that "riding" was once a common sexual verb; so that riding, be it the hobbyhorse or in Uncle Oscar's car, brings everybody into the family romance.

CHAPTER 5

1. "The Man Who Loved Islands" has frequently been read as a fable that satirizes sickness while pointing the reader toward health. See, for example, Leavis 1967, 324; see also Moynahan who argues that insight into sickness brings added insight into health (Moynahan 1972, 225); see also Turner who states that the tale "is both a powerful indictment of Christian bourgeois society for the schizoid disconnection that it breeds and an attempt to subvert it by the poetic recreation of that disconnection" (Turner 1983, 286); see also Marina S. Ragachewskaya who says that Cathcart's preoccupation with time and eternity presents the story as a metaphorical "journey into timelessness" (Ragachewskaya 2017, 1). Cathcart's misanthropy, or "androphobia," as Lawrence calls it, becomes a defense against death consciousness (Ragachewskaya 2017, 25). She argues that Cathcart's half-conscious quest for death is an attempt to master time, and that, as such it becomes "a drive towards immortality" (Ragachewskaya 2017, 21). But this drive toward immortality is a clear case of the pleasure principle overriding the death drive, even if death is the unconscious overriding goal. Unlike the woman who rode away, who is consciously escaping from the society of white men, Cathcart is also escaping from society unconsciously, or perhaps half-consciously. As Jill Franks points out, "islands exert a unique appeal because they are contained spaces, and therefore, theoretically at least, controllable" (Franks 2006, 7).

2. In an unpublished letter to Martin Secker, Lawrence wrote, "The Man Who Loved Islands has a philosophy behind him, and a real significance." This letter is in the Lawrence-Secker collection at the University of Illinois in Champaign-Urbana (qtd. in Turner 1983, 274).

3. According to Lacan "the Law appears to be giving the order, 'Jouis,' to which the subject can only reply 'J'ouis' (I hear), the *jouissance* being no more than understood" (Lacan 1977a, 319).

4. See Derrida 1987c, 257–410.

5. Turner argues cogently that Lawrence's tale not only describes the failure of Christianity and self-abnegation, but also prophesizes "the end of North European bourgeois society" (Turner 1983, 281). I find it difficult to agree with him, however, when he states that "The Man Who Loved Islands" is "an invitation to die with the dying and surrender ourselves to the processes of the disintegration within us," or that the extraordinariness of the islander's dissolution induces a like dissolution in

us (Turner 1983, 281). That might be true if we all loved islands and also refused to live elsewhere. The fact is that many of us like islands, and we are not trapped in the insular mode that characterizes Cathcart's unconscious trauma. Turner's essay is interesting because for him "The Man Who Loved Islands" is an open text that allows for two simultaneous and perhaps contradictory interpretations. In part one "The Tale as he argues that Cathcart's dissolution of self is subversive because it invites the reader to do likewise. In Cathcart's case, the pleasure principle, in concert with the death instinct, drives him to a premature demise. Every reader is of course free to draw whatever moral truths they infuse into the narrative, but I see the islander's choices as a fascinating account of actions emanating from an extreme primal split: he cannot adjust to the "normal" course of life as a deferral of death because, as Freud says, every organism wishes to die in its own way and in its own time: "The living organism muddles most energetically against events (dangers, in fact) which might help it to attain its life's aim rapidly [death]—by a kind of short-circuit" (Freud 1953a, 47); see also Jill Franks who argues that the negative ideals of Utopia, sex, and isolation explain Cathcart's island choices. His first island represents an "intentional community," based on hierarchy; the second one, a "personal resurrection through right sexual relations," but which, in his case, are not satisfactory; and the third one, his complete "independence from other people," an independence that leads to his death (Franks 2007, 150).

6. According to Freud, dreams are "The royal road to the unconscious" (qtd. in Lacan 1977b, 158).

7. See Turner's excellent analysis of the destructive love relationship between Cathcart and his housekeeper (Turner 1983, 275–78).

8. Moynahan states that, in general, the form of the fable offers little information into the causes of the passions it delineates (Moynahan 1972, 186). Turner, for whom the story is also a fable, concurs, adding that in this tale "Lawrence has not offered sufficient evidence for certainty" and that we must "search for a language capable of suggesting the cause in the effect" (Turner 1983, 270). I argue, on the contrary, that a Lacanian analysis of language in this text, when coupled with Cathcart's behavior, is sufficient to provide the cause in the effect, and that we need not look for certainty outside the story, either in Lawrence's pronouncements elsewhere, or in construing the tale as a "religious fable." Although many of his views on love, nature, and society are embedded in "The Man Who Loved Islands," knowing what Lawrence's views are on these matters, is not a *sine qua non* for a Lacanian or, for that matter, intelligent reading of the story. My own view on biographical criticism is that, although interesting, because we're always fascinated by a writer's life, the life itself is not a prerequisite to the elucidation of their fiction.

CHAPTER 6

1. "A sex story" is Linda Ruth Williams's alternative title to her article even as she pursues vampirism, the abject, and Freud's uncanny (Williams 1997–98, 235). She

concludes her essay by saying that "Glad Ghosts" "articulates Lawrence's masculine uncanny in all its exquisite ambivalence" (Williams 1997–98, 250–51).

2. See David J. Gordon, who says that Lawrence "read literature mainly as a diagnosis of our psychic illness" (Gordon 1966, 5). "Glad Ghosts" is indeed about the diagnosis and cure of an illness whose metaphors and metonyms are in plain view, if only we know where and how to look for them, that is, how to read the substitution of one signifier for another: ghost for repression, and the scent of plum-blossom for guest; see also Brooke Jarvis, "The Global Dream Lab," who quotes Deirdre Barrett: "Dreaming is, above all, a time when the unheard parts of ourselves are allowed to speak. We would do well to listen" (Jarvis 2021, 45). Barrett teaches in the psychiatry department at Harvard Medical School and edits the scientific journal *Dreaming.*

3. See Williams, who says, "Haunting as neurosis is spelled-out, catharsis and confrontation are prescribed" (Williams 1997–98, 248).

4. See Phillips, who says, "by finding the short-story writer included in his case history—what is perhaps revealed to Freud is that the short-story writer and the scientific psychiatrist share an assumption: both take for granted, in their very acts of exclusion, that we can describe only the unique and the repeatable, what is singular and what can be replicated. Freud's literary engagement draws his attention not merely to the opposition between the literary and the scientific but also to the position they share" (Phillips 2003, 17). Lawrence and Lacan exploit this shared position, and their works demonstrate that these positions are not mutually exclusive.

5. In interpreting Freud, Lacan discards the terminology for *id* and *ego* in favor of *it* and *I,* the same terms that Lawrence uses. Freud capitalizes *I* and *It,* as does Lawrence. Lacan does not capitalize the *ça,* that is, the *it.* See Lacan 1977a, 128–29.

6. In *Écrits* Lacan says, "The moment in which desire becomes human is also that in which the child is born into language" (Lacan 1977a, 103). He sees language and culture linked indissolubly, with desire as the nexus.

7. The antidote to hysteria, according to Morier, is wine, music, and dancing. They are the royal way to the unconscious. Lady Lathkill, however, has transformed Riddings into a "hollow and gruesome" house (Lawrence 1995d, 197). The weight of the "unliving" has crushed all warmth and vitality from the living, and this is why they smell of death. Hysteria is their death-in-life; see Matt Foley's article, "Living with Lawrence's silent ghosts: a Lacanian reading of 'Glad Ghosts,'" in which he contends that "Lawrence's staging of haunting, which emphasizes the role of the silent ghost, is symptomatic of the Lacanian barred subject's attempt to experience different registers of *jouissance.*" Although my reading of "Glad Ghosts" and Foley's reading of the story are different, we both agree that it has been vastly underappreciated (Foley 2011, 19).

CHAPTER 7

1. D.H. Lawrence's titles, *Psychoanalysis of the Unconscious and Fantasia of the Unconscious,* alert us to his knowledge of Freudian and Jungian theory, and his

attempts to accommodate the unconscious within his own writings. Indeed, in 1918, Lawrence wrote Katherine Mansfield that he had sent her the Jung book, probably *The Psychology of the Unconscious* (translated in 1916), in which, chapter six, "The Battle for Deliverance from the Mother," reflects many of Lawrence's attitudes concerning incest and the devouring mother, which, he says, can become an obsession. In *Fantasia of the Unconscious,* however, Lawrence denies that incest craving is a component of the unconscious, and he affirms instead an incest-aversion. Judith Ruderman, in *D.H. Lawrence and the Devouring Mother: The Search for a Patriarchal Ideal of Leadership,* notes that Lawrence wrote his essays on psychology "in order to define scientifically the 'kind of incest' that he wrote of incessantly and obsessively in his letters, poetry, and narrative prose—a pre-oedipal, pre-genital desire to merge with the caretaker mother" (Ruderman 1984, 24); see also Daniel J. Schneider, who, in *D.H. Lawrence: The Artist as Psychologist,* asserts that Lawrence recognized the desire in himself for the bliss of Nirvana in the womb/tomb of the female, but "fought against it, insisting that the healthy power impulse counters the desire for a regressive submission" (Schneider 1984, 250). From 1930 to the present, as Ruderman observes, writers who have discussed Lawrence's psyche, have shown a marked Oedipal bias, looking toward mother-love to explicate his work. The differences in their approach, according to Ruderman, and I agree with her, stem from two separate but related issues: "whether Lawrence retained his obsessional love for his mother or grew away from it, and whether his mother fixation was emotionally and artistically crippling or emotionally and artistically ennobling" (Ruderman 1984, 7).

2. "The Escaped Cock," in *The Virgin and the Gipsy and Other Stories.*

3. Lawrence's "quarrel with Freud," as well as the congruent ideas of both men, have been examined by a number of scholars, notably by Frederick J. Hoffman in *Freudianism and the Literary Mind;* Philip Rieff in "The Therapeutic as Mythmaker"; James Cowan in "Allusions and Symbols in D.H. Lawrence's *The Escaped Cock;* Daniel Weiss in *Oedipus in Nottingham: D.H. Lawrence.* Weiss refers to the Oedipal level in *The Escaped Cock;* also to Ruderman and Schneider, among others. For Lacanian studies of Lawrence's work see also Jewinski 1989, "The Phallus in D.H. Lawrence and Jacques Lacan"; see also Nelson 1990, "The Familial Isotopy in the Fox."

4. See Jacques Lacan, "The agency of the letter in the unconscious or reason since Freud," in Lacan 1977b, 146–78; "L'instance de la letter dans l'inconscient ou la raison depuis Freud," in Lacan 1966b, 249–89.

5. See "The mirror stage as formative of the function of the I" (Lacan 1977a, 1–7); "Le stade du miroir comme formateur de la function du Je" (Lacan 1966a, 89–100).

6. In this passage, Lacan is referring to the English translation of Freud. It should not be confused with Sheridan's translation of Lacan.

7. See Jane Gallop, *Reading Lacan.* She says: "Freud's discovery, as Lacan casts it, is that the center of the human being is not the ego, as we have long supposed, but what Lacan calls the subject, which sometimes but not always corresponds to what Freud called the id" (Gallop 1985, 96); see also Jean Laplanche, "The Ego and the Vital Order," in *Life and Death in Psychoanalysis* (Laplanche 1976, 48–65).

8. See Lacan, "The signification of the phallus," where he says, "We know that the unconscious castration complex has the function of a knot" ("On sait que le complexe de castration inconscient a une function de noeud" (Lacan 1977a, 281; Lacan 1971b, 103).

9. See *Sketches of Etruscan Places and Other Italian Essays.* Lawrence says, "To the Etruscan, all was alive: the whole universe lived: and the business of man was himself to live amid it all. [. . .] The cosmos was alive, like a vast creature. The whole thing breathed and stirred" (Lawrence 1992, 56–57).

References

Ali, Zahra A. Hussein. 2016. "Islomania, Deilettantism, and the Devolutioonary Vision of Lawrence's "The Man Who Loved Islands.'" *Horizons in the Humanities and Social Sciences: An Internation Refereed Journal* 1.

Balbert, Peter. 2020. "From Relativity to Paraphrenia in D.H. Lawrence's 'The Man Who Loved Islands': Speculations on Einstein, Freud, Gossamer Webs, and Seagulls." *Journal of Modern Literature* 43: 60–79.

Barthes, Roland. 1953. *Le Degré zéro de l'écriture*. Paris: Seuil.

_____. 1973. *Le Plaisir du texte*. Paris: Seuil.

_____. 1975a. *Roland Barthes*. Paris: Seuil.

_____. 1975b. *The Pleasure of the Text*. Translated by Richard Miller. New York: Hill and Wang.

Becket, Fiona. 2002. *D.H. Lawrence*. Abington, Oxfordshire and New York: Routledge.

Beauvoir, Simone de. 1960. *La Force de l'âge*. Paris: Gallimard.

_____. 1960. *The Second Sex*. Translated by J. M Parshley. London: Picador.

Bell, Michael. 1992. *Language and Being*. Cambridge: Cambridge University Press.

Bible, The Holy. Authorized King James' Version. Oxford: Oxford University Press, ndl.

Bonaparte, Marie. 1949. *The Life and Works of Edgar Allan Poe: A Psycho-Analytic Interpretation*. Foreword Sigmund Freud. Translated by John Rodker. London: Imago.

Brandào, Izabel F.O. 2013. "Lawrence and the Healing Italian 'Sun': Reweaving Links with the Body." In *Lake Garda Gateway to Lawrence's Voyage to the* Sun, edited by Nick Ceramella, 123–40. Newcastle: Cambridge Scholars Publishing.

Bricout, Shirley. 2012. "Le sacrifice du langage dans 'The Woman Who Rode Away' de D.H. Lawrence." *Études britanniques contemporaines* 42: 37–50.

Brooks, Peter. 1987. "The Idea of a Psychoanalytic Criticism." *Critical Inquiry* 13: 334–48.

Burden, Robert. 2000. *Radicalizing Lawrence: Critical Interventions in the Reading and Reception of D.H. Lawrence's Narrative Fiction*. Amsterdam and Atlanta: Rodopi.

Butler, Judith. 1994. "Gender as Performance: An Interview with Judith Butler." Interview by Peter Osborne and Lynne Segal. *Radical Philosophy* 67: 32–39.

Camus, Albert. 1988. *The Stranger.* Translated by Matthew Ward. New York: Knopf.

_____. 2006a. "Le Mythe de Sisyphe." In *Oeuvres complètes* Vol. 1, edited by Jacqueline Lévi-Valensi, 217–315. Paris: Gallimard-Pléiade.

_____. 2006b. *L'Étranger.* In *Oeuvres complètes* Vol. 1, edited by Jacqueline Lévi-Valensi, 141–213. Paris: Gallimard-Pléiade.

_____. 2006c. "Survey on the American Novel." *Combat*, Jan. 17, 1947. Reprint of *Les Nouvelles littéraires*, no. 954, in *Oeuvres complètes* Vol. 2.

Chamberlain, John R. 1928. "D.H. Lawrence Shows Himself More Prophet than Artist." *New York Times,* June 3, 1928. BR2.

Con Davis, Robert. 1983. "Introduction." In *Lacan and Narration: The Psychoanalytic Difference in Narrative Theory,* 849–59. Baltimore: Johns Hopkins University Press.

Contreras, Sheila. 1993/94. "'These Were Just Natives to Her': Chilchui Indians and 'The Woman Who Rode Away.'" *D.H. Lawrence Review* 25, 1–3: 91–103.

Costin, Jane. 2012. "Lawrence's 'Best Adventure': Blood-Consciousness and Cornwall." *Études Lawrenciennes*, 43: 151–72.

_____. 2013. "Lawrence's Italy: An Adventure Down Old Religious Pathways." In *Lake Garda: Gateway to Lawrence's Voyage to the Sun*, edited by Nick Ceramella, 260–70. Newcastle upon Tyne: Cambridge Scholars Publishing.

Cowan, James C. 1970. *D.H. Lawrence's American Journey: A Study in Literature and Myth.* Cleveland, OH: Press of Case Western Reserve University.

_____. 1988. "Allusions and Symbols in D.H. Lawrence's *The Escaped Cock.*" In *Critical Essays on D.H. Lawrence*, edited by Dennis Jackson and Fleda Brown Jackson, 174–88. Boston: G.K. Hall.

_____. 1990. *D.H. Lawrence and the Trembling Balance.* University Park and London: The Pennsylvania State University Press.

Cushman, Keith. 1978. *D.H. Lawrence at Work: The Emergence of the* Prussian Officer *Stories.* Charlottesville: University of Virginia Press.

DeLia, D. 2020. "Bridled Rage: Pre-oedipal Theory and 'The Rocking-Horse Winner," In *Short Story Criticism: Criticism of the Works of Short Fiction Writers* Vol. 281, 218–26. Edited by Rebecca Parks. Farmington Hills, MI: Gale.

Derrida, Jacques. 1967a. *De la grammatologie.* Paris: Minuit.

_____. 1967b. *L'Écriture et la différence.* Paris: Seuil.

_____. 1972. *La Dissémination.* Paris: Seuil.

_____. 1974. *Glas.* Paris: Galilée.

_____. 1987a. "Le Facteur de la vérité." In *The Post Card: From Socrates to Freud and Beyond.* Translated by Alan Bass, 411–96. Chicago: The University of Chicago Press.

_____. 1987b. *The Post Card: From Socrates to Freud and Beyond.* Translated by Alan Bass. Chicago: The University of Chicago Press.

_____. 1987c. "To Speculate on 'Freud.'" In *The Post Card: From Socrates to Freud and Beyond.* Translated by Alan Bass, 257–409. Chicago: The University of Chicago Press.

_____. 1992. "That Strange Institution Called Literature: An Interview with Jacques Derrida." In *Acts of Literature*. Edited and introduced by Derek Attridge. New York and London: Routledge.

"D.H. Lawrence." *Gale Literature Resource Center—Advanced Research* 1–37. Gale Group 23. February, 232003.

Draper, Ronald P. 1964. "The Tales." In *D.H. Lawrence*, 119–48. New York: Twayne.

Felman, Shoshana. 1983. "Beyond Oedipus: The Specimen Story of Psychoanalysis." In *Lacan and Narration: The Psychoanalytic Difference in Narrative Theory*, edited by Robert Con Davis, 1021–53.

_____. 1988. "On Reading Poetry: Reflections on the Limits and Possibilities of Psychoanalytic Approaches." In *The Purloined Poe: Lacan, Derrida and Psychoanalytic Readings*, edited by John P. Muller and William J. Richardson, 147–48. Baltimore: Johns Hopkins University Press.

Fernihough, Anne. 1993. *D.H. Lawrence: Aesthetics and Ideology.* Oxford: Clarendon.

Fjågesund, P. 1991. *The Apocalyptic World of D.H. Lawrence.* London and Drammen, Norway: Norwegian University Press.

Foley, Matt. 2011. "Living with Lawrence's Silent Ghosts: a Lacanian Reading of 'Glad Ghosts.'" *The Linguistic Academy Journal of Interdisciplinary Language Studies* 1: 19–31.

_____. 2017. "The Blood-Consciousness and Lawrence's Silent Ghosts." In *Haunting Modernisms,* 169–73. New York: Palgrave Macmillan.

Fox, Elizabeth M. (2009). "André Green's 'The Dead Mother' and D.H. Lawrence's 'The Rocking-Horse Winner.'" *Études Lawrenciennes* 39: 151–61.

Freije, George F. 1989. "Equine Names in 'The Rocking-Horse Winner.'" *CEA Critic* 51: 75–84.

Franks, Jill. 2006. *Islands and the Modernists: The Allure of Isolation in Art, Literature and Science.* Jefferson, North Carolina: McFarland and Company.

_____. 2007. "'To Make a World of His Own': Psychoanalysis and Weltanschauung in 'The Man Who Loved Islands.'" *D.H. Lawrence Studies* 15: 147–57.

Freud, Sigmund. 1953a. *Beyond the Pleasure Principle.* Vol. 18 of *The Standard Edition of the Complete Psychological Works.* Translated by James Strachey et al. Edited by James Strachey. London: Hogarth.

_____. 1953b. *The Interpretation of Dreams.* Vol. 4 of *The Standard Edition of the Complete Psychological Works.* Translated by James Strachey et al. Edited by James Strachey. London: Hogarth.

_____. 1953c. *Jokes and Their Relation to the Unconscious.* Vol. 8 of *The Standard Edition of the Complete Psychological Works.* Translated by James Strachey et al. Edited by James Strachey. London: Hogarth.

_____. 1953d. *Studies on Hysteria.* Vol. 2 of *The Standard Edition of the Complete Psychological Works.* Translated by James Strachey et al. Edited by James Strachey. London: Hogarth.

_____. 1985. "The Uncanny." In *Art and Literature.* Harmondsworth: Penguin.

Gallop, Jane. 1985. *Reading Lacan.* Ithaca: Cornell University Press.

Girard, René. 1977. *La Violence et le sacré.* Paris: Grasset.

Gordon, David J. 1966. *D.H. Lawrence as a Literary Critic.* New Haven: Yale University Press.

Gouirand, Jacqueline. 2000. "D.H. Lawrence After a Phallic Christ: The Resurrection into Touch in 'The Man Who Died.'" *Études Lawrenciennes* 23: 45–55.

Granon-Lafont, Jeanne. 1985. *La Topologie ordinaire de Jacques Lacan.* Paris: Points Hors Lignes.

Gutierrez, Donald. 1976. "DHL's Golden Age." *D.H. Lawrence Review* 9: 377–408.

Harris, Janice Hubbard. 1984. *The Short Fiction of D. H. Lawrence.* New Brunswick: Rutgers University Press.

Hemingway, Ernest. 1926. *The Sun Also Rises.* New York: Scribner.

_____. 1932. *Death in the Afternoon.* New York: Scribner.

_____. 1959. *The Dangerous Summer.* New York: Scribner.

_____. 1987a. "Big Two-Hearted River." In *The Complete Short Stories of Ernest Hemingway*, 161–80. New York: Scribner.

_____. 1987b. "Hills Like White Elephants." In *The Complete Short Stories of Ernest Hemingway*, 161–80. New York: Scribner.

Hoffman, Frederick J. 1957. *Freudianism and The Literary Mind.* Baton Rouge: Louisiana State University Press.

Holland, Norman. 1970. "The 'Unconscious' of Literature." *Contemporary Criticism,* edited by Norman Bradbury and David Palmer, 131–54. New York: St. Martin's.

Hough, Graham. 1956. *The Dark Sun: A Study of D.H. Lawrence.* New York: Capricorn.

Hyde, Virginia. 2004. "What the Parrots Said: Fable, Myth, and History in *Mornings in Mexico.*" *D.H. Lawrence Studies* 12: 105–34.

Ingarden, Roman. 1973. *The Literary Work of Art: An Investigation on the Borderlines of Ontology, Logic and Theory of Literature.* Translated by with an introduction by George Grabowicz. Evanston: Northwestern University Press.

Ingersoll, Earl G. 2001. *D.H. Lawrence, Desire, and Narrative.* Gainseville: University Press of Florida.

Jakobson, Roman. 1990. *On Language*, edited by Linda R. Waugh and Monique Monville-Burston. Cambridge, MA: Harvard University Press.

Jarvis, Brooke. 2021. "The Global Dream Lab." *The New York Times Magazine.* Nov. 7: 23–29, 45.

Jewinski, edited by. 1989. "The Phallus in D.H. Lawrence and Jacques Lacan." *D.H. Lawrence Review* 21: 7–24.

Johnson, Barbara. 1980. *The Critical Difference: Essays in the Contemporary Rhetoric of Reading.* Baltimore: Johns Hopkins University Press.

Jones, Ernest. 1986. *Hamlet and Oedipus.* New York: Norton.

Josephs, Allen. 1986. "*Toreo:* The Moral Axis of *The Sun Also Rises.*" *Hemingway Review* 6, 1: 88–99.

Kearney, Martin F. 1998. *Major Short Stories of D.H. Lawrence: A Handbook.* New York and London: Garland.

Kermode, Frank. 1973. *Lawrence.* London: Fontana Press.

Kinkead-Weekes, Mark. 2004. "A Lawrence Who Love Islands," edited by Simoneta de Filippis and Nick Ceramella. In *D.H. Lawrence and literary genres.* Napoli: Loferedo Editore. 187–94.

Lacan, Jacques. 1966a. *Écrits I.* Paris: Seuil.

_____. 1971a. *Écrits II.* Paris: Seuil.

_____. 1971b. "La Signification du phallus." In *Écrits II,* 103–19. Paris: Seuil.

_____. 1966b. "L'Instance de la lettre dans l'inconscient, ou la raison depuis Freud." In *Écrits I,* 249–89. Paris: Seuil.

_____. 1977a. *Écrits: A Selection.* Translated by Alan Sheridan. New York: Norton.

_____. 1977b. "The Agency of the Letter in the Unconscious or Reason Since Freud." In *Écrits: A Selection,* 146–78. Translated by Alan Sheridan. New York: Norton.

_____. 1981. *The Four Fundamental Concepts of Psycho-Analysis.* Translated by Alan Sheridan. New York: Norton.

_____. 1988. "Seminar on 'The Purloined Letter.'" Translated by Jeffrey Mehlman. In *The Purloined Poe: Lacan, Derrida, and Psychoanalytic Reading*, edited by John P. Muller and William J. Richardson, 28–54. Baltimore: Johns Hopkins University Press.

Lamson, Roy. 1949. "A Critical Analysis of 'The Rocking-Horse Winner.'" In *The Critical Reader*, edited by Roy Lamson, Douglas Wallace, and Hallett Smith. New York: Norton.

Laplanche, Jean. 1976. "The Ego and the Vital Order." In *Life and Death in Psychoanalysis*, 48–65. Translated by Jeffrey Mehlman. Baltimore: Johns Hopkins University Press.

Lawrence, D.H. 1936. *Phoenix: The Posthumous Papers of D H. Lawrence.* Edited by E. D. McDonald. New York: Viking.

_____. 1969. *Reflections on the Death of a Porcupine and Other Essays.* Bloomington and London: Indiana University Press.

_____. 1988a. *Aaron's Rod,* edited by Mara Kalnins. Cambridge: Cambridge University Press.

_____. 1972. *John Thomas and Lady Jane.* New York: Viking.

_____. 1979. *Apocalypse and the Writings on Revelation*, edited by Mara Kalnins. Cambridge: Cambridge University Press.

_____. 1985. *Study of Thomas Hardy and Other Essays.* Cambridge: Cambridge University Press.

_____. 1987a. "Glad Ghosts." In *The Woman Who Rode Away and Other Stories.* Cambridge: Cambridge University Press.

_____. 1992. *Sketches of Etruscan Places and Other* Essays, edited by Simonetta de Filippis. Cambridge: Cambridge University Press.

_____. 1993. *Lady Chatterley's Lover and A Propos of* 'Lady Chatterley's Lover,' edited by Michael Squires. Cambridge: Cambridge University Press.

_____. 1994. *Kangaroo*, edited by B. Steele. Cambridge: Cambridge University Press.

_____. 1995a. *"None of That!"* In *The Woman Who Rode Away and Other Stories*, edited by Dieter Mehl and Christa Jansohn, 211–29. Cambridge: Cambridge University Press.

_____. 1995b. "Sun." In *The Woman Who Rode Away and Other Stories*, edited by Dieter. Mehl and Christa Jansohn, 19–38. Cambridge: Cambridge University Press.

_____. 1988b. *Reflections on the Death of a Porcupine and Other Essays*, edited by Michael Herbert. Cambridge: Cambridge University Press.

_____. 1999. *The First and Second Lady Chatterley Novels.* Eds. Dieter Mehl and Crista Jansohn. Cambridge: Cambridge University Press.

_____. 2002. *Sketches of Etruscan Places and Other Italian Essays,* edited by Simonetta de Filippis. Cambridge: Cambridge University Press.

_____. 2004a. *Late Essays and Articles* edited by James T. Boulton. Cambridge: Cambridge University Press

_____. 2004b. *Psychoanalysis and the Unconscious and Fantasia of the Unconscious*, edited by Bruce Steele. Cambridge: Cambridge University Press. (*Psychoanalysis and Fantasia;* also *FU*).

_____. 2005a. "Review of *In Our Time,* by Ernest Hemingway." *Introductions and Reviews*, edited by N. H. Reeve and Jon Worthen, 311–112. Cambridge: Cambridge University Press.

_____. 2005b. "The Escaped Cock." In *The Virgin and the Gipsy and Other Stories*, edited by Michael Bethan Jones and Lindeth Vasey, 123–63. Cambridge: Cambridge University Press.

_____. 2009. *Mornings in Mexico and Other* Essays, edited by Virginia Crosswhite Hyde. Cambridge: Cambridge University Press.

_____. 2013. Poems, edited by Christopher Pollnitz. 2 vols. Cambridge: Cambridge University Press.

_____. 2014. *Studies in Classic American Literature.* Cambridge: Cambridge University Press.

_____. 1995c. "'Sun.' Variants between the two versions." In *The Woman Who Rode Away and Other Stories*, edited by Dieter Mehl   and Christa Jansohn, 275–82. Cambridge: Cambridge University Press.

_____. 1964. *The Complete Poems of D.H. Lawrence.* Vol. 2, edited by Vivian de Sola Pinto and Warren Roberts. New York: Viking.

_____. 1987b. *The Plumed* Serpent, edited by L. D. Clark. Cambridge: Cambridge University Press.

_____. 1995d. *The Woman Who Rode Away and Other Stories.* Edited by Dieter Mehl and Christa Jansohn. Cambridge: Cambridge University Press.

Leavis, F. R., 1955. *D.H. Lawrence Novelist.* London: Chatto & Windus.

Leitch, Vincent B. 1983. *Deconstructive Criticism: An Advanced Introductioon.* New York: Columbia University Press.

Lemaire, Anika. 1977. *Jacques Lacan.* Translated by David Macey. London: Routledge and Kegan Paul.

Lévi-Strauss, Claude. 1955. *Tristes Tropiques.* Paris: Plon.

MacCannell, Juliet F. 1986. *Figuring Lacan: Criticism and the Cultural Unconscious.* Lincoln: University of Nebraska Press.

MacLeod, Sheila. 1985. *Lawrence's Men and Women.* Londoon: Paladin.

Maekawa, Toshihiro. 2001. "Hemingway's Iceberg Theory." *North Dakota Quarterly* 68 (2–3): 37–48.

Magny, Claude-Edmonde. 1948. *L'Âge du roman américain.* Paris: Seuil.

Marks, W.S. III. 1965–66. "The Psychology of the Uncanny in Lawrence's 'The Rocking-Horse Winner." *Modern Fiction Studies* 11 (4): 381–392.

Martin, Wendy. 1987. "Brett Ashley as New Woman in *The Sun Also Rises.*" In *New Essays on* The Sun Also Rises, edited by Linda Wagner-Martin, 65–82. Cambridge: Cambridge University Press.

Martinez, I. 2009. "Ego Readings vs. Reading for Psyche." *Journal for Jungian Scholarly Studies* 5 (2): 1–17.

Mehl, Dieter and Christa Jansohn. 1995. "Introduction." *The Woman Who Rode Away and Other Stories,* edited by Dieter Mehl and Christa Jansohn, xxxi–lxv. Cambridge: Cambridge University Press.

Mellard, James M. 1991. *Using Lacan, Reading Fiction.* Urbana: University of Illinois Press.

Meyers, J. 1982. *D.H. Lawrence and the Experience of Italy.* Philadelphia and London: University of Pennsylvania Press.

_____. 2020. "D.H. Lawrence's Children." In *Short Story Criticism: Criticism of the Works of Short Fiction Writers* Vol. 281. 212–18, edited by Rebecca Parks. Farmington Hills, MI: Gale.

Millet, K. 1969. *Sexual Politics.* New York: Columbia University Press.

Moore, Harry T. 1951. *The Life and Work of D.H. Lawrence.* London: George Allen & Unwin.

Moynahan, Julian. 1972. *The Deed of Life: The Novels and Tales of D.H. Lawrence.* Princeton: Princeton University Press.

Muratore, M.J.. 2016. *Hermeneutics of Textual Madness: Re-Readings.* Fasano: Schena Editore.

Nancy, J-L. and Philippe Lacoue-Labarthe. 1992. *The Title of the Letter: A Reading of Lacan, trans. François Raffoul and David Pettigrew. Albany: State University of New York Press.*

Nelson, Jane A. 1990. "The Familial Isotopy in *The Fox.*" In *The Challenge of D.H. Lawrence*, edited by Michael Squires and Keith Cushman, 129–43. Madison: University of Wisconsin Press.

Partridge, Eric. 1958. *Origins: A Short Etymological Dictionary of Modern English.* New York: MacMillan.

Pascal, Blaise. 1982. *Les Pensées.* Paris: Editions du Cerf. 152.

Perry, Seamus. 2021. "With a Da bin ich!" *London Review of Books.* September 9, vol. 43, no. 17: 23–26.

Phillips, Adam. 2003. "Making the Case: Freud's Literary Engagements." *Profession*: 10–20. The Modern Language Association of America.

Pinion, F.B. 1978. "Shorter Stories." In *A D.H. Lawrence Companion: Life, Thought, and Works*, 218–48. London: Macmillan.

Plimpton, George. 1958. "Ernest Hemingway: The Art of Fiction XXXI." *The Paris Review* 18: 60–89.

Raffoul, F. and David Pettigrew. 1992. "Translators' Preface." In *The Title of the Letter: A Reading of Lacan, vii–xxx. Albany: State University of New York Press.*

Ragachewskaya, Marina S. 2017. "The Man Who Loved Islands" and "The Woman Who Rode Away": Turning a Moment into Eternity," *Études Lawrenciennes* 48: 1–29.

_____. 2013. "The Voyage in D.H. Lawrence's Cosmological Symbolism in Psychological Terms." In *Lake Garda: Gateway to Lawrence's Voyage to the Sun*, edited by Nick Ceramella, 89–99. Newcastle upon Tyne: Cambridge Scholars Publishing.

Ragland-Sullivan, Ellie. 1984. "The Magnetism Between Reader and Text: Prolegomena to a Lacanian Poetics." *Poetics* 13: 381–406.

Reeve, N. 2003. *Reading Late Lawrence.* London: Palgrave.

Rieff, Philip. 1968. "Introduction." *Psychoanalysis and the Unconscious* and *Fantasia of the Unconscious*, vii–xxiii. by D.H. Lawrence. New York: Viking.

_____. 1966. "The Therapeutic as Mythmaker." In *The Triumph of the Therapeutic: Uses of Faith after Freud.* New York: Harper.

Ruderman, Judith. 1984. *D.H. Lawrence and the Devouring Mother: The Search for a Patriarchal Ideal of Leadership.* Durham, NC: Duke University Press.

Sartre, Jean-Paul. 1966. "American Novelists in French Eyes." *The Atlantic Monthly* 178 (2): 114–18.

_____. 1957. "Camus' *The Outsider.*" In *Literary Essays*, 21–41. Translated by Annette Michelson. New York: Philosophical Library.

Saussure, Ferdinand de. 1967. *Cours de linguistique générale,* 3rd. ed. Paris: Payot.

Scheckner, Peter. 1985. *Class, Politics, and the Individual: A Study of the Major Works of D.H. Lawrence.* Rutherford, Madison, Teaneck, NJ: Fairleigh Dickinson University Press.

Schneider, Daniel J. 1984. *D.H. Lawrence: The Artist as Psychologist.* Lawrence: University of Kansas Press.

Sheed, Wilfrid. 1977. "Desperate Character." Review of *L'Étranger* by Albert Camus. *The New York Review of Books*, May 12, 1977: 31–34.

Snodgrass, W. D. 1963. "A Rocking-Horse: The Symbol, the Pattern, the Way to Love." In *D.H. Lawrence: A Collection of Critical Essays.* Englewood Cliffs, NJ: Prentice-Hall.

Spilka, Mark. 1962. "The Death of Love in *The Sun Also Rises.*" In *Hemingway: A Collection of Critical Essays*, edited by Robert Weeks, 127–38. Englewood Cliffs, N.J.: Prentice-Hall.

Stanton, Edward F. 1989. *Hemingway and Spain: A Pursuit.* Seattle: University of Washington Press.

Stewart, Jack. 2003. "Lawrence's Ontological Vision in *Etruscan Places, The Escaped Cock* and *Apocalypse.*" *D.H. Lawrence Review* 31 (2): 43–58.

Stoltzfus, Ben. 1996a. "D.H. Lawrence: *The Escaped Cock.*" In *Lacan and Literature: Purloined Pretexts*, 19–31. Albany: SUNY Press.

_____. 1996b. "D.H. Lawrence: 'The Rocking-Horse Winner." In *Lacan and Literature: Purloined* Pretexts, 32–49. Albany: SUNY Press.

_____. 2010. *Hemingway and French Writers.* Kent, OH: Kent State University Press.

_____. 2009. "Hemingway's Iceberg: Camus' *L'Étranger* and *The Sun Also Rises.*" *North Dakota Quarterly* 76 (1–2): 22–39.

_____. 1996c. *Lacan and Literature: Purloined Pretexts.* Albany: SUNY Press.

_____. 2000. "'The Man Who Loved Islands': A Lacanian Reading." *D.H. Lawrence Review* 29: 27–38.

Stoneback, H.R. 2007. *Reading Hemingway's* The Sun Also Rises: *Glossary and Commentary.* Kent, OH: Kent State University Press.

Sutherland, Romy. 2013. "From D.H. Lawrence to the Language of Cinema: Chaste Sacrifices in *The Woman Who Rode Away* and *Picnic at Hanging Rock* 44: 241–51.

Swerdlow, Noel. 1991. "Review Article: On the Cosmical Mysteries of Mithras." *Classical Philology* 86: 48–63.

Thornton, Weldon. 1993. *D.H. Lawrence: A Study of The Short Story.* New York: Twayne.

Todd, Olivier. 1966. *Albert Camus: Une vie.* Paris: Gallimard.

Torgovnick, Marianna. 1990. *Gone Primitive: Savage Intellects, Modern Lives.* Chicago: University of Chicago Press.

Turner, John. 2020. *D.H. Lawrence and Psychoanalysis.* New York & London: Routledge.

Turner, John F. 1983. "The Capacity to be Alone and Its Failure in D.H. Lawrence's 'The Man Who Loved Islands.'" *D.H. Lawrence Review* 16: 259–89.

Weiss, Daniel A. 1962. *Oedipus in Nottingham: D.H. Lawrence.* Seattle: University of Washington Press.

Welty, Eudora. 1949. "The Reading and Writing of Short Stories." *The Atlantic Monthly* (March): 47–48.

Whitaker, T. R. 1961. "Lawrence's Western Path: *Mornings in Mexico.*" *Criticism* 3: 219–36.

Widmer, Kingsley. 1962. *The Art of Perversity: D.H. Lawrence's Shorter Fictions.* Seattle: University of Washington Press.

Widdowson, Peter. 1992. "Post-Modernizing Lawrence." Introduction to the *Longman Critical Reader: D.H. Lawrence.* Harlow: Longman.

Williams, Linda Ruth. 1997. *D.H. Lawrence.* Plymouth: Northcote House.

_____. 1997–98. "'We've been forgetting that we're flesh and blood, Mother': 'Glad Ghosts' and Uncanny Bodies." *D.H. Lawrence Review* 27: 232–53.

Wilson, Edmund. 1952. *The Shores of Light: A Literary Chronicle of the Twenties and Thirties.* New York: Farrar, Straus, & Young.

Worthen, John. 1991. *D.H. Lawrence.* London: Edward Arnold.

_____. 1979. *D.H. Lawrence and the Idea of the Novel.* London: Macmillan.

Young, Richard O. 1980. "'Where Even the Trees Come and Go': D.H. Lawrence and the 'Fourth Dimension.'" *D.H. Lawrence Review* 13: 30–44.

Index

Leavis, F.R., 3, 55, 70, 108
Leitch, Vincent, 82
Lemaire, Anika, 17
letter of the law, 98
Lévi-Strauss, Claude, 18, 19, 22
The Life and Work of D.H. Lawrence
    (Moore), 105
The Life and Works of Edgar Allan Poe
    (Bonaparte), 22
linguistic analyses, 115
linguistic comedy, 77
linguistic dissemination, 82
linguistics, 18, 90, 95
loss of sexual desire (*aphanasis*), 93, 95
Lucifer, 82, 83, 84
luck, 74, 75–77, 78–79, 80, 88
lucre, wordplay with luck, 74, 76–77,
    78–79, 80, 88
luna, 83
lūx, 83

MacCannell, Juliet Flower, 17, 22
machine-technology, 37
machine-worship, 38
MacLeod, Sheila, 11, 60
macrotext, 21
madness, 36, 48, 50, 57–58, 75,
    83; collective, 47; hysteria and,
    109; of industrialized society,
    43, 46; rejection of, 37; of the
    world, 2, 24, 91
Maekawa, Toshihiro, 32
magical writing pad, 81. *See also* traces
Magna Graecia, 34
"The Magnetism Between Reader and
    Text" (Ragland-Sullivan), 17, 20
Magny, Claude-Edmonde, 31
Major Short Stories of D.H. Lawrence
    (Kearney), 13
"Making the Case" (Phillips), 106
Malabar, 83–84, 86–87, 88, 89, 90–91
Le Malin (the devil), 84, 85
manifest content, 18, 21, 89, 115. *See
    also* latent content
The Man Who Died (Lawrence), 69

"The Man Who Loved Islands"
    (Lawrence), 14, 15, 93–102, 117
"Market Day" (Lawrence), 116
Marks, W. S., 74
Martin, Wendy, 64
Martinez, Inez, 15, 16
materialism, 6
McLeod, Arthur, 134
"Mechanism of Pleasure and the
    Psychogenesis of Jokes" (Freud), 79
mechanization, 1, 3, 6
méconnaissance (misrecognition),
    87, 94, 99
Mellard, James, 17, 20
Melville, Herman, 49
mendacity, 6, 8, 71, 74, 83
mental consciousness, 40
mercantilism, 46, 53
metaphor, 18, 20, 21, 90, 95, 121;
    discourse of the Other and, 111;
    floating signifiers and, 105; hysteria
    and, 108; production of, 100;
    symptomatic behavior as, 101; of
    unconscious, 113–14
metaphorical slippage, 105
metonymy, 18, 20, 21, 90, 95, 100, 101,
    121; discourse of the Other and,
    111; floating signifiers and, 103;
    hysteria and, 110
Meyers, Jeffrey, 46, 78
microtext, 21
military-industrial complex, 57, 131
Millet, Kate, 11, 58, 60
Mind, 2, 3–4, 6, 50, 133; *Blood* and, 38;
    blood-Mind dichotomy, 65; blood-
    sense and, 48; deleterious effects of,
    73; desire and, 8; unbridled, 37
mind-consciousness, 4
mirror phase, 87, 96, 122. *See also*
    mirror stage
mirror stage, 20, 95, 96, 132
misanthropy, 26, 95, 98
misogyny, 11, 12
misrecognition (*méconnaissance*),
    87, 96, 99

"Shorter Stories" (Pinion), 9
short story form, 5, 70, 133
significance, 89, 90
signification, 89
signifieds, 19, 86, 90
signifier, 19, 86, 90; floating, 81, 103;
   free play of the, 89; human condition
   and, 100; Lacan on, 120; "The
   Rocking-Horse Winner" and, 85;
   transparency and opacity of, 82
Sketches of Etruscan Places (Lawrence),
   1, 33, 34, 40, 46, 51, 52, 54, 60, 134
Snodgrass, W. D., 74
society, 102, 112; disenchantment with,
   98; inherently evil, 95
Sons and Lovers (Lawrence), 11
Sophocles, 107
spiritual bankruptcy, 131
spiritualism, 110, 112, 113
spirituality, 122
splitting of the self, 98, 101. *See also*
   mirror phase; mirror stage
Spotnitz, Hymon, 74
Stein, Gertrude, 35
Stewart, Jack, 34, 52, 56
Studies in Classic American Literature
   (Lawrence), 13
Studies on Hysteria (Freud), 5, 70, 106
*Study of Thomas Hardy and Other
   Essays* (Lawrence), 141
submerged portion stories, 4–5
substitution, 86, 115
sun, image of, 4, 5, 38, 42, 45, 50, 63
"Sun" (Lawrence), 6, 14, 31, 32–33,
   46–47, 50, 133; Becket on, 41;
   Etruscans and, 40; irony and, 35;
   Lady Chatterley's Lover and, 36;
   parable of, 52; phallic power and,
   38–39; unconscious and, 139; *The
   Woman Who Rode Away* and, 51
The Sun Also Rises (Hemingway), 30,
   35, 63; bullfighting and, 67–68; man-
   woman relationships and, 65–66, 70
Sutherland, Romy, 59
Symbolic, 19, 96

symbolic castration, 99
symbolic displacement, 101
symbolic lesions, 85
symbolic phallus, 46
symbolic slippages, 101
synecdoche, 121

"The Tales" (Draper), 9
talking Cure, 26, 112, 109
tangle, 107
teenage suicide, 3
ternary concept, 102, 117
textuality, 99
Thanatos, 124
theological idealism, 122
"The Thorn in the Flesh"
   (Lawrence), 10
Thornton, Weldon, 13
*La Topologie ordinaire de Jacques
   Lacan* (Granon-Lafont), 110
Torgovnick, Marianna, 11
traces, 21, 80, 81, 82, 121
transference, 23
Tristes tropiques (Lévi-Strauss), 19
tropes, 31, 34, 35, 50, 81, 111, 115, 117;
   dreams as, 18; "Glad Ghosts" and,
   111; male-female, 57; mechanisms
   of language found in, 17; networks
   of interrelated, 71; play of, 77;
   traces and, 21
tropological weave, 126
Turner, John, 11, 110

uncanniness, 105
unconscious, 17, 88, 95, 100, 121, 123,
   131, 133; collective, 15; conscious
   contact with, 114; desire, 111; erotic
   spirit of, 116; *It*, 115; language and,
   120, 132; letter of, 86–87, 119;
   metaphors of, 113–14; as power of
   affect, 23; sexuality of, 127; veiled
   nature of, 101; voice of, 6, 132
"The 'Unconscious' of Literature"
   (Holland), 23
unconscious speech, 18

166

Index

About the Author

Ben Stoltzfus is professor emeritus of comparative literature, creative writing, and French at the University of California, Riverside. He is a novelist, translator, literary critic, and inter-arts scholar. He has published many articles on twentieth-century French, English, and American writers, 12 monographs of literary criticism on Chennevière, Robbe-Grillet, Gide, Lacan, and others, as well as books on Hemingway, Magritte, and Jasper Johns. An award-winning writer, he has received a fair share: Fulbright, Camargo, Gradiva, Humanities, Creative Arts, and MLA. He has published six novels and two collections of short stories. *Romoland,* a pictonovel, written in collaboration with Judith Palmer, the artist, was published in 2017. The collection *Falling and Other Stories* was published in 2018. The novel, *Dumpster for God's Sake,* was published in 2019. *Alliecats,* text by Ben Stoltzfus, illustrations by Allie Kirschner, his granddaughter. *Alliecats* is a collection of 53 graphic tales and word-puns about cats beginning with the prefix *cat: catalog, catsup, catwalk,* etc., published in 2019. The novel, *Transgression: Hitler, Mirka, Mireille, and Me,* will be published in 2022. Stoltzfus lives in Riverside, California, with his artist wife, Judith Palmer.

Also by Ben Stoltzfus

NOVELS

The Eye of the Needle
Black Lazarus
Red White & Blue
Valley of Roses
Cat O'Nine Tails (short stories)
Romoland (a pictonovel; art by Judith Palmer)
Falling and Other Stories
Dumpster for God's Sake
Alliecats (53 graphic tales in collaboration with Allie Kirschner, the artist)
Transgression: Hitler, Mirka, Mireille and Me

TRANSLATIONS

La Belle Captive (Alain Robbe-Grillet)
The Target (Alain Robbe-Grillet)

POETRY

The Puma Drinks the New Moon

MONOGRAPHS

Georges Chennevière et l'unanimisme

174

Also by Ben Stoltzfus

Alain Robbe-Grillet and the New French Novel
Gide's Eagles
Gide and Hemingway: Rebels Against God
Alain Robbe-Grillet: The Body of the Text
Postmodern Poetics: Nouveau Roman *and Innovative Fiction*
La Belle Captive: A Novel. Alain Robbe-Grillet and René Magritte
Lacan and Literature: Purloined Pretexts
The Target: Alain Robbe-Grillet and Jasper Johns
Hemingway & French Writers
Magritte and Literature: Elective Affinities